GERMAN IS FUN ★ BOOK 1

LIVELY LESSONS FOR BEGINNERS

Elsie M. Szecsy

Foreign Language Department
Garden City (NY) Public Schools

AMSCO

When ordering this book, please specify *either* **R 559 W**
or GERMAN IS FUN, BOOK 1

AMSCO SCHOOL PUBLICATIONS, INC.
315 Hudson Street / New York, N.Y. 10013

Cassettes

The cassette program comprises six two-sided cassettes. The voices are those of native speakers of German.

Each of the twenty-four lessons in the book includes the following cassette materials:

Oral exercises in four-phased sequences: cue—pause for student response—correct response by native speaker—pause for student repetition.

The narrative or playlet at normal listening speed.

Questions or completions based on the narrative or playlet in four-phased sequences.

The conversation, first at normal listening speed, then by phrases with pauses for student repetition.

The Cassettes (ordering Code N 559 C), with accompanying script, are available separately from the publisher.

For Elsie U. and Alek B. Szecsy

ISBN 0-87720-580-9

Printed in the United States of America

1 2 3 4 5 6 7 8 9 10   99 98 97 96 95 94 93 92

Preface

GERMAN IS FUN, BOOK 1 offers an introductory program that makes language acquisition a natural, personalized, enjoyable, and rewarding experience. The book provides all the elements for a one-year course.

GERMAN IS FUN, BOOK 1 is designed to help students attain an acceptable level of proficiency in four basic skills—speaking, listening, reading, and writing—developed through simple materials in visually focused topical contexts that students can easily relate to their own experiences. Students are asked easy-to-answer questions that require them to speak about their daily lives, express their opinions, and supply real information.

GERMAN IS FUN, BOOK 1 consists of six parts. Each part contains four lessons followed by a *Wiederholung*, in which structure is recapitulated and practiced through various *Übungen*. These include games and puzzles as well as more conventional exercises.

Each lesson includes a step-by-step sequence of elements designed to make the materials immediately accessible as well as give students the feeling that they can have fun learning and practicing their German. To further this objective, topics of high frequency and student interest are presented early in the course: Numbers, Telling Time, Clothing and Colors, Weather.

Vocabulary

Each lesson begins with topically related sets of drawings that convey the meanings of new words in German without recourse to English. This device enables students to make a direct and vivid association between the German terms and their meanings. The *Übungen* also use pictures to practice German words and expressions.

To facilitate comprehension, the book uses cognates of English words wherever suitable, especially in the first lesson. Beginning a course in this way shows the students that German is not so "foreign" after all and helps them overcome any fears they have about the difficulty of learning a foreign language.

Structures

GERMAN IS FUN, BOOK 1 uses a simple, straightforward, guided presentation of new structural elements. These elements are introduced in small learning components—one at a time—and are directly followed by appropriate activities, many of them visually cued, personalized, and in a communicative framework. Students thus gain a feeling of accomplishment and success by making their own discoveries and formulating their own conclusions.

Conversation

To encourage students to use German for communication and self-exprression, each lesson (after the first) includes a conversation—sometimes practical, sometimes humorous. All conversations are illustrated in cartoon-strip fashion to provide a sense of realism. Conversations are followed by dialog exercises, with students filling empty "balloons" with appropriate bits of dialog. These dialogs serve as springboards for additional personalized conversation.

Reading

Each lesson (after the first) contains a short, entertaining narrative or playlet that features new structural elements and vocabulary and reinforces previously learned grammar and expressions. These passages deal with topics that are related to the everyday experiences of today's student generation. Cognates and near-cognates are used extensively.

Culture

Each lesson is followed by a *Kulturecke*. These twenty-four *Kulturecken*, many of them illustrated, offer students picturesque views and insights into well-known and not so well-known aspects of German culture.

Techer's Manual and Key; Testing

A separate *Teacher's Manual and Key* provides suggestions for teaching all elements in the book, additional oral practice materials, and a complete Key to all exercises and puzzles.

The *Manual* also includes a Quiz for each lesson, a Unit Test for each part, and two Achievement Tests. These tests are designed to be simple in order to give all students a sense of accomplishment. The tests use a variety of techniques through which mastery of structure and vocabulary as well as comprehension may be evaluated. Teachers may use them as they appear or modify them to fit particular needs. Keys are provided for all test materials.

E. M. S.

Contents

Dritter Teil

Vierter Teil

Fünfter Teil

Sechster Teil

DÄNEMARK

Nordsee

Ostsee

Nord-
Ostsee-
Kanal

Kiel

SCHLESWIG-
/HOLSTEIN

Stralsund

Greifswald

Cuxhaven

Lübeck

Rostock

HAMBURG

Schwerin

MECKLENBURG-
VORPOMMERN

Bremerhaven

Hamburg

Neubrandenburg

Lüneburg

BREMEN

Lüneburger
Heide

Elbe

BRANDENBURG

Havel

POLEN

Bremen

Weser

SACHSEN-
ANHALT

BERLIN

Berlin

Ems

NIEDERSACHSEN

Oder

Osnabrück

Hannover

Mittellandkanal

Brandenburg

Potsdam

Frankfurt/Oder

Braunschweig

Magdeburg

Spree

TEUTOBURGER
WALD

Münster

HARZ

Wittenberg

BROCKEN

Neiße

Göttingen

Dessau

Essen

Dortmund

Saale

Halle

Düsseldorf

NORDRHEIN-
WESTFALEN

Kassel

Eisenach

Leipzig

Meißen

Aachen

Köln

Wartburg

Weimar

SACHSEN

Bonn

HESSEN

Erfurt

Jena

Dresden

EIFEL

Rhein

Marburg

THÜRINGEN

Gera

Chemnitz

Gießen

Suhl

VOGELSBERG

THÜRINGER
WALD

ERZGEBIRGE

Koblenz

RHEINLAND-
PFALZ

Wiesbaden

TAUNUS

RHÖN

FICHTELGEBIRGE

LUX.

Mosel

Frankfurt

Main

BÖHMERWALD

Trier

HUNSRÜCK

Mainz

Bayreuth

TSCHECHOSLOWAKEI

Worms

Würzburg

SAARLAND

Speyer

Rothenburg

Nürnberg

Saarbrücken

Heidelberg

BAYERISCHER WALD

Karlsruhe

Heilbronn

BAYERN

FRÄNKISCHE
ALB

Regensburg

BADEN-

Stuttgart

Baden-Baden

WÜRTTEMBERG

Eßlingen

Donau

Isar

Passau

Tübingen

Nürtingen

Rottweil

Ne kar

Ulm

Augsburg

Inn

Donau

Brigach

SCHWÄBISCHE

ÖSTERREICH

FRANKREICH

SCHWARZWALD

Breg

ALB

Sigmaringen

München

Freiburg

Donaueschingen

Konstanz

Chiemsee

Berchtesgaden

Bodensee

BAYERISCHE ALPEN

Königsee

LIECHTENSTEIN

Garmisch-
Partenkirchen

ZUGSPITZE

SCHWEIZ

Genfer See

Rhein

Rhône

ITALIEN

MATTERHORN

DEUTSCHLAND

☆ Staatshauptstadt

● Landeshauptstädte

Kilometer

0   50   100

Meilen

0   50   100

Erster
Teil

1 Deutsch und Englisch

Words That Are Similar in German and English; How to Say "The" in German

German is spoken by about 120 million people as their mother tongue. Can you name the countries where German is spoken? Where are they?

You'll have fun learning German, and it will probably be easier than you think. Do you know why? Well, first of all, German and English are both members of the same family of languages: German and English are both Germanic languages. So there are lots of words that are identical or nearly identical in both German and English. In time, you will come to see the similarities between German and English in words that, on first glance, do not look similar at all. Also, there are many German words that have a slightly different spelling but can be recognized instantly by anyone who speaks English.

Let's look at some German words and pronounce them the German way. Your teacher will show you how.

1 Words that are exactly the same in English and German:

blond	der **Arm**	die **Bank**	das **Auto**
elegant	der **Ball**	die **Garage**	das **Baby**
gold	der **Bus**	die **Giraffe**	das **Hotel**
intelligent	der **Finger**	die **Hand**	das **Radio**
modern	der **Hunger**	die **Nation**	das **Restaurant**
normal	der **Motor**	die **Party**	das **Sandwich**
warm	der **Name**	die **Person**	das **Sofa**
wild	der **Paragraph**	die **Tour**	das **Taxi**
	der **Park**	die **Vase**	das **Tennis**
	der **Plan**		das **Theater**
	der **Pullover**		das **Tunnel**
	der **Ring**		das **Zebra**
	der **Sport**		
	der **Tiger**		
	der **Tourist**		
	der **Winter**		
	der **Wolf**		
	der **Zoo**		

2 Here are some German words that look or sound almost like English words. Repeat them aloud after your teacher:

blau	der **Amerikaner**	die **Biologie**	das **Bett**
braun	der **Balkon**	die **Bluse**	das **Bier**
dick	der **Bruder**	die **Erde**	das **Buch**
dumm	der **Elefant**	die **Familie**	das **Haus**
dünn	der **Fisch**	die **Frucht**	das **Programm**
grün	der **Freund**	die **Gitarre**	das **Telefon**
hier	der **Garten**	die **Klarinette**	das **Wasser**
interessant	der **Kaffee**	die **Klasse**	das **Wetter**
jung	der **Mann**	die **Lampe**	das **Zentrum**
kalt	der **Onkel**	die **Liste**	
kühl	der **Präsident**	die **Maschine**	
lang	der **Salat**	die **Maus**	
laut	der **Schuh**	die **Mathematik**	
reich	der **Sommer**	die **Milch**	
rot	der **Wein**	die **Musik**	
rund		die **Nummer**	
imitieren		die **Schule**	
reparieren		die **Schwester**	
schwimmen		die **Sekretärin**	
singen		die **Suppe**	
studieren		die **Tomate**	
tanzen		die **Trompete**	
trinken		die **Universität**	
		die **Violine**	

3 Some German letters have two dots, ¨, called **Umlaut** (vowel change). The letters **ä, ö, ü** are pronounced differently from **a, o, u.** Listen carefully to your teacher when you learn to pronounce words with an **Umlaut.**

4 Of course, there are many words that are quite different from the English words that have the same meaning. These words you must memorize. You will probably be able to learn many of them easily by connecting them with some related English word. For example, **der Hund** (*dog*) is related to *hound*; **die Platte** (*record*) is related to *plate*, a fairly flat round object; **das Schwein** (*pig*) is related to *swine*.

Here are some more words to add to your German vocabulary:

die Bibliothek

das Kino

die Zeitung

die Blume

der Junge

das Mädchen

der Mann

die Frau

die Schule

der Stuhl

 Well, so much for vocabulary. Let's learn a little German grammar. Did you notice the words **der, die,** and **das** before all of the nouns? These three words are the German words for "the." That's right. German has three words for "the" in the singular: **der, die,** and **das.** The reason is that all German nouns, unlike English nouns, have GENDER. Nouns are either MASCULINE (m.), FEMININE (f.), or NEUTER (n.): **der** is used before masculine singular nouns; **die** is used before feminine singular nouns; **das** is used before neuter singular nouns.

How do you tell which words are masculine, which are feminine, and which are neuter. With some words, it's very easy. Obviously, **Mutter** (*mother*), **Schwester** (*sister*), and **Frau** (*woman*) are feminine; **Vater** (*father*), **Bruder** (*brother*), and **Mann** (*man*) are masculine; **Buch** (*book*), **Heft** (*notebook*), and **Haus** (*house*) are neuter. But why is **Salat** masculine and **Tomate** feminine? And why is **Mädchen** neuter? There really is no logical reason. So, the only way to learn German nouns is with the word for *the.* You don't memorize **Tiger** but **der Tiger,** not **Musik** but **die Musik,** not **Haus** but **das Haus,** and so on.

Did you notice anything else that's special about German nouns? That's right. German nouns begin with a capital letter regardless of where they appear in the sentence.

Now that you have learned some German words and grammar, let's see if you can figure out the meaning of these ten sentences. Repeat them aloud after your teacher:

1. **Das Hotel ist modern.**

2. **Die Klasse ist intelligent.**

3. Das Buch ist gut.

4. Das Tunnel ist lang.

5. Der Präsident ist blond.

6. Die Familie ist reich.

7. Der Elefant ist dick.

8. Die Giraffe ist dünn.

9. Die Trompete ist laut.

10. Der Kaffee ist braun.

Ausgezeichnet! Here are ten more:

1. Die Milch ist kalt.

2. Der Tiger ist wild.

3. Der Salat ist grün.

4. Die Tomate ist rot.

5. Das Theater ist elegant.

6. Die Suppe ist warm.

7. Die Garage ist klein.

8. Die Liste ist lang.

9. Das Programm ist interessant.

10. Die Frage ist schwer.

__ ÜBUNGEN

A. Match the following words with the correct pictures:

das Baby	das Buch	die Bluse
der Elefant	der Garten	die Giraffe
die Gitarre	der Hund	die Tomate
das Kino		

1. _____

2. _____

3. _____

4. _____

5. _____

6. _____

7. _____

8. _____

9. _____

10. _____

B. Label the following pictures. Make sure to use **der, die,** or **das:**

1. _____

2. _____

3. _____

4. _____

5. _____

6. _____

7. _____

8. _____

9. _____

10. _____

11. _____

12. _____

13. _____

14. _____

15. _____

16. _____

17. _____

18. _____

19. _____

20. _____

C. Write the German word for *the* (**der, die, das**) before each noun:

1. _____ Park

2. _____ Elefant

3. _____ Sport

4. _____ Person

5. _____ Restaurant

6. _____ Universität

7. _____ Stuhl

8. _____ Baby

9. _____ Tunnel

10. _____ Familie

11. _____ Mädchen

12. _____ Klasse

13. _____ Mann

14. _____ Auto

15. _____ Theater

16. _____ Salat

17. _____ Bruder

18. _____ Bluse

19. _____ Kino

20. _____ Garten

D. Ja (*yes*) **oder nein** (*no*). If the statement is true, write **richtig** (*correct*). If it is false, write **falsch** (*false*):

1. Der Elefant ist dünn. _____

2. Das Schwein ist intelligent. _____

3. Der Kaffee ist braun. _____

4. Das Bier ist warm. _____

5. Der Sommer ist kalt. _____

6. Die Schule ist populär. _____

7. Der Ball ist rund. _____

8. Das Tunnel ist lang. _____

9. Der Tiger ist dumm. _____

10. Die Tomate ist blau. _____

E. Give your opinion by completing each sentence with one or more of the adjectives listed at right. (There may be several possible correct answers.)

1. Der Ball ist _____ .

2. Das Auto ist _____ .

3. Der Wein ist _____ .

4. Der Bus ist _____ .

5. Der Präsident ist _____ .

6. Die Sekretärin ist _____ .

7. Das Hotel ist _____ .

8. Das Wetter ist _____ .

9. Der Mann ist _____ .

10. Das Buch ist _____ .

blond
blau
lang
warm
modern
interessant
dünn
rund
intelligent
kalt

Here is something else to remember about German nouns. German can string together words to form a new compound noun. Some compound nouns consist of several words strung together. Sometimes letters are added or left off words to make the compound sound better, but the gender of the compound is always the same as the last noun in the string. Examples:

> **das Telefon + das Buch = das Telefonbuch**
> **das Telefon + die Nummer = die Telefonnummer**
> **die Tomate + n + die Suppe = die Tomatensuppe**
> **rot + der Wein = der Rotwein**
> **der Winter + der Sport + das Programm = das Wintersportprogramm**

Can you figure out the meanings of the compound nouns?

__ ÜBUNG

F. Now let's see how well you can make compound nouns and guess their meanings:

1. das Tennis + der Ball = _____

    _____

2. die Hand + der Schuh = _____

    _____

3. das Radio + das Programm = _____

    _____

4. das Gold + der Fisch = _____

    _____

5. der Sommer + die Schule = _____

    _____

6. die Mathematik + das Buch = _____

    _____

7. das Haus + die Nummer =   _____

_____

8. die Schule (omit **e**) + der Freund =   _____

_____

9. das Haus + die Mutter =   _____

_____

10. das Hotel + das Telefon + die Nummer =   _____

_____

_____ **DU** _____

Choose the words from the list that will tell others about you:

dumm	blond	modern
reich	intelligent	interessant
dick	dünn	jung

1. Ich bin ___Dick___.

2. _____

3. _____

4. _____

5. _____

KULTURECKE

Die deutschsprechende Welt (The German-speaking world)

Where do people speak German? Most people would say Germany. German is the official language not only of Germany but also of Austria and the principality of Liechtenstein. German is also one of the official languages of Switzerland and of Luxembourg. In addition, many older ethnic Germans living in areas adjacent to and at one time or another part of Germany (such as Alsace in France, Bohemia in Czecho-slovakia, and Silesia in Poland) consider German their mother tongue.

2 *Die Familie*

How to Make Things Plural

Wortschatz

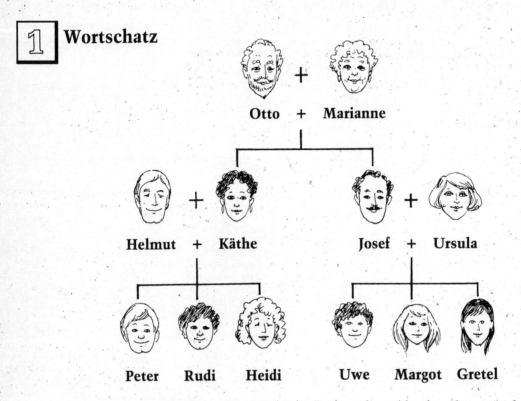

Otto + Marianne

Helmut + Käthe   Josef + Ursula

Peter   Rudi   Heidi   Uwe   Margot   Gretel

Here we have a big happy family. It's obvious from the family tree who all the members are. Let's take a closer look:

Otto und Marianne sind die Großeltern. Otto ist der Opa, und Marianne ist die Oma. Opa und Oma sind Kosenamen für Großvater und Großmutter. Helmut und Käthe sind die Eltern. Josef und Ursula sind auch Eltern.

sind *are*
die Großeltern *the grandparents*
Kosenamen *nicknames*
die Eltern *the parents*
auch *also*

Peter und Rudi sind Brüder. Sie sind Helmuts und Käthes Söhne. Margot und Gretel sind Schwestern. Sie sind Josefs und Ursulas Töchter. Käthe ist Josefs Schwester, Peters, Emils und Heidis Mutter und Uwes, Margots und Gretels Tante. Josef ist Käthes Bruder, Uwes, Margots und Gretels Vater und Peters, Rudis und Heidis Onkel.

die Brüder *the brothers*
die Schwestern *the sisters*
die Töchter *the daughters*

die Tante *the aunt*

Peter ist Uwes, Margots und Gretels Vetter. Heidi ist die Kusine. Es gibt auch Haustiere. Der Hund heißt Waldi, und die Katze heißt Schatzi. Die Familie Schmidt wohnt in München. Was für eine nette Familie!

der Vetter *the cousin*
es gibt *there are*
  Haustiere *pets*
heißt *is named*
wohnt *lives*
was für eine . . . *what a . . .*
nett *nice*

NOTE: The symbol ß is used instead of **ss** after a long vowel or diphthong: **Großeltern, heißt.** It is also used after a short vowel at the end of a syllable: **Kuß** (*kiss*). When writing German, ß may be replaced by **ss**. When capitalizing, ß is always replaced by **SS: KUSS.**

__ ÜBUNGEN __

A. Following the family tree of the Schmidts, complete each sentence with the correct words:

1. Käthe ist Peters, Rudis und Heidis __

2. Josefs und Ursulas Kinder sind _____ , _____

    und _____ .

3. Rudis Bruder ist __ __ .

4. Peter und Rudi sind __ __ .

5. Uwes Schwestern sind __ __ und _____ .

6. Waldi ist _____ .

7. Schatzi ist _____ .

8. Margot und Gretel sind Josefs und Ursulas _____ .

9. Heidi ist Gretels _____ .

10. Uwe ist Rudis _____ .

B. **Ja oder nein.** Tell whether each statement is true (**richtig**) or false (**falsch**). If your answer is **falsch**, give the correct answer:

1. Die Katze ist **ein Haustier.**

_____

2. Der Opa ist Helmuts **Bruder.**

_____

3. Gretel und Heidi sind **Schwestern.**

_____

4. Die Katze ist Waldi.

_____

5. Rudi und Peter sind **Brüder.**

_____

6. Gretel ist Käthes **Sohn.**

_____

7. Der Hund ist Schatzi.

_____

8. Peter ist Helmuts **Sohn.**

_____

9. Rudi und Gretel sind **die Eltern.**

_____

10. Die Familie wohnt **in München.**

_____

C. Identify the members of the Schmidt family, matching the words with the pictures:

die Mutter   der Vater   der Hund
die Oma   der Opa   die Katze
die Schwestern   die Brüder   die Großeltern
die Eltern

1. _____   2. _____

3. _____   4. _____

5. _____   6. _____

7. _____   8. _____

9. _____   10. _____

2 There are many people in the Schmidt family. When we speak about more than one person or thing, we must use the PLURAL. How do we change nouns from the singular to the plural in German? See if you can figure out the easy rules for most nouns. Look carefully:

I	II
der Vater	die Väter
der Sohn	die Söhne
der Opa	die Opas
der Onkel	die Onkel
der Vetter	die Vettern
die Mutter	die Mütter
die Schwester	die Schwestern
die Katze	die Katzen
die Oma	die Omas
das Baby	die Babys
das Tier	die Tiere
das Kind	die Kinder

Now compare the two groups of nouns. Underline all the words in Group I that mean "the." Look carefully at Group II, do the same, and complete the rule:

The plural form of **der** is _____ .

The plural form of **die** is _____ .

The plural form of **das** is _____ .

Remember, in English we have only one word for "the." How many ways are

there to say "the" in German? There are _____ .

When do you use **der**? _____

         die? 1. _____

               2. _____

         das? _____

3 Look again at the two groups of words. Circle all the nouns in Groups I and II.

What happens to the nouns in the plural? _____ .

That's right! Almost all of them change. Sometimes you add an UMLAUT (the two dots ¨ over **a, o,** or **u**), or you add a plural ending (the most common plural endings are **-e, -er, -n, -nen,** and **-s**). Sometimes you add both an umlaut and an ending, and sometimes there is no change at all. Each noun is different.

The way to remember the plural of a noun in German is to memorize it as you learn the noun. You don't memorize only **der Vater;** you memorize **der Vater, die Väter;** not **die Mutter,** but **die Mutter, die Mütter;** not **das Kind,** but **das Kind, die Kinder.** The bigger your vocabulary gets, the easier the plural forms will become.

___ ÜBUNGEN _____

D. Fill in the correct word for *the* in German:

1. _____ Hunde		11. _____ Schwester
2. _____ Bruder		12. _____ Onkel
3. _____ Familie		13. _____ Katzen
4. _____ Schule		14. _____ Stühle
5. _____ Mann		15. _____ Klasse
6. _____ Freunde		16. _____ Hand
7. _____ Parks		17. _____ Hotel
8. _____ Auto		18. _____ Bibliotheken
9. _____ Restaurant		19. _____ Väter
10. _____ Telefone		20. _____ Bücher

E. Make the following nouns plural. Use the correct form of *the*:

1. die Mutter   _____

2. der Vater   _____

3. der Finger   _____

4. das Haus   *die Häuser*

5. die Kusine   *die Kusinen*

6. die Tochter   *die Töchter*

7. der Sohn   *die Söhne*

8. die Platte   _____

9. das Taxi   _____

10. der Vetter   *die Vettern*

11. das Mädchen   *die Mädchen*

12. der Junge   *die Jungen*

13. die Gitarre   *die Gitarren*

14. die Freundin   *die Freundinen*

15. der Arm   *die arme*

16. die Lampe   *die Lampen*

17. das Theater   *die Theater*

18. der Ball   *die Bälla*

19. der Schuh   *die Schuha*

20. die Blume   *die Blumen*

GESPRÄCH

Wortschatz

guten Tag *hello*
Wie heißt du? *What's your name?*
ich heiße *my name is*
Wie geht's? *How are you?*
danke *thanks*
gut *fine*
Und dir? *And you?*

sehr *very*
Wo wohnst du? *Where do you live?*
ich wohne *I live*
da *there*
also *well, then*
auf Wiedersehen *good-bye*
Bis später dann. *See you later.*

DIALOG

You are the second person in the dialog. Complete it with responses chosen from the following list:

Danke, sehr gut. Und dir? Ich heiße Susanne.
Guten Tag! Bis später, Roger.

_____ **DU** _____

The Census Bureau is taking a survey. Fill out the information about the members of your family:

Ich heiße: _____

Vater: _____

Mutter: _____

Bruder/Brüder: _____

Schwester(n): _____

Opa(s): _____

Oma(s): _____

Onkel: _____

Tante(n): _____

Vetter(n): _____

Kusine(n): _____

Hund(e): _____

Katze(n): _____

KULTURECKE

Guten Tag! Ich heiße . . . (Hi! My name is . . .)

Here is a list of popular German first names. Your teacher will help you pronounce them:

JUNGEN

Alexander	Johann
Alois	Jürgen
Anton	Karl
Bernd	Kurt
Christian	Ludwig
Daniel	Markus
Dirk	Michael
Emil	Oliver
Erich	Otto
Frank	Paul
Franz	Richard
Fritz	Rudi
Hans	Thomas
Holger	Thorsten
Jens	Udo

MÄDCHEN

Andrea	Margot
Christine	Marianne
Claudia	Martina
Elise	Monika
Erika	Nicole
Gretel	Petra
Heike	Sabine
Ilse	Silke
Karin	Simone
Kerstin	Stefanie
Luise	Susanne
Maria	Ulrike

3 *Die Schule und die Klasse*

Indefinite Articles

Wortschatz

Say the following words after your teacher:

der Lehrer

die Lehrerin

das Buch

der Schüler

die Schülerin

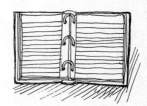

das Heft

das Papier

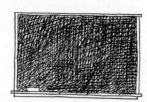

die Tafel

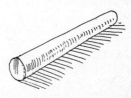

die Kreide

der Kuli   der Bleistift   die Note

___ ÜBUNG _____

A. It's the first day of the new school year. Identify what you see in the classroom:

1. _____

2. _____

3. _____

4. _____

5. _____

6. _____

7. _____

8. _____

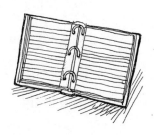

9. _____

10. _____

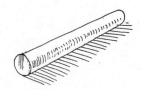

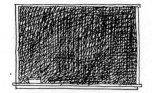

11. _____

12. _____

Here are some more words for you to say aloud:

das Wörterbuch   **das Lineal**   **der Radiergummi**

der Schwamm   **die Landkarte**   **der Schreibtisch**

das Fenster   **die Tür**   **der Stuhl**

ÜBUNGEN

B. Identify:

1. _____   2. _____

3. _____

4. _____

5. _____

6. _____

7. _____

8. _____

9. _____

10. _____

C. Give the correct definite article:

1. _____ Schüler	10. _____ Lehrerinnen
2. _____ Heft	11. _____ Kulis
3. _____ Wörterbuch	12. _____ Radiergummi
4. _____ Schülerin	13. _____ Tafel
5. _____ Schule	14. _____ Fenster
6. _____ Tür	15. _____ Schwamm
7. _____ Papier	16. _____ Bücher
8. _____ Lineal	17. _____ Landkarte
9. _____ Lehrer	18. _____ Schreibtisch

3 Now that you know all of the new words, read the following story and see if you can understand it:

Die Schule hat eine Deutschklasse. Die Klasse ist interessant. Der Lehrer heißt Herr Schulz. Herr Schulz ist sehr intelligent. Die Schüler benutzen Kulis, Bleistifte, Hefte und Bücher. Herr Schulz benutzt Kreide und die Tafel. Es gibt auch ein Wörterbuch. Das Wörterbuch ist sehr groß.

benutzen *use*

Viele Schüler lernen Deutsch. Roger ist ein Schüler in der Deutschklasse. Er ist beliebt, denn er ist nett und intelligent. Monika ist eine Schülerin. Sie ist beliebt, denn sie ist hübsch und auch sehr intelligent.

viele *many*
beliebt *popular*
nett *nice*
denn *because*
hübsch *pretty*

Die Schüler haben Deutsch gern. Deutsch ist beliebt, und Herr Schulz ist intelligent und nett.

haben ... gern *like*

___ ÜBUNGEN _____

D. Complete each statement about the story:

1. Die _____ ist interessant.

2. Der Lehrer heißt _____.

3. Der Lehrer ist _____.

4. Die Schüler benutzen _____, _____,

   _____ und _____ .

5. Das Wörterbuch ist _____.

6. Ein Schüler heißt _____.

7. Roger ist _____.

8. Eine Schülerin heißt _____.

9. Monika ist _____ und _____.

10. Die Schüler haben _____ gern.

11. Deutsch ist _____.

12. Herr Schulz ist _____ und _____.

E. **Ja oder nein.** Read the story again. If a statement is true, write **richtig**. If it is false, write **falsch** and correct the statement:

1. Die Schule hat eine Spanischklasse.

   _____

2. Der Lehrer heißt Herr Meyer.

   _____

3. Herr Schulz benutzt ein Textbuch.

   _____

4. Roger ist ein Lehrer in der Deutschklasse.

   _____

5. Monika ist dumm.

_____

6. Deutsch ist beliebt.

_____

F. How would you describe the people and things in the story? Form sentences by matching the adjectives with the nouns they describe. Write the answers in the spaces provided:

EXAMPLE: Das Buch / blau   Das Buch ist blau.

1. Roger _____.   groß
                                                                                            interessant
2. Herr Schulz _____.   beliebt
                                                                                            hübsch
3. Monika _____.   nett
                                                                                            intelligent
4. Die Klasse _____.

5. Das Wörterbuch _____.

6. Deutsch _____.

4 Look at the story again. There are two little words that appear many times.

What are these two new words? _____ That's right! **Ein** and **eine** both mean _a_ or _an_ in German. Can you figure out when to use **ein** and when to use **eine**. Look carefully:

I	II
der Lehrer	_ein_ Lehrer
der Schüler	_ein_ Schüler
der Arm	_ein_ Arm

Let's start by comparing the two groups of words. In Group I, are the nouns

singular or plural? _____ How do you know? _____

Are the nouns in Group I masculine, feminine, or neuter? _____

How do you know? _____

What does **der** mean? _____ Now look at Group II. Which word has

replaced **der**? _____ What does **ein** mean? _____

5　Now look at these examples:

I	II
die Lehrerin	*eine* **Lehrerin**
die Landkarte	*eine* **Landkarte**
die Tafel	*eine* **Tafel**

Are the nouns in Group I singular or plural? _____

How do you know? _____

Are the nouns in Group I masculine, feminine, or neuter? _____

How do you know? _____

What does **die** mean? _____ Now look at Group II. Which word has

replaced **die**? _____ What does **eine** mean? _____

6　Here's another group:

I	II
das Auto	*ein* **Auto**
das Buch	*ein* **Buch**
das Mädchen	*ein* **Mädchen**

Are the nouns in Group I singular or plural? _____

How do you know? _____

Are the nouns in Group I masculine, feminine, or neuter? _____

How do you know? _____

What does **das** mean? _____ Now look at Group II. Which word has

replaced **das**? _____ What does **ein** mean? _____

7　Let's summarize:

_____ is used before masculine singular nouns to express *a* or *an*.

_____ is used before feminine singular nouns to express *a* or *an*.

_____ is used before neuter singular nouns to express a or an.

__ ÜBUNGEN __

G. Here are some people and things you find in the classroom. Match the description with the pictures:

ein Papier   ein Heft   ein Lineal
ein Schüler   ein Schreibtisch ein Lehrer
ein Fenster   eine Tür   ein Bleistift
ein Radiergummi

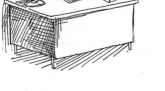

1. _____   2. _____

3. _____   4. _____

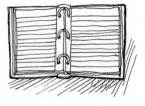

5. _____   6. _____

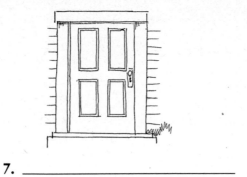

7. _____ 8. _____

9. _____ 10. _____

H. Substitute **ein** or **eine** for **der, die**, or **das**:

1. der Hund _____

2. die Mutter _____

3. das Mädchen _____

4. der Junge _____

5. das Wörterbuch _____

6. die Familie _____

7. der Tisch _____

8. der Freund _____

9. die Lehrerin _____

10. das Radio _____

I.   Now try some on your own. Fill in **ein** or **eine**:

1. ___eine___ Schwester   6. _____ Katze

2. _____ Baby   7. _____ Klasse

3. _____ Freundin   8. _____ Bruder

4. _____ Buch   9. _____ Kusine

5. _____ Schüler   10. _____ Bleistift

J.   While you are walking down the street, you point out all the things you see:

     EXAMPLE: Mann   Da ist ein Mann.

1. Auto _____

2. Frau _____

3. Park _____

4. Tier _____

5. Theater _____

6. Blume _____

7. Haus _____

8. Schule _____

9. Hund _____

10. Familie _____

K.   Underline the expression that does NOT belong in each group:

1. eine Tür, ein Fenster, ein Lehrer, ein Haus

2. der Bleistift, der Kuli, das Heft, der Kaffee

3. intelligent, nett, beliebt, richtig

4. der Großvater, die Tante, die Musik, der Sohn

5. die Frau, die Frucht, die Tomate, die Suppe

6. die Schule, der Park, die Universität, die Klasse

7. ein Hund, eine Platte, eine Katze, ein Tiger

8. die Sekretärin, der Lehrer, der Tourist, die Garage

⟨8⟩ Let's look at these questions and the two possible responses for each one:

Ist hier *ein* Buch?	*Is a book here?*
Ja, hier ist *ein* Buch.	*Yes, here is a book.*
Nein, hier ist *kein* Buch.	*No, here is no book.*
Ist hier *eine* Tafel?	*Is a blackboard here?*
Ja, hier ist *eine* Tafel.	*Yes, here is a blackboard.*
Nein, hier ist *keine* Tafel.	*No, here is no blackboard.*

What do **kein** and **keine** mean? _____ That's right! They mean *no* and are used to negate the noun that follows them. The endings of **kein** and **keine** always follow the same patterns as **ein** and **eine**.

___ ÜBUNG ___

L. **Was ist auf dem Bild?** (*What is in the picture?*) *Do at Home*

Look at the picture. Then complete each statement about it, using the correct form of **ein** or **kein**:

1. _____ Kreide ist auf dem Bild.

2. _____ Lehrerin ist auf dem Bild.

3. _____ Schüler ist auf dem Bild.

4. _____ Buch ist auf dem Bild.

5. _____ Lineal ist auf dem Bild.

_____ *DU* _____

List eight items you keep in your locker in school or in your desk at home:

1. _____

2. _____

3. _____

4. _____

5. _____

6. _____

7. _____

8. _____

GESPRÄCH

Wortschatz

Wie geht es Ihnen . . . ? *How are you . . . ?*	**schwer** *difficult*
heute *today*	**leicht** *easy*
und dir *and you*	**bist du** *are you*
wir haben *we have*	**vorbereitet** *prepared*
morgen *tomorrow*	**natürlich** *of course*
es ist ganz egal *it doesn't matter at all*	**mein Lieblingsfach** *my favorite subject*
ja *(here) certainly*	**viel Glück** *good luck*

DIALOG

Complete the dialog with expressions chosen from the following list:

Sehr gut   Danke
Viel Glück!   morgen
es ist ganz egal   vorbereitet
Aber natürlich   schwer
geht es Ihnen   mein Lieblingsfach
es ist sehr leicht ein Examen

KULTURECKE

Das deutsche Schulsystem

German children are required by law to attend school from age six to fifteen. As in the United States, the organization of the school systems is the responsibility of the **Bundesländer** (*states*).

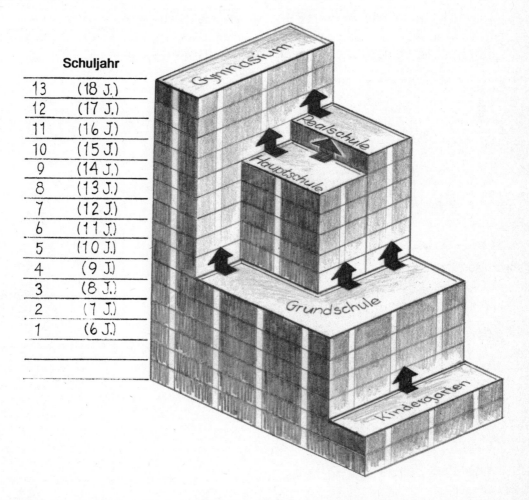

Schuljahr	
13	(18 J.)
12	(17 J.)
11	(16 J.)
10	(15 J.)
9	(14 J.)
8	(13 J.)
7	(12 J.)
6	(11 J.)
5	(10 J.)
4	(9 J.)
3	(8 J.)
2	(7 J.)
1	(6 J.)

Though not mandatory, many children attend **Kindergarten** before they begin first grade in the **Grundschule** (*elementary school*), which all children are required to attend.

Upon leaving the **Grundschule**, students attend one of three types of secondary schools:

The **Hauptschule** specializes in preparing students for trades. After five years of formal education, **Hauptschule** graduates can continue on to the **Berufsschule** (*trade school*) or they may serve an apprenticeship under a skilled craftsman in their field.

The **Realschule** prepares students for more highly skilled positions. Graduates from the **Realschule** may go on to further their education in a **Fachschule** (*technical college*).

The **Gymnasium** (*academic high school*) prepares students to continue their education in the **Universität** (*university*). Students must pass a special test, the **Abitur**, at the end of their studies at the **Gymnasium** in order to qualify for a place in the university. Students in the **Gymnasium** who complete the university program can pursue careers in the professions, such as medicine, law, and education.

Of course, students may switch their educational path, should such a change be considered desirable. In addition, opportunities exist for adults to continue their education in order to open more career opportunities to them.

4 *Die Verben*

How to Express Actions; How to Ask Questions and Say No in German; Question Words

1 Wortschatz

gehen

lernen

schreiben

schwimmen

singen

üben

2 Many people and things will be involved in the story later in this lesson. Who are they?

ich (*I*)

wir (*we*)

du (*you*)

ihr (*you*)

Sie (*you*)

Sie (*you*)

er (*he*)

sie (*she*)

sie (*they*)

es (*it*)

These words are called subject pronouns. Subject pronouns refer to the persons or things doing the action. Did you notice that **du, Sie,** and **ihr** all mean *you?*

du is used when you are speaking to a friend, a close relative, or a child — someone with whom you are familiar.

Sie is used when you are speaking to a stranger or a grown-up — a person or persons with whom you are or should be formal.

ihr is used when you are speaking to friends, close relatives or children — people with whom you are familiar.

__ ÜBUNG _____

A. Write the subject pronoun you would use if you were speaking to the following people. Would you use **du, Sie,** or **ihr**?

1. der Lehrer _____
2. Paul _____
3. Frau Müller _____
4. Ilse und Susanne _____

5. die Großeltern _____
6. die Mutter _____
7. ein Baby _____
8. Herr Becker _____

3 Which pronoun would you use if you want to speak about **Karl** without using his name? _____

Which pronoun would you use if you want to speak about **Maria** without using her name? _____

Which pronoun would replace **Karl und Paul**? _____ **Maria und Anna**? _____ **Maria und Paul**? _____

Er and **sie** also mean *it*. Which pronoun would you use to refer to **der Tisch**? _____ **die Tafel**? _____

Which pronoun would you use to replace **das Buch**? _____ **die Bücher**?

_____

Let's summarize:

> **er** replaces a masculine name or noun;
> **sie** replaces a feminine name or noun;
> **es** replaces a neuter noun;
> **sie** replaces all plural names or nouns.

__ ÜBUNG _____

B. Supply the pronoun you would use to substitute for each name or noun:

1. Peter ist intelligent. _____ ist intelligent.

2. Herr und Frau Gärtner sind aus München. _____ sind aus München.

3. Die Tiere sind wild. _____ sind wild.

4. Das Wörterbuch ist dick. _____ ist dick.

5. Die Suppe und der Fisch sind kalt. _____ sind kalt.

6. Die Lehrerin ist beliebt. _____ ist beliebt.

7. Das Hotel ist modern. _____ ist modern.

8. Der Ball ist rund. _____ ist rund.

---

4 Here's a story using verbs you have just learned. Can you spot them?

Frau Schmidt ist Lehrerin. Ihr Fach ist Deutsch. **Die Schüler lernen** Deutsch, Englisch, Mathe und andere Fächer. **Frau Schmidt schreibt** mit Kreide an die Tafel. **Die Schüler schreiben** in die Hefte. **Sie lernen** gut.

ihr *her*
das Fach *the subject*
andere *other*
die Fächer *the subjects*
mit *with*

Frau Schmidt fragt: Jürgen, was machst du nach der Schule?
JÜRGEN: **Ich schwimme.** Und du, Helmut?
HELMUT: **Ich singe** im Chor. Uschi und Marianne, **ihr spielt** Tennis, nicht wahr?
USCHI UND MARIANNE: Nein, **wir spielen** nicht Tennis. **Wir telefonieren** mit Gabi.
FRAU SCHMIDT: Ja, **Gabi geht** nach Hause und **übt** Klavier. Sie ist sehr fleißig.

machst du *do you do*

nicht wahr? *don't you?*

nach Hause *home*
das Klavier *the piano*
fleißig *diligent*

Was macht Frau Schmidt nach der Schule? **Sie korrigiert** die Aufgaben und **schreibt** die Pläne für den nächsten Schultag.

korrigiert *corrects*
die Pläne *the plans*
für *for*
den nächsten *the next*
der Schultag *the schoolday*

___ ÜBUNG _____

C. Ja oder nein. Tell whether each statement is true (**richtig**) or false (**falsch**). If your answer is **falsch,** give the correct answer:

1. Frau Schmidt ist Englischlehrerin.

_____

2. Frau Schmidt schreibt mit Kreide an die Tafel.

_____

3. Jürgen schwimmt nach der Schule.

_____

4. Helmut singt im Chor nach der Schule.

_____

5. Uschi und Marianne spielen Tennis nach der Schule.

_____

6. Gabi übt Klavier nach der Schule.

_____

7. Frau Schmidt spielt Tischtennis.

_____

5 | Now that you know the subject pronouns, you are ready to learn the CON-JUGATION of verb forms.

CONJUGATION, what's that? CONJUGATION refers to changing the ending of the verb so that the verb agrees with the subject. We do the same in English without even thinking about it. For example, we say *I play* but *he plays*. Look carefully at the verbs in bold type in our story and see if you can answer this question:

To conjugate a verb (making subject and verb agree), which letters are dropped

from the infinitive? _____ Using **spielen** as an example, let's see how it works. If you want to say *I play*, take **ich**, remove **-en** from **spielen,** and add the ending **-e:**

| | spiel ~~en~~ | to play |
| ich | spiel e | I play, I am playing |

Do the same for all the other subjects:

du	spiel st	you play, you are playing
er		he
sie }	spiel t	she } plays, is playing
es		it
wir	spiel en	we play, we are playing
ihr	spiel t	you play, you are playing
sie	spiel en	they play, they are playing
Sie	spiel en	you play, you are playing

NOTE: There are two possible meanings for each verb form: **ich spiele** may mean *I play* or *I am playing*; **du lernst** may mean *you learn* or **you are learning**; and so on.

Now you do one. Take the verb **lernen** (*to learn*). Remove the **-en,** look at the subjects, and add the correct endings:

ich lern _____   wir lern _____

du lern _____   ihr lern _____

er lern _____   sie lern _____

sie lern _____   Sie lern _____

es lern _____

ÜBUNGEN

D. Conjugate these verbs: *do at home*

	gehen	schreiben	singen	üben
ich	_____	_____	_____	_____
du	_____	_____	_____	_____
er	_____	_____	_____	_____

sie	_____	_____	_____	_____
es	_____	_____	_____	_____
wir	_____	_____	_____	_____
ihr	_____	_____	_____	_____
sie	_____	_____	_____	_____
Sie	_____	_____	_____	_____

E. A reporter for the school newspaper is asking what you do in your German class. Tell him:

EXAMPLE: lernen/Deutsch   Ich lerne Deutsch.

1. schreiben / in das Heft _____

2. üben / die Verben _____

3. singen / ,,Die Lorelei'' _____

4. korrigieren / die Aufgaben _____

F. Your friends are telling you what they do in their spare time:

EXAMPLE: gehen / nach Hause   Wir gehen nach Hause.

1. singen / im Chor _____

2. spielen / Tennis _____

3. telefonieren / mit Freunden _____

4. schwimmen / nach der Schule _____

G. Say to a friend what she does on weekends:

EXAMPLE: gehen / ins Kino   Du gehst ins Kino.

1. telefonieren / mit Uschi _____

2. spielen im Park _____

3. schreiben / die Aufgaben _____

4. singen / im Chor _____

H. Tell what the members of the Ehrhardt family are doing:

> EXAMPLE: Georg / gehen / ins Theater
> Georg geht ins Theater.

1. Kerstin und Alois / spielen / Tennis

_____

2. der Vater / üben / Klavier

_____

3. der Onkel und die Tante / telefonieren / mit Freunden

_____

4. die Mutter / singen / im Chor

_____

5. die Großeltern / lernen / Deutsch

_____

6. die Tochter / schreiben / die Aufgaben

 Here are some more activities:

antworten   **arbeiten**   **besuchen**

fragen

kaufen

kommen

tanzen

trinken

Let's take a closer look at the verbs **tanzen** and **arbeiten**:

tanz	arbeit ⬛
ich tanz*e*	ich arbeit*e*
du tanz*t*	du arbeit*est*
er ⎫	er ⎫
sie ⎬ tanz*t*	sie ⎬ arbeit*et*
es ⎭	es ⎭
wir tanz*en*	wir arbeit*en*
ihr tanz*t*	ihr arbeit*et*
sie tanz*en*	sie arbeit*en*
Sie tanz*en*	Sie arbeit*en*

Circle the form of **tanzen** that does not follow the rule. What form did you

circle? _____ If you circled and wrote **du tanzt,** you are correct.
It's unnecessary to use the **-s** of the **-st** ending in **du tanzt** because **tanz-** already
contains the **s**-sound.

Now circle the forms of **arbeiten** that do not follow the rule. Which forms did

you circle? _____ _____ _____.

How do the **du, er, sie** (*she*), **es** and **ihr** forms differ from the rule? We put an extra **e** before the ending in order to make it easier to pronounce the verb. What other new verb in this lesson needs the extra **e** for these forms?

_____. Correct, **antworten** (*to answer*) follows the same pattern as **arbeiten**.

Tanzen, arbeiten, and **antworten** belong to a group of verbs showing similar differences from the pattern. As you learn each new verb, take special note of these differences.

do at home

I. Here are ten German "action words." Tell who is "doing the action" by writing every pronoun that can be used with the verb. Then write what each verb means. Follow the example:

wir, sie Sie	spielen	we play, they play, you play

1. _____ singe _____

2. _____ arbeitest _____

3. _____ antwortet _____

4. _____ kaufen _____

5. _____ geht _____

6. _____ kaufe _____

7. _____ trinken _____

8. _____ besucht _____

9. _____ telefonierst _____

10. _____ schreibt _____

ÜBUNGEN

J. Match the descriptions with the correct pictures:

Die Mädchen singen.
Die Schüler lernen Mathe.
Die Frau telefoniert mit Hans.
Heidi übt Klavier.
Der Mann arbeitet viel.

Wir spielen Tennis.
Die Jungen gehen nach Hause.
Der Freund trinkt Milch.
Die Lehrerin fragt die Klasse.
Die Kinder schreiben in die Hefte.

1. _____

2. _____

3. _____

4. _____

5. _____

6. _____

7. _____

8. _____

9. _____   10. _____

K. Write the form of the verb that is used with each subject:

   EXAMPLE: spielen: ich _____spiele_____

   1. (kommen) du _____

   2. (schreiben) wir _____

   3. (tanzen) er _____

   4. (singen) du _____

   5. (gehen) sie (*she*) _____

   6. (üben) er _____

   7. (fragen) die Lehrerinnen _____

   8. (spielen) der Junge _____

   9. (lernen) die Klasse _____

   10. (antworten) die Eltern _____

L. Here's a description of what some people are doing. Complete the sentences by adding the correct German verb form:

   1. (learn) Ich _____ Deutsch.

   2. (telephone) Du _____ mit meiner Freundin.

   3. (dances) Otto _____ gut.

4. (sings)   Das Mädchen _____ auf deutsch.

5. (buy)   Wir _____ viel.

6. (go)   Die Schüler _____ nach Hause.

7. (practices)   Der Bruder _____ die Trompete.

8. (plays)   Die Schwester _____ Klavier.

9. (writes)   Er _____ die Aufgabe.

10. (answers)   Die Schülerin _____.

11. (drink)   Die Eltern _____ Kaffee.

12. (visit)   Ich _____ die Schule.

13. (work)   Alois und Werner _____ hier.

14. (learns)   Hans _____ Mathe.

15. (comes)   Der Onkel _____ später.

7 Now look at these sentences: *do at home*

I	II
Ich komme.	Ich komme *nicht*.
Herbert tanzt.	Herbert tanzt *nicht*.
Wir antworten.	Wir antworten *nicht*.

How are the sentences in Group II different from the sentences in Group I?

_____

Which little word is used in German to make a sentence negative? _____

Where do you put **nicht** in relation to the verb? _____
What do the sentences in Group II above mean in English? Each sentence has two meanings. What are they?

1. _____

_____

2. _____

_____

3. _____

_____

No matter what we say in English (*don't, doesn't, aren't, isn't,* and the like), in German the rule is always the same. To make a sentence negative, use **nicht** at the end of the sentence:

Ich tanze *nicht*. $\begin{cases} \textit{I don't dance.} \\ \textit{I'm not dancing.} \end{cases}$

Er schwimmt *nicht*. $\begin{cases} \textit{He doesn't swim.} \\ \textit{He's not swimming.} \end{cases}$

Wir arbeiten *nicht*. $\begin{cases} \textit{We don't work.} \\ \textit{We're not working.} \end{cases}$

___ ÜBUNG _____

M. You like to contradict your brother. Make the following statements negative and write the English meanings of each negative sentence on the line below it:

1. Paul tanzt. _____

_____

2. Die Mädchen singen. _____

_____

3. Sie arbeiten. _____

_____

4. Du fragst. _____

_____

5. Sie kommen. _____

_____

6. Wir spielen. _____

_____

7. Er antwortet. _____

_____

8. Ich übe. _____

_____

8 | Let's see what happens in a longer sentence:

I   II

I	II
Johanna spielt gut.	**Johanna spielt *nicht* gut.**
Herr Müller ist mein Lehrer.	**Herr Müller ist *nicht* mein Lehrer.**
Mutter ist zu Hause.	**Mutter ist *nicht* zu Hause.**

Can you give the meanings of the sentences in Group II?

1. _____

_____

2. _____

_____

3. _____

_____

Look again at the German sentences in Group II.

Where is **nicht** in the first sentence? _____

Where is **nicht** in the second sentence? _____

Where is **nicht** in the third sentence? _____

In German, if you want to negate a particular part of a sentence, put **nicht** directly before that part of the sentence.

__ ÜBUNG _____

N. Make the following sentences negative:

1. Die Eltern gehen in den Park.

_____

2. Ursula singt im Chor.

_____

3. Frau Schmidt korrigiert die Aufgaben.

_____

4. Wir kaufen das Wörterbuch.

_____

5. Du antwortest sehr gut.

_____

6. Ihr übt viel Klavier.

_____

Ausgezeichnet! You now know how to make a German sentence negative. Let's see how to ask a question in German:

I	II
Ich tanze.	**Tanze ich?**
Du kommst.	**Kommst du?**
Wir arbeiten.	**Arbeiten wir?**
Er geht.	**Geht er?**

What did we do to all the statements in Group I to form the questions in Group

II? _____
That's right! We reversed the order of the subject and the verb.

What do the sentences in Group II above mean in English?

1. _____

2. _____

3. _____

4. _____

Observe that we do not use _do, does, is, am, are_ when forming questions in German. Questions like those above normally call for **Ja** (_yes_) or **Nein** (_no_) as part of the answer.

__ ÜBUNGEN _____

O. You have an earache and can't hear very well today. Change the following statements to questions and tell what they mean:

1. Der Arzt kommt. _____

   _____

2. Die Gitarre ist alt. _____

   _____

3. Er plant (*plans*) eine Party. _____

   _____

4. Sie arbeiten zu Hause. _____

   _____

5. Die Jungen lernen Deutsch. _____

   _____

6. Du liebst Deutsch. _____

   _____

7. Wir spielen Tennis. _____

   _____

P. Answer the following questions about Hans and Johanna in the affirmative:

1. Ist Hans Deutscher?

   _____

2. Wohnt er in Deutschland?

   _____

3. Lernt er Deutsch?

   _____

4. Ist Johanna schön?

   _____

5. Ist sie beliebt?

   _____

Q. Change the answers in Übung O to the negative:

1. _____

2. _____

3. _____

4. _____

5. _____

10 Let's look at these questions:

Wo spielt er?	*Where does he play?*
Was spielt er?	*What does he play?*
Wie spielt er?	*How does he play?*

In German, if you want more information than a yes-or-no answer, begin a question with a question word. Here are the most common question words:

wann? ~~where?~~ *when*	**wieviel?** *how much?*
warum? *why?*	**wie viele?** *how many?*
was? *what?*	**wo?** *where?* *state of being*
wer? *who?*	**wohin?** *where to?* *direction toward something*
wie? *how?*	**Woher** ~~from what~~ *where from*

___ ÜBUNGEN ___

R. What's the question? Complete the questions with the correct question word corresponding to the answer in the right column:

1. _WANN_ kommt der Lehrer?   Der Lehrer kommt jetzt.

2. _WO_ ist das Buch?   Hier ist das Buch.

3. _WAS_ ist das?   Das ist ein Wörterbuch.

4. _Wu_ ist das?   Das ist meine Mutter.

5. _____ gehen wir?   Wir gehen nach Hause.

6. _Wie_ geht's?   Danke, gut.

7. _WARUM_ lernst du Deutsch?   Deutsch ist nicht schwer.

8. _Wer_ besucht die Familie?   Die Großeltern besuchen die Familie.

GESPRÄCH

Wortschatz

Tag! = Guten Tag!
Na ja, es geht *Well, yes, so-so*
jeden *every*
Hast du Deutsch gern? *Do you like German?*

sehr gern *I like it a lot*
meine *my*
im Krankenhaus *in the hospital*
Das tut mir leid. *I'm sorry (about that).*
Tschüs *Good-bye*

_____ PERSÖNLICHE FRAGEN _____

1. Tanzt du gut?

_____

2. Singt ihr in der Klasse?

_____

3. Spielst du Tennis?

_____

4. Übst du Deutsch zu Hause?

_____

5. Telefonierst du viel?

_____

_____ DU _____

List four things you do from the time you get home from school until dinner is ready, in German, of course.

1. _____

2. _____

3. _____

4. _____

do at home

DIALOG

Fill in what the second person would say. Choose from the following list:

Auf Wiedersehen, Heidi.
Ja, die Schüler gehen jetzt
   in die Klasse.
Sehr gern.

Hier ist dein Buch.
Danke, gut. Und dir?
Ja, wir üben Deutsch jeden Tag.

KULTURECKE

Die Jugendherberge (Youth hostel)

There are about 500 youth hostels in Germany, 100 in Austria, and 75 in Switzerland. They are meeting places for young travelers from all over the world. In addition to providing inexpensive food and lodging for students, they offer a variety of courses and organized trips.

Membership in the AYH (American Youth Hostels) entitles the cardholder to privileges in hostels all over the world. To apply for membership, write to:

American Youth Hostels Association
P.O. Box 37613
Washington, D.C. 20013-7613

Wiederholung I (Aufgaben 1–4)

Aufgabe 1

There are three ways to say "the" in German in the singular:

der is used before masculine singular nouns: *der* **Vater**

die is used before feminine singular nouns: *die* **Mutter**

das is used before neuter singular nouns: *das* **Kind**

Aufgabe 2

The definite article **die** (*the*) is used before all plural nouns. Plural nouns are formed by adding an umlaut, a plural ending, or both to the singular. Some nouns do not change at all:

SINGULAR	PLURAL
der Vater	die Väter
der Opa	die Opas
der Onkel	die Onkel
die Schwester	die Schwestern
die Lehrerin	die Lehrerinnen
das Tier	die Tiere
das Kind	die Kinder
das Buch	die Bücher

Memorize the plural form with each noun you learn.

Aufgabe 3

There are two ways to say *a* or *an* in German:

ein is used before masculine and neuter singular nouns:

ein **Vater**   *ein* **Kind**

eine is used before feminine singular nouns:

eine **Mutter**

Aufgabe 4

a. The subject pronouns are:

ich (*I*)		**wir** (*we*)
du (*you*)	**Sie** (*you*)	**ihr** (*you*)
er (*he*)		
sie (*she*)		**sie** (*they*)
es (*it*)		

b. In order to have a correct verb form with each subject, the infinitive of the verb is changed so that the verb form agrees with the subject pronoun or noun. To conjugate a verb in the present tense, drop **-en** from the infinitive and add the endings. This step is called CONJUGATION:

EXAMPLE: **spielen**

If the subject is		add e	to the remaining stem:		
	ich	**e**		**ich**	**spiele**
	du	**st**		**du**	**spielst**
	er	**t**		**er**	**spielt**
	sie	**t**		**sie**	**spielt**
	es	**t**		**es**	**spielt**
	wir	**en**		**wir**	**spielen**
	ihr	**t**		**ihr**	**spielt**
	sie	**en**		**sie**	**spielen**
	Sie	**en**		**Sie**	**spielen**

c. Each verb form has two possible meanings:

ich spiele   *I play*
             I am playing

d. Special verbs, like **tanzen**, drop the **s** in the **du**-form ending because **du tanzt** already has an **s**-sound.

Special verbs like **arbeiten** and **antworten** have an extra **e** before the endings **-st** and **-t** to make it easier to pronounce the verb form:

du	**arbeitest**	**du**	**antwortest**
er ⎱		**er** ⎱	
sie ⎬	**arbeitet**	**sie** ⎬	**antwortet**
es ⎰		**es** ⎰	
ihr	**arbeitet**	**ihr**	**antwortet**

e. To make a sentence negative in German, that is, to say that a subject does NOT do something, put **nicht** at the end of the sentence:

Ich besuche meine Tante *nicht*.

To negate a particular part of the sentence, put **nicht** directly before that part of the sentence:

> **Frau Schmidt ist *nicht* meine Lehrerin.**
> **Karl ist *nicht* sehr fleißig.**

f. To ask a yes/no question, put the subject after the verb:

> ***Singst du* im Chor?**
> ***Schwimmt er* viel?**

To ask for information, use a question word at the beginning of a question:

> ***Wo* arbeitet er?**
> ***Warum* lernt er Deutsch?**

The most common question words are:

wann? *when?*	**wieviel?** *how much?*
warum? *why?*	**wie viele?** *how many?*
was? *what?*	**wo?** *where?*
wer? *who?*	**wohin?** *where to?*
wie? *how?*	

___ ÜBUNGEN _____

A. Using the clues on the left, write German words that begin with the letters in the word **FERNSEHER** (*TV set*):

1. family   F __ __ __ __ __ __

2. he   E __

3. pencil eraser   R __ __ __ __ __ __ __ __ __

4. no   N __ __ __

5. school   S __ __ __ __ __

6. parents   E __ __ __ __ __

7. house   H __ __ __

8. it   E __

9. round   R __ __ __

B. How many words describing the pictures in the puzzle do you remember? Fill in the German words, then read down the boxed column to find out what we use to communicate with each other:

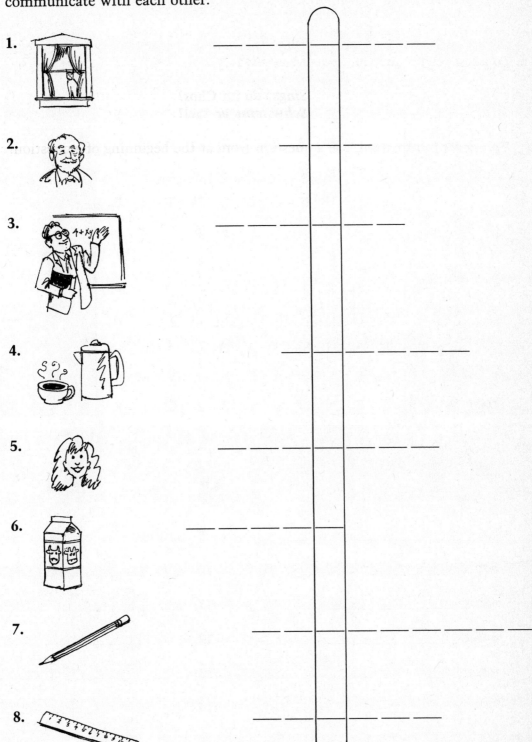

1.

2.

3.

4.

5.

6.

7.

8.

C. Worträtsel (*Word puzzle*). Find 16 German nouns hidden in the puzzle. Circle them in the puzzle and list them below. The words may be read from left to right, right to left, up or down, or diagonally:

```
L R E T S E W H C S E
T N B Ü T G T C R O T
K U L R I W A M E N T
L J U N G E F N T B E
A A M O E S E A H R N
V S E S R H L S C U I
I O C B A O C H O D R
E H D H R U E D T E A
R N U S U A H C Ä R L
I R T W A L K A V M K
L E N N U T E Z C T R
```

1. _____   9. _____

2. _____   10. _____

3. _____   11. _____

4. _____   12. _____

5. _____   13. _____

6. _____   14. _____

7. _____   15. _____

8. _____   16. _____

D. **Das Fundbüro** (*Lost and Found*). You are working in the lost-and-found office. The following objects have been brought in. List them below in German:

1. _____
2. _____
3. _____
4. _____
5. _____
6. _____
7. _____
8. _____
9. _____
10. _____
11. _____
12. _____
13. _____
14. _____
15. _____
16. _____

E. Here are ten pictures of people doing things. Describe each picture, using the correct form of one of the following verbs:

arbeiten	imitieren	schreiben	tanzen
besuchen	kaufen	schwimmen	telefonieren
fragen	kommen	singen	trinken
gehen	lernen	spielen	üben

1. Der Schüler _____
Deutsch.

2. Die Schüler _____
die Lehrerin.

3. Wir _____.

4. Die Frauen _____
im Chor.

5. Ich _____.

6. _____ du
Tennis?

7. Die Frau _____
eine Lampe.

8. Der Mann _____
im Restaurant.

9. Der Hund _____
ins Haus.

10. Der Junge _____
Klavier.

F. Picture Story. Can you read this story? Much of it is in picture form. Whenever you come to a picture, read it as if it were a German word:

Die [Familie] hat auch zwei Haustiere: Waldi und Schatzi. Waldi ist ein

[Hund], und Schatzi ist eine [Katze]. Karl lernt in einer großen [Schule].

Die [Schüler] benutzen [Kugelschreiber], [Bleistift], [Heft] und [Bücher]

in der [Klasse]. Eine [Tafel], ein [Schwamm] und [Kreide] sind auch in der

[Klasse].

Zweiter Teil

5 *Eins, zwei, drei . . .*

How to Count in German

1 Repeat the numbers aloud after your teacher:

0	null				
1	eins	11	elf	21	einundzwanzig
2	zwei	12	zwölf	22	zweiundzwanzig
3	drei	13	dreizehn	23	dreiundzwanzig
4	vier	14	vierzehn	24	vierundzwanzig
5	fünf	15	fünfzehn	25	fünfundzwanzig
6	sechs	16	sechzehn	26	sechsundzwanzig
7	sieben	17	siebzehn	27	siebenundzwanzig
8	acht	18	achtzehn	28	achtundzwanzig
9	neun	19	neunzehn	29	neunundzwanzig
10	zehn	20	zwanzig	30	dreißig

ÜBUNGEN

A. Match the German number with the numeral and write it in the space provided:

1. drei	_____	9. eins	_____	14	
				3	
2. vierzehn	_____	10. fünf	_____	20	
				16	
3. sieben	_____	11. fünfzehn	_____	11	
				2	
4. zehn	_____	12. zwei	_____	8	
				10	
5. zwanzig	_____	13. zwölf	_____	1	
				15	
6. einundzwanzig	_____	14. neunzehn	_____	21	
				7	
7. acht	_____	15. elf	_____	5	
				19	
8. sechzehn	_____			12	

B. Lohre wants to play the lottery and has made a list of her lucky numbers. Write them out in German in the spaces provided:

7 _____

11 _____

12 _____

29 _____

26 _____

15 _____

2 _____

16 _____

23 _____

21 _____

14 _____

13 _____

18 _____

4 _____

3 _____

C. The telephone operator would like you to repeat some numbers in German:

1. 456-3278　vier-fünf-sechs-drei-zwei-sieben-acht

2. 879-4621 _____

3. 737-3456 _____

4. 455-6743 _____

5. 620-2987 _____

6. 080-2539 _____

7. 435-8723 _____

D. Your teacher will read some numbers to you. Write the numerals for the number you hear:

EXAMPLE: You hear: zwanzig. You write: 20.

1. _30_

2. _5_

3. _17_ (16)

4. _25_

5. _80_ (18) ✓

6. _11_

7. _31_

8. _7_

9. _12_

10. _23_

E. You will hear a number in English. Write the number in German:

1. _____

2. _____

3. _____

4. _____

5. _____

6. _____

7. _____

8. _____

9. _____

10. _____

2 Now that you know the numbers from 0–30, let's try some arithmetic. First you must memorize the following expressions:

und *plus* (+)
weniger/minus *minus* (−)
durch *divided by* (÷)

mal *times* (×)
ist *equals* (=)

EXAMPLES:
$2+2=4$ **zwei und zwei ist vier**
$5-4=1$ **fünf weniger (minus) vier ist eins**
$3\times3=9$ **drei mal drei ist neun**
$12\div6=2$ **zwölf durch sechs ist zwei**

___ ÜBUNGEN _____

F. Read the following examples in German. Then write out each problem in numerals:

1. Fünf und fünf ist zehn. _____

2. Zwanzig minus fünf ist fünfzehn. _____

3. Neun mal zwei ist achtzehn. _____

4. Vier durch zwei ist zwei. _____

5. Sechs und drei ist neun. _____

6. Siebzehn minus sechzehn ist eins. _____

7. Elf mal eins ist elf. _____

8. Zwanzig durch fünf ist vier. _____

9. Achtzehn weniger zwei ist sechzehn. _____

10. Zehn und sechs ist sechzehn. _____

G. Read the following examples in German and then write them in German:

1. $2+3=5$ _____

2. $9-2=7$ _____

3. $4 \times 4=16$ _____

4. $8-2=6$ _____

5. $12+3=15$ _____

6. $30-5=25$ _____

7. $6 \times 5=30$ _____

8. $36 \div 3=12$ _____

9. $10+13=23$ _____

10. $12-7=5$ _____

H. Complete in German:

1. Dreizehn und sieben ist _____ .

2. Dreißig minus elf ist _____ .

3. Vier mal sechs ist _____ .

4. Fünfzehn durch fünf ist _____ .

5. Zehn und sechs ist _____ .

6. Neunundzwanzig weniger sechzehn ist _____ .

7. Zwanzig minus zwölf ist _____ .

8. Sieben mal drei ist _____ .

9. Sechzehn weniger zwölf ist _____ .

10. Zwanzig und zehn ist _____ .

3 Study and practice the numbers to 100:

40	vierzig	70	siebzig	90	neunzig
50	fünfzig	80	achtzig	100	hundert
60	sechzig				

___ ÜBUNGEN _____

I. Read the following numbers aloud and place the correct numerals in the spaces provided:

1. zweiundvierzig _____   7. einundsiebzig _____

2. achtundfünfzig _____   8. vierundachtzig _____

3. neununddreißig _____   9. dreiundneunzig _____

4. achtzig _____   10. achtunddreißig _____

5. siebenundneunzig _____   11. vierundfünfzig _____

6. fünfundsechzig _____   12. sechsundsiebzig _____

The scene of this story is a grocery store, where Robert and his sister Rita want to buy some candy. Read on to find out how they do. But first make sure to know your numbers, because there are many in the story:

PERSONEN: Robert, ein Junge von 11 Jahren
Rita, ein Mädchen von 9 Jahren
ein Verkäufer

der Verkäufer *the sales clerk*

Robert und Rita gehen in den Laden.

in den Laden *into the store*

VERKÄUFER: Guten Tag, Kinder. Was möchtet ihr?

möchten *to want*

ROBERT: Wir möchten eine große Tafel Schokolade.

die Tafel *the bar*

VERKÄUFER: Sie kostet eine Mark achtzig.
ROBERT: Eine Mark achtzig? Das ist sehr teuer.

teuer *expensive*

VERKÄUFER: Aber die Schokolade ist ausgezeichnet.
ROBERT: Na gut, hier ist eine Mark fünfzig. Ich brauche dreißig Pfennig. (Er zählt.) Fünf und fünf ist zehn und zehn ist zwanzig. Ich habe zwanzig Pfennig. Nehmen Sie eine Mark und siebzig Pfennig?

na gut *well, then*
brauchen *to need*
   zählen *to count*
nehmen *to take*

VERKÄUFER: Es tut mir leid. Die Schokolade kostet eine Mark achtzig.
RITA: Sieh mal! Ich habe etwas Geld hier.

Sieh mal! *Look here!*

ROBERT: Prima! Siebzig, einundsiebzig, zweiundsiebzig, dreiundsiebzig, vierundsiebzig, fünfundsiebzig und fünf ist achtzig.

Prima! *Super!*

VERKÄUFER: Richtig. Vielen Dank, Kinder.
ROBERT UND RITA: Bitteschön. Auf Wiedersehen!

vielen Dank *many thanks*
Bitteschön *You're welcome*
Auf Wiedersehen!
   Good-bye.

___ ÜBUNGEN ___

J. Complete these sentences based on the conversation you have just read:

1. Robert ist ein Junge von _____ Jahren.

2. Rita ist ein Mädchen von _____ Jahren.

3. Der Verkäufer fragt: _____ ?

4. Robert antwortet: _____ .

5. Die Schokolade kostet _____ .

6. Robert fragt den Verkäufer: _____ ?

7. Robert zählt: siebzig, einundsiebzig, _____

_____ .

8. Robert und Rita kaufen _____ .

K. You have been asked to make a list of the number of students in your classes. How many students are there in each class? How many boys and girls? Write the numbers in German:

KLASSE	SCHÜLER	JUNGEN	MÄDCHEN
Mathe	29	15	14
Deutsch	25	6	19
Englisch	26	13	13
Biologie	21	11	10
Geschichte (*History*)	30	18	12
Musik	17	9	8

GESPRÄCH

Wortschatz

noch *still, another*   **Gehen wir** *Let's go*
prima *super*

_____ PERSÖNLICHE FRAGEN _____

1. Wie viele Platten hast du?

_____

2. Wie viele Bücher kaufst du?

_____

_____ DU _____ *do at home* _____

Complete the following information about yourself in German. Write out all numbers:

1. Ich bin _____ Jahre alt.

2. Ich habe _____ Brüder.

3. Ich habe _____ Schwestern.

4. Meine Familie hat _____ Personen.

5. Meine Telefonnummer ist _____ .

6. Meine Hausnummer ist _____ .

7. Im Hause sind _____ Tiere.

do at home

DIALOG

You are the second person in this dialog. Complete it using some of the following expressions:

Ich brauche Geld.
Gehen wir in den Laden!
Prima!

Das ist eine gute Idee.
Hier, ich habe das Geld.
Eine Mark.

Das Geld (Money)

If you want to buy something in the United States, you use dollars (**Dollar**). If you are traveling to a German-speaking country, you will have to find out what the national currency is. Though they share the same language, the German-speaking countries do not share the same currency. Here are the names of the monetary units of the German-speaking world:

(die) Mark (DM)	Germany
(der) Schilling (S)	Austria
(der) Schweizer Franken (sFr)	Switzerland and Liechtenstein

Check your local newspaper for the latest information on how much each currency is worth today in U. S. dollars.

Foreign Exchange

	Fgn. currency in dollars		Dollar in fgn. currency	
f-Argent (Austral)	.000101	.000101	9905.0	9905.0
Australia (Dollar)	.7677	.7633	1.3026	1.3101
Austria (Schilling)	.0936	.0931	10.68	10.74
c-Belgium (Franc)	.0320	.0319	31.22	31.35
Brazil (Cruzeiro)	.0010	.0010	1002.30	1002.30
Britain (Pound)	1.8740	1.8780	.5336	.5325
30-day fwd	1.8633	1.8672	.5367	.5356
60-day fwd	1.8540	1.8579	.5394	.5382
90-day fwd	1.8439	1.8481	.5423	.5411
Canada (Dollar)	.8757	.8750	1.1420	1.1428
30-day fwd	.8730	.8726	1.1455	1.1460
60-day fwd	.8709	.8703	1.1483	1.1490
90-day fwd	.8690	.8684	1.1508	1.1515
y-Chile (Peso)	.002750	.002750	363.68	363.68
Colombia (Peso)	.001761	.001761	568.00	568.00
Denmark (Krone)	.1697	.1686	5.8931	5.9295
z-Ecudr (Sucre)	.000804	.000804	1244.01	1244.01
ECU	1.33697	1.32280	.7480	.7560
d-Egypt (Pound)	.3003	.3003	3.3305	3.3305
Finland (Mark)	.2428	.2430	4.1190	4.1150
France (Franc)	.1899	.1899	5.2665	5.2665
Germany (Mark)	.6579	.6596	1.5199	1.5160
30-day fwd	.6548	.6564	1.5272	1.5235
60-day fwd	.6519	.6534	1.5339	1.5300
90-day fwd	.6490	.6507	1.5409	1.5369
Greece (Drachma)	.005703	.005722	175.35	174.75
Hong Kong (Dollar)	.1290	.1290	7.7545	7.7545
y-India (Rupee)	.0386	.0386	25.907	25.907
Indnsia (Rupiah)	.000504	.000504	1985.03	1985.03
Ireland (Punt)	1.7500	1.7500	.5714	.5714
Israel (Shekel)	.4478	.4478	2.2329	2.2329
Italy (Lira)	.000871	.000869	1148.00	1151.25

	Fgn. currency in dollars		Dollar in fgn. currency	
Japan (Yen)	.008022	.008068	124.65	123.95
30-day fwd	.008015	.008061	124.77	124.06
60-day fwd	.008008	.008053	124.87	124.11
90-day fwd	.008000	.008047	125.00	124.27
Jordan (Dinar)	1.4859	1.4859	.67300	.67300
Lebanon (Pound)	.001138	.001138	879.00	879.00
Malaysia (Ringgit)	.3693	.3691	2.7080	2.7090
z-Mexico (Peso)	.000326	.000324	3068.00	3089.00
Nethrinds (Guilder)	.5857	.5826	1.7075	1.7165
N. Zealand (Dollar)	.5475	.5457	1.8265	1.8325
Norway (Krone)	.1674	.1667	5.9720	5.9997
Pakistan (Rupee)	.0407	.0407	24.60	24.60
y-Peru (New Sol)	.9358	.9500	1.0700	1.0500
z-Philpins (Peso)	.0382	.0382	26.15	26.15
Portugal (Escudo)	.007576	.007544	132.00	132.55
Saudi Arab (Riyal)	.2667	.2667	3.7495	3.7494
Singapore (Dollar)	.6161	.6161	1.6230	1.6230
So. Korea (Won)	.001314	.001315	761.00	760.60
So. Africa (Rand)	.3654	.3654	2.7370	2.7370
Spain (Peseta)	.010392	.010341	96.23	96.70
Sweden (Krona)	.1808	.1800	5.5320	5.5545
Switzerlnd (Franc)	.7368	.7443	1.3572	1.3435
30-day fwd	.7343	.7417	1.3618	1.3482
60-day fwd	.7321	.7394	1.3660	1.3524
90-day fwd	.7296	.7369	1.3707	1.3570
Taiwan (NT $)	.0391	.0392	25.56	25.49
Thailand (Baht)	.03965	.03945	25.22	25.35
Turkey (Lira)	.000196	.000199	5100.01	5037.00
U.A.E. (Dirham)	.2723	.2723	3.6727	3.6727
f-Uruguay (Peso)	.000401	.000407	2493.77	2457.00
z-Venzuel (Bolivar)	.0161	.0162	61.9600	61.6800
Yugoslav (Dinar)	.05018	.05018	19.93	19.93

If you go shopping in Germany, you may see labels like these:

If they look strange, it's because German uses a comma where English uses a decimal point and a decimal point where English uses a comma:

(German usage) **1.746,70 DM**   (U.S. usage) *$1,746.70*

6 *Wieviel Uhr ist es?*

Telling Time in German

1 **Wieviel Uhr ist es?**

Es ist zwölf Uhr.
Es ist Mittag.
Es ist Mitternacht.

Es ist ein Uhr.

Es ist zwei Uhr.

Es ist drei Uhr.

Es ist vier Uhr.

Es ist fünf Uhr.

Now see if you can do the rest:

_____   _____   _____

_____   _____   _____

2 How do you say "What time is it?" in German? _____

How do you say "it is"? _____

How do you express the time? _____

How do you say "it is noon"? _____

How do you say "it is midnight"? _____

For "noon" and "midnight," which word do you leave out? _____

Now study these:

Es ist fünf nach eins.

Es ist fünf vor eins.

Es ist fünf nach zwei.

Es ist fünf vor zwei.

Es ist fünf nach drei.

Es ist fünf vor drei.

Es ist fünf nach vier.

Es ist fünf vor vier.

Continue writing these times:

How do you express time after the hour? _____

How do you express time before the hour? _____

How would you say?

 _____

 _____

 _____

 _____

 _____

 _____

 _____

 _____

_____

_____

_____

_____

 Now study these:

Es ist Viertel nach eins.

Es ist Viertel vor eins.

Es ist Viertel nach zwei.

Es ist Viertel vor zwei.

Es ist Viertel nach drei.   **Es ist Viertel vor drei.**

What is the special word for "quarter"? _____

How do you say "a quarter after"? _____

How do you say "a quarter before"? _____

How would you say:

 _____

 _____

 _____

 _____

 _____

 _____

 _____

 _____

 _____

5 Now study these:

Es ist halb zwei.

Es ist halb drei.

Es ist halb vier.

Es ist halb fünf.

What is the special word for "half past"? _____

How do you say "half past the hour"? _____

When telling time, what does **halb** mean? _____

How would you say:

5:30 _____

6:30 _____

7:30 _____

8:30 _____

___ ÜBUNGEN ___

A. Write out these times as numbers:

    EXAMPLE: Es ist ein Uhr.   1:00

  1. Es ist Viertel vor neun. _____

  2. Es ist halb sieben. _____

  3. Es ist zehn nach vier. _____

  4. Es ist fünf vor drei. _____

  5. Es ist Viertel nach zwölf. _____

  6. Es ist zwanzig nach zwei. _____

7. Es ist zehn vor zehn. _____

8. Es ist zwanzig vor elf. _____

9. Es ist fünf nach acht. _____

10. Es ist fünfundzwanzig vor eins. _____

B. Write out these times in German:

1. 10:20 _____

2. 7:55 _____

3. 11:20 _____

4. 6:45 _____

5. 4:35 _____

6. 8:25 _____

7. 12:50 _____

8. 2:40 _____

9. 9:16 _____

10. 3:42 _____

C. Here are some clocks. What time does each one show?

1. _____   2. _____

3. _____

4. _____

5. _____

6. _____

7. _____

8. _____

9. _____   **10.** _____

D. Here are some broken clocks. Each one has the minute hand missing. Can you replace it according to the correct time?

1. Es ist zwei Uhr.   **2.** Es ist halb fünf.   **3.** Es ist Viertel nach drei.

4. Es ist elf nach neun.   **5.** Es ist fünf nach elf.   **6.** Es ist zehn vor fünf.

7. Es ist Viertel nach eins.

8. Es ist fünfundzwanzig vor sechs.

9. Es ist Mittag.

 Now you know what to say when someone asks **Wieviel Uhr ist es?** But how do you reply if someone asks **Um wieviel Uhr?** (*At what time?*) Look at these questions and answers:

Um wieviel Uhr ißt du das Abendessen?	*At what time do you eat dinner?*
Ich esse das Abendessen *um sechs Uhr.*	*I eat dinner at six o'clock.*
Um wieviel Uhr machst du die Aufgaben?	*At what time do you do your homework?*
Ich mache die Aufgaben *um acht Uhr.*	*I do my homework at eight o'clock.*

If you want to express "at" a certain time, which German word do you use

before the time? _____

 If you want to be more specific about the time of day, here is what you do:

Ich esse das Frühstück um acht Uhr *morgens.*	*I eat breakfast at eight o'clock in the morning (8:00 a.m.)*
Ich esse das Mittagessen um ein Uhr *nachmittags.*	*I eat lunch at one o'clock in the afternoon (1:00 p.m.).*
Ich esse das Abendessen um sieben Uhr *abends.*	*I eat dinner at seven o'clock in the evening (7:00 p.m.).*

How do you express "in the morning" or "a.m." in German? _____

How do you express "in the afternoon" or "p.m." in German? _____

How do you express "in the evening"? _____

NOTE ALSO: **um zwölf Uhr mittags** *at twelve o'clock noon*
         um zwölf Uhr nachts *at twelve o'clock midnight*

ÜBUNGEN

E. Here are some daily activities. Choose the most likely answer to the question **Um wieviel Uhr?**:

Um halb zwei nachmittags.
Um sieben Uhr morgens.
Um drei Uhr nachmittags.

1. _____ 7:00 a.m. _____

Um sieben Uhr abends.
Um vier Uhr nachmittags.
Um halb acht morgens.

2. _____

Um zehn nach acht morgens.
Um elf Uhr abends.
Um Viertel nach eins nachmittags.

3. _____

Um sechs Uhr abends.
Um zwei Uhr nachmittags.
Um zwölf Uhr mittags.

4. _____

Um halb zwölf morgens.
Um drei Uhr nachmittags.
Um zwanzig vor elf abends.

5. _____

Um acht Uhr abends.
Um halb sechs morgens.
Um Viertel vor zwei nachmittags.

6. _____

Um halb drei nachmittags.
Um fünf nach acht abends.
Um zehn vor neun morgens.

Um sechs Uhr abends.
Um zehn vor zehn abends.
Um ein Uhr morgens.

7. _____

8. _____

Um zehn vor vier nachmittags.
Um zwölf Uhr mittags.
Um Viertel nach zehn abends.

Um Mitternacht.
Um fünf nach zehn morgens.
Um halb drei nachmittags.

9. _____

10. _____

F. You do certain things at a certain time every day. Express at what time you usually do the following:

EXAMPLE: gehen/in die Schule
Ich gehe um acht Uhr in die Schule.

1. kommen/in die Deutschklasse

_____

2. schreiben/die Aufgaben

_____

3. singen/im Chor

_____

4. telefonieren/ mit der Freundin

_____

5. üben/Klavier

_____

6. spielen/Tennis

_____

7. besuchen/die Großeltern

_____
_____

⑧ Now read this dialog and answer the questions that follow:

ANDREAS: Mutti, wieviel Uhr ist es?
MUTTI: Das Radio sagt, es ist halb zehn.
ANDREAS: Halb zehn? Unmöglich! Auf meiner Uhr ist es zehn nach acht.
MUTTI: Deine Uhr ist kaputt. Kauf dir eine neue!
ANDREAS: Ja, ja. Jetzt aber habe ich Verspätung.
MUTTI: Aber nein! Heute ist Sonntag. Heute ist keine Schule.
ANDREAS: Es ist Sonntag? Was für eine Überraschung! Gott sei Dank!

unmöglich _impossible_
auf _on_
kaputt _broken_
eine neue _a new one_
Verspätung haben _to be late_
keine _no_
die Überraschung _the surprise_
Gott sei Dank! _Thank God!_

__ÜBUNG__

G. Antworte auf deutsch!

1. Wer spricht mit Mutti?

_____

2. Was fragt Andreas?

_____

3. Was sagt das Radio?

_____

4. Warum geht Andreas' Uhr nicht?

_____

5. Warum ist keine Schule?

_____

GESPRÄCH

Wortschatz

schon *already*
warum denn? *why (in the world)?*
Samstag *Saturday*

doch *definitely*
Freitag *Friday*

PERSÖNLICHE FRAGEN

1. Wieviel Uhr ist es?

_____

2. Um wieviel Uhr ißt du das Frühstück?

_____

3. Um wieviel Uhr kommst du zur Schule?

_____

4. Um wieviel Uhr beginnt die Deutschklasse?

_____

5. Um wieviel Uhr endet der Schultag?

_____

DU

Complete each sentence with an appropriate time:

1. Ich komme zur Schule um _____ .

2. Die Deutschklasse beginnt um _____ .

3. Ich mache die Aufgaben um _____ .

4. Ich sehe fern (*I watch TV*) um _____ .

5. Ich esse das Mittagessen um _____ .

do at home

DIALOG

Complete the dialog with expressions chosen from the following list:

Heute ist Freitag.   Warum denn?
Ich habe Verspätung.   Es ist dreiviertel acht.
Wann ist die Party?   Die Uhr ist kaputt.

KULTURECKE

Die Uhr (Time)

Germany, like European countries in general, uses the 24-hour system for official time: schedules for planes, trains, radio and television programs, movies, sports events, and the like:

CONVENTIONAL TIME	OFFICIAL TIME
Noon	12 Uhr
1:15 p.m.	13 Uhr 15
5:30 p.m.	17 Uhr 30
9:45 p.m.	21 Uhr 45
Midnight	24 Uhr
10 past midnight	00 Uhr 10

Official time may also be written as 12.00, 13.15, 17.30, etc.

To calculate official time, add 12 to the conventional time for the hours between noon and midnight:

3:45 a.m.	03 Uhr 45
3:45 p.m.	15 Uhr 45

To calculate the conventional time, subtract 12 from the official time for the hours between noon and midnight:

14 Uhr 30   2:30 p.m.

7 Kleidung und Farben

How to Describe Things in German

 Can you guess the meanings of these new words?

die Kleidung

der Hut

der Mantel

der Anzug

die Hose

die Jacke

das Hemd

die Krawatte

die Schuhe

der Gürtel

die Badehose

die Socken

___ ÜBUNG ___

A. Karl-Heinz just went shopping. Identify the new clothes in his closet:

1. _____

2. _____

3. _____

4. _____

5. _____

6. _____

7. _____

8. _____

9. _____

10. _____   11. _____

2 Now try to figure out the meanings of these words:

das Kleid

die Bluse

der Rock

der Pullover

die Handschuhe

der Regenmantel

die Strümpfe

der Schal

der Badeanzug

— ÜBUNGEN

B. Anna has also bought some new clothes. Identify her purchases:

1. _____

2. _____

3. _____

4. _____

5. _____

6. _____

7. _____

8. _____

9. _____

C. Robert has just gotten a job in a clothing store. The boss asks him to pin labels on the models so that the prices can be put on later. Can you help him?

das Hemd	der Rock	der Mantel
die Schuhe	die Bluse	der Hut
die Hose	die Handschuhe	der Pullover
die Krawatte	der Anzug	der Gürtel
die Strümpfe	das Kleid	

D. You are making a list of new clothes you want to buy. Write the names of the items in German:

1. the socks _____

2. the shirt _____

3. the blouse _____

4. the jacket _____

5. the pants _____

6. the tie _____

7. the overcoat _____

8. the dress   _____

9. the hat   _____

10. the suit   _____

11. the skirt   _____

12. the belt   _____

13. the gloves   _____

14. the shoes   _____

15. the bathing suit   _____

16. the clothing   _____

17. the stockings   _____

3 Can you understand these two stories?

Bernd ist Schweizer. Er wohnt in der Schweiz. Er ist groß und blond. Er ist sehr stark. Er ist auch elegant. Er lernt Deutsch. Er liebt Deutsch, denn Deutsch ist nicht langweilig. Er ist sehr intelligent, interessant und beliebt. Er ist perfekt.

Schweizer *Swiss*
Schweiz *Switzerland*

langweilig *boring*

Johanna ist Deutsche. Sie wohnt in Deutschland. Sie ist klein und brünett. Sie ist besonders schön, wenn sie tanzt. Sie tanzt sehr gut. Sie lernt auch Deutsch. Sie ist interessant und sehr intelligent. Sie liebt die Jungen, aber sie ist ein bißchen schüchtern. Sie ist beliebt. Sie ist auch perfekt.

besonders *especially*

ein bißchen *a little*
schüchtern *shy*

___ ÜBUNGEN ___

E. Change all of the words in bold type to make the sentences true:

1. Bernd ist **Amerikaner.** _____

2. Bernd ist **sehr schwach.** _____

3. Er ist **klein und braun.** _____

4. Er liebt **Johanna**. _____

5. Er ist **häßlich**. _____

6. Johanna ist **Schweizerin**. _____

7. Sie ist **blond und groß**. _____

8. Sie **singt** sehr gut. _____

9. Sie lernt **Mathematik**. _____

10. Sie liebt **die Lehrer**. _____

F. Make a list from the story of all the adjectives that describe Bernd:

1. _____   **5.** _____

2. _____   **6.** _____

3. _____   **7.** _____

4. _____   **8.** _____

G. Make a list from the story of all the adjectives that describe Johanna:

1. _____   **5.** _____

2. _____   **6.** _____

3. _____   **7.** _____

4. _____   **8.** _____

4 Colors are adjectives, too. Can you figure out the color of each subject:

Die Tomate ist rot.

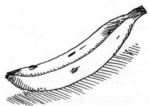

Die Banane ist gelb.

Die Katze ist schwarz.

Die Milch ist weiß.

Der Kaffee mit Milch ist braun.

Der Himmel ist blau.

Der Baum ist grün.

Die Rose ist rosa.

Die Orange ist orange.

Die Trauben sind lila.

Der Elefant ist grau.

Die Fahne ist rot, weiß und blau.

__ ÜBUNGEN _____

H. Identify the articles of clothing purchased by the Schiller family. Follow the example:

1. _____Der Rock ist blau._____
(blue)

2. _____
(black)

3. _____
(green)

4. _____
(red)

5. _____
(pink)

6. _____
(white)

7. _____   8. _____
     (brown)   (yellow)

I. Describe in German ten articles of clothing you bought recently by referring to their colors:

   EXAMPLE: Das Kleid ist schwarz.

   1. _____

   2. _____

   3. _____

   4. _____

   5. _____

   6. _____

   7. _____

   8. _____

   9. _____

   10. _____

Colors are not the only adjectives that describe people and things. Here are a few more. Can you guess their meanings?

groß

klein

schön

häßlich

stark

schwach

reich

arm

dick

dünn

$$5762.03$$
$$\times 382.96$$

schwer

$$1+3=$$

leicht

alt

jung

neu

ÜBUNG

J. You are asked to give your opinion about some people and things. Complete the sentence with the correct German adjective:

1. (big) Das Hotel ist _____ .

2. (modern) Der Regenmantel ist _____ .

3. (difficult) Die Frage ist nicht _____ .

4. (small) Der Garten ist sehr _____ .

5. (thin) Meine Schwester ist _____ .

6. (easy) Die Aufgabe ist _____ .

7. (thick) Das Wörterbuch ist _____ .

8. (ugly) Die Krawatte ist _____ .

9. (young) Das Mädchen ist _____ .

PERSÖNLICHE FRAGEN

1. Wer ist beliebt in der Schule?

_____

2. Wer ist intelligent?

_____

3. Was ist interessant?

_____

4. Welche Farbe hat das Deutschbuch?

_____

5. Was ist deine Lieblingsfarbe?

_____

_DU_

You are editor of the school yearbook. Fill in the students' names and describe each of them by using three adjectives:

Er ist   **Sie ist**

_____   _____

Sie sind

_____

GESPRÄCH

Wortschatz

welche *which* **na** *well*
was für *what* **die Kunst** *(the) art*
toll(e) *crazy*

DIALOG

You are the first person in this dialog, the one asking all the questions:

KULTURECKE

Die Größen (Sizes)

If you should buy a German article of clothing, don't be too frightened or too overjoyed by the sizes:

GIRLS — SKIRTS, DRESSES, COATS, PANTS

USA	3/4	5/6	7/8	9/10	11/12	13/14	15/16
Germany	32	34	36	38	40	42	44

GIRLS — BLOUSES

USA	30	32	34	36	38	40
Germany	38	40	42	44	46	48

GIRLS — SHOES

USA	4–4½	5–5½	6–6½	7–7½	8–8½	9–9½	10–10½
Germany	35	36	37	38	39	40	41

BOYS — SUITS, PANTS, COATS

USA	26	28	30	32	34	36	38	40
Germany	36	38	40	42	44	46	48	50

BOYS — SHIRTS

USA	14	14½	15	15½	16	16½	17
Germany	36	37	38	39	40	41	42

BOYS — SHOES

USA	7	7½	8	8½	9–9½	10–10½	11–11½
Germany	39	40	41	42	43	44	45

Which sizes do you wear?

German sizes are based on the metric system:

1 Meter = 39.37 inches	1 foot = 0.3 meters
3.28 feet	1 yard = 0.9 meters
1.09 yards	

How tall are you in meters? Check the chart:

FEET/INCHES	METERS/CENTIMETERS
5	1.52
5.1	1.54
5.2	1.57
5.3	1.59
5.4	1.62
5.5	1.64
5.6	1.68
5.7	1.70
5.8	1.73
5.9	1.75
5.10	1.78
5.11	1.80
6	1.83

How much do you weigh metrically?

1 kilo(gram) = 2.2 pounds
1 pound   = 0.45 kilograms

POUNDS	KILOGRAMS
90	40.5
100	45
110	49.5
120	54
130	58.5
140	63
150	67.5
160	72
170	76.5
180	81
190	85.5
200	90

8 *Sein oder nicht sein*

Professions and Trades; the Verb **sein;** Possessive Adjectives

 Wortschatz

der Lehrer

die Lehrerin

der Arzt

die Ärztin

der Zahnarzt

die Zahnärztin

129

der Sekretär

die Sekretärin

der Künstler

die Künstlerin

der Schauspieler

die Schauspielerin

der Krankenpfleger

die Krankenpflegerin

der Rechtsanwalt

die Rechtsanwältin

der Polizist

die Polizistin

der Briefträger

die Briefträgerin

der Feuerwehrmann

ÜBUNGEN

A. Wer ist es? (*Who is it?*) The people in your family have different professions. Match the occupation with the correct picture:

eine Zahnärztin   eine Lehrerin
ein Polizist   eine Rechtsanwältin
eine Schauspielerin   ein Krankenpfleger
ein Arzt   ein Feuerwehrmann
ein Sekretär   eine Briefträgerin

1. _____

2. _____

3. _____

4. _____

5. _____

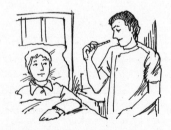

6. _____

7. _____

8. _____

9. _____

10. _____

B. Now identify these professions:

1. _____

2. _____

3. _____

4. _____

5. _____ 6. _____

7. _____ 8. _____

9. _____ 10. _____

 Read the following conversation and see if you can answer the questions about it. All of the verbs in bold type are some form of the verb **sein** (*to be*):

EMIL: Guten Tag, Robert! Guten Tag, Hans! Warum **seid ihr** hier?

HANS: Wir warten auf Frau Fuchs.

ROBERT: Hans interviewt sie für unsere Zeitung.

EMIL: Da kommt euere Frau Fuchs.

FRAU FUCHS: Guten Tag, Klasse. Hans, **bist du** fertig?

HANS: **Ich bin** bald fertig, Frau Fuchs. Robert holt jetzt sein Heft.

ROBERT: Hier **ist es.** Frau Fuchs, seit wann **sind Sie** Deutschlehrerin?

warten auf *wait for*
unsere *our*
   die Zeitung *the newspaper*
euere *your*
fertig *ready*
bald *soon*
   holt *is getting*
sein *his*
seit wann *since when*

FRAU FUCHS: Seit zehn Jahren.

ROBERT: **Ist Ihre Mutter** auch Lehrerin?

FRAU FUCHS: Nein. **Meine Mutter ist** Hausfrau, aber **ihr Bruder ist** Mathematiklehrer.

HANS: Haben Sie Geschwister?

FRAU FUCHS: Ja. Wir haben eine große Familie. Ich habe zwei Brüder und zwei Schwestern.

HANS: Was tun die Brüder?

FRAU FUCHS: **Sie sind** Mechaniker. Sie haben ihre eigene Garage.

ROBERT: Und die Schwestern?

FRAU FUCHS: **Beide sind** Krankenpflegerinnen. Sie arbeiten im Krankenhaus.

HANS: **Das ist** sehr interessant, Frau Fuchs. Vielen Dank.

FRAU FUCHS: Bitteschön. Hoffentlich **ist dein Artikel** gut, Hans.

seit *for*
Ihre *your*
die Hausfrau *the housewife*
ihr *her*
haben *to have*
  die Geschwister *brothers and sisters*

der Mechaniker *the mechanic*
eigene *own*

beide *both*

hoffentlich *hopefully*

C. Beantworte die Fragen!

1. Warum sind Hans und Robert da?

   _____

2. Was holt Robert?

   _____

3. Seit wann ist Frau Fuchs Deutschlehrerin?

   _____

4. Was ist ihre Mutter von Beruf?

   _____

5. Wer ist Mathematiklehrer?

   _____

6. Hat Frau Fuchs Geschwister?

   _____

7. Wie viele Brüder hat Frau Fuchs?

   _____

8. Wie viele Schwestern hat Frau Fuchs?

   _____

9. Was tun die Brüder?

_____

10. Was tun die Schwestern?

_____

11. Wo arbeiten die Schwestern?

_____

3 In the conversation you have just read, did you notice something special about these sentences?

> **Ihr Bruder ist _Mathematiklehrer._**
> **Frau Fuchs, seit wann sind Sie _Deutschlehrerin?_**

That's right. We do not use **ein** or **eine** with a profession, trade, or occupation after a form of the verb **sein.**

___ ÜBUNG ___

D. Choose eight people you know and write their professions. Write complete sentences:

EXAMPLE: Tom Cruise ist Schauspieler.

1. _____

2. _____

3. _____

4. _____

5. _____

6. _____

7. _____

8. _____

There is a new verb in our conversation — **sein** (*to be*). **Sein** is the infinitive. No other German verb is conjugated like **sein**. For this reason, **sein** is called irregular. Can you pick out the forms of **sein** from the conversation to match the following subjects?

ich ___*biN*___   wir ___*SiNd*___

du ___*bist*___   ihr ___*seid*___

er
sie } ___*isT*___   sie ___*SiNd*___
es

                         Sie ___*SiNd*___

Memorize all the forms of **sein**.

ÜBUNGEN

E. Here are some sentences in which a form of **sein** is used. Match the sentences with the pictures they describe:

Schnauzi ist ein Hund.   **Die Großeltern sind Schauspieler.**
Das Haus ist alt und häßlich.   **Horst ist groß und dünn.**
Ich bin Klassenpräsidentin.   **Sie ist eine beliebte Künstlerin.**
Karla ist Polizistin   **Sie sind sehr intelligent.**
Wir sind Freundinnen.   **Du bist stark.**

1. _____   2. _____

3. _____

4. _____

5. _____

6. _____

7. _____

8. _____

9. _____

10. _____

F. You have a pen pal in Germany who wants to know details about your family. Complete these sentences with the correct form of the verb **sein:**

1. Mein Vater _____ Rechtsanwalt.

2. Mein Bruder und ich _____ blond.

3. Meine Eltern _____ auch blond.

4. Wir _____ nicht groß.

5. Ich _____ dünn, aber mein Bruder _____ dick.

6. Meine Schwestern _____ Lehrerinnen; sie

   _____ sehr intelligent.

7. _____ du groß oder klein, dick oder dünn?

8. Du _____ mein Freund. Du _____ Deutscher;

   ich _____ Amerikaner.

---

5 Let's look at the conversation on pages 134–135 one more time. Can you find

all the German words that show possession? _____

_____

That's right. In the conversation, **mein, dein, sein, ihr, ihre, unsere, euere,** and **Ihre** are possessive adjectives. Possessive adjectives express ownership. Did you notice that some possessive adjectives end in **e** and some do not? Can you

guess why? _____
You are correct if you wrote that the noun following the possessive determines

whether or not to add an **e** ending. When do you add **e**? _____

_____

That's right. The feminine singular possessive and the plural possessive take an **e** ending; that is, whenever the definite article would be **die,** add **e** to the possessive.

Let's summarize all of the possessive adjectives:

mein, meine	*my*
dein, deine	*your* (familiar singular)
sein, seine	*his, its*
ihr, ihre	*her*
unser, unsere	*our*
euer, euere	*your* (familiar plural)
ihr, ihre	*their*
Ihr, Ihre	*your* (formal singular and plural)

6 Did you notice that **dein/deine, euer/euere,** and **Ihr/Ihre** all mean *your*? On the basis of what you already know about **du, ihr,** and **Sie,** use **dein/deine** when you talk to someone you would address as **du, euer/euere** when you talk to a group you would address as **ihr,** and **Ihr/Ihre** when you talk to a person or people you would address more formally as **Sie.**

7 Did you also notice that the word **ihr** now has four meanings? What are they?

_____

How do you know what **ihr** means? _____
That's right. You can tell what **ihr** means by the way it is used in a sentence. The context will give you the clues to help you figure out whether **ihr** means *you, your, her,* or *their.*

__ ÜBUNGEN _____

G. Supply the correct German form of the possessive in parentheses:

EXAMPLE: (my) _____ meine _____ Mutter

1. (my) _____ Vater

2. (your) _____ Tante

3. (his) _____ Kinder

4. (our) _____ Bücher

5. (your) _____ Autos

6. (their) _____ Lehrer

7. (your) _____ Mann

8. (her) _____ Bruder

9. (its) _____ Haus

10. (your) _____ Onkel

H. Match the English in the right column with the German in the left column. Write the matching letter in the space provided:

1. unsere Zeitung _____

2. euere Lehrerin _____

3. sein Heft _____

4. Ihre Mutter _____

5. meine Mutter _____

6. ihr Bruder _____

7. ihre Tante _____

8. deine Ärztin _____

9. seine Nummer _____

a. your mother
b. her brother
c. his notebook
d. their aunt
e. its number
f. our newspaper
g. your doctor
h. my mother
i. your teacher

GESPRÄCH

Wortschatz

willst du *do you want*   **mir gefallen** *I like*
vielleicht *perhaps*   **braunhaarig** *brown-haired*
mutig *brave*   **besser** *better*
Schade! *Too bad!*

_____ PERSÖNLICHE FRAGEN _____

1. Bist du Sekretärin?

_____

2. Bist du stark?

_____

3. Bist du groß oder klein?

_____

4. Bist du glücklich?

_____

5. Was ist dein Vater von Beruf?

_____

_____ DU _____

List in German five professions that interest you. Next to each profession, write a sentence that describes the person involved in that profession and say something about the profession.

EXAMPLE: Arzt   Der Arzt ist intelligent.

1. _____

2. _____

3. _____

4. _____

5. _____

DIALOG

Complete the dialog with suitable expressions of your own choice:

Das belegte Brot (German sandwich)

Bread, sausage, and cheese are the main components of a typical German sandwich.
Let's see how it's put together.

There are approximately two hundred kinds of bread and thirty kinds of rolls in the
German-speaking world. The main types of German bread are:

das Weißbrot (similar to U.S. white bread)
das Graubrot (wheat and rye mixture)
das Schwarzbrot, das Roggenbrot (whole rye or cracked rye/wheat combination)
der Pumpernickel (heavy, dark bread)

Germans like their bread **belegt** (*covered*) with any of the 1400 kinds of **Wurst** (*sausage*) and/or with **Käse** (*cheese*). The most important kinds of **Wurst** are:

die Mettwurst (ground pork sausage)
die Leberwurst (liverwurst)
die Blutwurst (blood sausage)
die Fleischwurst (baloney)
die Bratwurst (fried pork sausage)
die Frankfurter Würstchen (frankfurters)
die Wiener Würstchen (wieners)

The German **Belegte Brot** (open-faced sandwich) is similar to the American sandwich.
Unlike the American variety, however, the **Belegte Brot** has only one slice of bread
and is sometimes eaten with knife and fork.

Wiederholung II
(Aufgaben 5–8)

Aufgabe 5

0	null	13	dreizehn	26	sechsundzwanzig
1	eins	14	vierzehn	27	siebenundzwanzig
2	zwei	15	fünfzehn	28	achtundzwanzig
3	drei	16	sechzehn	29	neunundzwanzig
4	vier	17	siebzehn	30	dreißig
5	fünf	18	achtzehn	40	vierzig
6	sechs	19	neunzehn	50	fünfzig
7	sieben	20	zwanzig	60	sechzig
8	acht	21	einundzwanzig	70	siebzig
9	neun	22	zweiundzwanzig	80	achtzig
10	zehn	23	dreiundzwanzig	90	neunzig
11	elf	24	vierundzwanzig	100	hundert
12	zwölf	25	fünfundzwanzig		

+ und   − weniger/minus   × mal   ÷ durch   = ist

Aufgabe 6

a. Time is expressed as follows:

Wieviel Uhr ist es?	*What time is it?*
Es ist ein Uhr.	*It's one o'clock.*
Es ist fünf nach zwei.	*It's 2:05.*
Es ist Viertel nach drei.	*It's 3:15.*
Es ist halb vier.	*It's 3:30.*
Es ist fünfundzwanzig vor fünf.	*It's 4:35.*
Es ist Viertel vor sechs.	*It's 5:45.*
Es ist Mittag.	*It's 12:00 noon.*
Es ist Mitternacht.	*It's 12:00 midnight.*

b. To express "at" a specific time, use **um**:

Um **wieviel Uhr beginnt die Schule?**	*At what time does school begin?*
Die Schule beginnt *um* **8.**	*School begins at 8.*

146

Aufgabe 7

Adjectives describe people and things. Some common adjectives are:

rot	groß	klein
schwarz	schön	häßlich
braun	stark	schwach
grün	reich	arm
gelb	dick	dünn
weiß	schwer	leicht
blau	alt	neu
rosa	blond	jung
orange	elegant	intelligent
lila	interessant	langweilig
grau	beliebt	braunhaarig
schüchtern	gut	schlecht

Aufgabe 8

a. The verb **sein** (*to be*) is irregular. Memorize all of its forms:

ich bin	wir sind
du bist	ihr seid
er	
sie } ist	sie sind
es	
	Sie sind

b. The indefinite article (**ein, eine**) is omitted after forms of **sein** before the name of a profession or trade:

Herr Schmidt ist *Mechaniker.*	*Mr. Schmidt is a mechanic.*
Ilse ist *Briefträgerin.*	*Ilse is a letter carrier.*

c. The possessive adjectives are used to express that something belongs to someone:

mein, meine	(*my*)
dein, deine	(*your*)
sein, seine	(*his, its*)
ihr, ihre	(*her, their*)
unser, unsere	(*our*)
euer, euere	(*your*)
Ihr, Ihre	(*your*)

The gender and number of the noun following the possessive adjective determines which form to use. Masculine and neuter nouns use the form without the ending; feminine and plural nouns use the form with the **e** ending.

__ ÜBUNGEN _____

A. Write the German word next to the English word. Then circle the German word in the puzzle. The words may be read from left to right, right to left, up or down, or diagonally across:

strong _____   twenty _____   red _____

false _____   coat _____   two _____

pink _____   eleven _____   pants _____

dentist _____   black _____   skirt _____

policeman _____ milk _____   blouse _____

necktie _____   mailman _____   scarf _____

suit _____   rich _____   yellow _____

thirteen _____   purple _____   poor _____

```
A  N  Z  L  A  H  C  S  N  Z  T
R  H  O  B  L  U  S  E  A  W  O
S  E  R  E  I  C  H  H  N  A  R
E  Z  G  E  L  B  N  E  Z  N  S
L  I  B  Ä  C  A  P  E  U  Z  M
E  E  R  A  R  M  T  R  G  I  I
T  R  H  Z  S  T  A  R  K  G  L
N  D  T  C  A  L  F  L  E  P  C
A  N  Z  W  S  R  S  E  S  O  H
M  G  A  P  O  L  I  Z  I  S  T
U  R  W  C  R  Ä  A  O  W  R  Ä
K  A  K  R  G  H  L  F  P  E  B
T  S  C  H  W  A  R  Z  H  R  I
```

B. All of the following people are saying some numbers. What are they?

1. _____

2. _____

3. _____

4. _____

5. _____

6. _____

C. Write the times in German:

1. _____

2. _____

3. _____

4. _____

5. _____

6. _____

7. _____

8. _____

D. Would you like to know your future? Follow these simple rules to see what the cards have in store for you. Choose a number from two to eight. Starting in the upper left corner and moving from left to right, write down all the letters that appear above that number:

drei R	vier G	acht V	sieben E	fünf G	sechs G	drei E
vier E	fünf R	zwei G	sechs U	drei I	sieben W	zwei U
zwei T	vier S	sieben I	drei C	acht I	fünf O	acht E
sechs T	fünf S	acht L	zwei E	fünf S	sieben G	vier U
vier N	drei H	sieben E	fünf E	sechs E	zwei N	acht G
sechs F	acht L	vier D	drei T	sieben L	fünf F	sechs R
sieben I	fünf A	zwei O	sechs E	fünf M	drei U	acht Ü
sechs U	vier H	fünf I	sieben E	sechs N	vier E	zwei T
sieben B	zwei E	sechs D	vier I	acht C	fünf L	drei M
fünf I	sieben E	acht K	sechs E	fünf E	vier T	zwei N

E. This puzzle contains seven useful expressions. Fill in the German words, then read down the boxed column and find out to whom you would say them:

1.   ___ ___ ___ ___ ___ ___ ___ ___ ___ ___ ___ ___
2.   ___ ___ ___
3.   ___ ___ ___ ___ ___
4.   ___ ___ ___ ___ ___ ___
5.   ___ ___ ___
6.   ___ ___ ___ ___
7.   ___ ___ ___ ___ ___ ___ ___

1. Good-bye.
2. Super!
3. How are you?
4. Hello.

5. Thanks.
6. Too bad.
7. See you later.

F. Kreuzworträtsel:

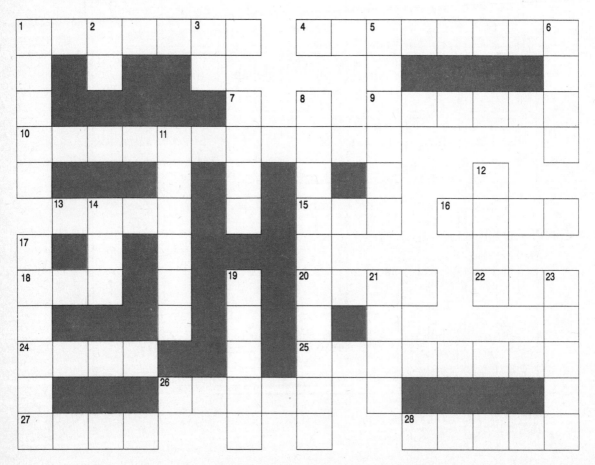

WAAGERECHT

1. _____ Uhr ist es?
4. Sein Bruder ist _____ . Er arbeitet am Schreibtisch.
9. Der Schal ist kurz (*short*), aber die _____ sind lang.
10. Er ist nicht dumm; er ist _____ .
13. "German Is Fun" ist ein interessantes _____ .
15. Der _____ ist sehr elegant.
16. Mein Vater ist _____ ; er arbeitet im Krankenhaus.
18. Inge ist Künstlerin; _____ Bruder ist Künstler.
20. Zwanzig weniger zwanzig ist _____ .
22. Acht _____ vier ist zwölf.
24. Die amerikanische Fahne ist rot, weiß und _____ .
25. Picasso ist _____ .
26. Ist das deine Jacke oder _____ Jacke?
27. Es ist zehn Minuten _____ elf.
28. Er hat viel Geld; er ist _____ .

SENKRECHT

1. Er spielt nicht viel; er spielt ein _____ .
2. Hans ist nicht groß; _____ ist klein.
3. Wieviel Uhr ist _____ ?
5. Wieviel _____ die Bluse?
6. Die Rose ist _____ .
7. _____ du Feuerwehrmann?
8. Dieter arbeitet in einer Garage. Er ist _____ .
11. Herr Meyer ist _____ . Ich bin in seiner Deutschklasse.
12. Elefanten sind _____ .
14. Es ist acht _____ .
17. Zwanzig weniger dreizehn ist _____ .
19. Mein Bruder ist _____ ; er ist nicht groß.
21. Mein Rock ist zu kurz, und mein Schal ist zu _____ .
23. Achtzehn _____ neun ist zwei.

G. Picture Story. Can you read this story? Much of it is in picture form. Whenever you come to a picture, read it as if it were a German word:

Es ist Samstag. Heute ist keine . Erika ist ein . Sie ist 12

Jahre alt. Heute geht sie in die Stadt einkaufen. Ihre und kommen

mit. Ihr [img] kommt nicht mit — er ist [img] und muß im [img]

arbeiten. Der [img] geht heute in die [img], denn er studiert an der

[img] .

Es ist [img] . Erika, ihre [img] und ihre [img] fahren mit dem

[img] in die Stadt. Erika braucht [img] . Sie kauft ein Paar [img] .

Die [img] sind schwarz. Dann kauft sie ein schönes [img] . Es ist blau.

Ihre [img] braucht eine neue [img] . Sie findet keine in der richtigen

Farbe. Alle sind rosa. Für den Bruder kaufen sie ein [img] .

Jetzt fahren sie nach Hause. Alle haben etwas Neues. Und der [img] hat die
Rechnung.

Wortschatz

die Stadt *the city*	**finden** *to find*	**die Rechnung** *the bill*
fahren *to travel*	**für** *for*	

Dritter Teil

9 _Sport und Spiel_

What to Say When You Like Something: **gern, lieber, am liebsten;** the Verb **haben**

1 Can you guess the meanings of these popular games?

das Fußballspiel
der Fußball

das Basketballspiel
der Basketball

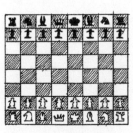

das Schachspiel
Schach

das Tennis

das Tischtennis

die Karten

das Baseballspiel
der Baseball

das Volleyballspiel
der Volleyball

__ ÜBUNGEN _____

A. Match the words with the correct pictures:

das Basketballspiel   das Fußballspiel
das Tennis   das Schachspiel
die Karten   das Tischtennis

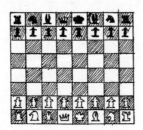

1. _____

2. _____

3. _____

4. _____

5. _____

6. _____

B. Was spielen wir? Wir spielen . . .

1. _____

2. _____

3. _____

4. _____

5. _____

6. _____

 Was machen wir? (*What are we doing?*)

Wir schwimmen.

Wir wandern.

Wir turnen.

Wir reiten.

Wir laufen Ski.

ÜBUNG

C. Was machen sie?

1. Sie _____ .

2. Sie _____ .

3. Sie _____ .

4. Sie _____ .

5. Sie _____ .

3 Now let's see if you can understand this story about Germans and their sports:

Die Deutschen haben Sport und Spiel sehr gern. Es gibt Sportvereine für alle — Kinder und Erwachsene.

Welchen Sport treiben die Deutschen am liebsten? Bei gutem Wetter spielen sie gern Fußball oder Tennis. Wenn es besonders warm ist, schwimmen sie auch gern. Aber am liebsten wandern sie, denn dafür braucht man nur gute Schuhe und keine besondere Ausrüstung.

Wenn das Wetter schlecht oder kalt ist, spielen die Deutschen auch gern Basketball. Sie schwimmen dann auch, aber im Hallenbad, nicht im Freien. Andere spielen Karten, Schach oder Tischtennis.

Wir fragen Hans, was er gern spielt. Er antwortet, er spielt Fußball am liebsten, aber er hat auch Tischtennis gern. Er sagt, er hat Tischtennis lieber als Schulaufgaben.

haben . . . gern *like*
der Sportverein *the sports club*
alle *everybody*
Erwachsene *adults*
welchen *which*
Sport treiben *to engage in a sport*
am liebsten *best of all*
bei gutem Wetter *in good weather*
wenn *whenever*
dafür *for that*
brauchen *to need*
man *one*
nur *only*
besondere *special*
die Ausrüstung *the equipment*
das Wetter *the weather*
das Hallenbad *the indoor pool*
im Freien *outdoors*
andere *others*
hat . . . lieber *prefers*
als *than*

ÜBUNG

D. **Beanworte die Fragen!**

1. Was haben die Deutschen gern?

2. Was gibt es für alle?

3. Was tun sie bei gutem Wetter?

_____

4. Was spielen sie bei schlechtem Wetter?

_____

5. Was spielt Hans am liebsten?

_____

6. Was spielt er auch noch gern?

_____

7. Macht er die Schulaufgaben gern?

_____

 In the story you just read, you learned about Germans' likes and dislikes in sports. Let's take a closer look at how we say that we like or dislike something in German:

First you need to know a special verb, **haben** (_to have_):

ich	habe	_I have_
du	hast	_you have_
er		_he_
Sie}	hat	_she} has_
es		_it_
wir	haben	_we have_
ihr	habt	_you have_
sie	haben	_they have_
Sie	haben	_you have_

Which forms of **haben** follow a different pattern from the regular verbs you know? That's right! The **du**-form is **hast** and the **er, sie, es**-form is **hat;** the **b** of **haben** was dropped. Otherwise, **haben** is pretty easy.

___ ÜBUNG _____

E. Complete the sentences with the correct forms of **haben:**

1. Ich _____ Fußball gern.

2. Meine Mutter _____ zwei Schwestern.

3. Was _____ du?

4. Hans und Otto _____ heute keine Aufgaben.

5. Wir _____ das Wörterbuch.

6. Sie _____ eine nette Familie, Frau Braun.

⑤ Now let's get back to liking something. There are three degrees of liking in German:

> **Ich** *habe* **Biologie** *gern.*   *I like biology.*
> **Ich** *habe* **Mathe** *lieber.*   *I like math better. I prefer math.*
> **Ich** *habe* **Deutsch** *am liebsten.*   *I like German best (of all).*

When you like something, which word do you add to the sentence?

_____ When you like something better than something else, which

word do you add? _____ When you like something best of all,

which words do you add to the sentence? _____ Which

verb do you use when you like something? _____

⑥ Let's see what happens when you like DOING something:

> **Ich schwimme** *gern.*   *I like swimming. I like to swim.*
> **Monika lernt** *gern* **Deutsch.**   *Monika likes learning German.*
> **Er spielt** *gern* **Tischtennis.**   *He likes playing table tennis.*

When you like doing something, you use the verb that expresses that action instead of **haben.**

How would you say *I like swimming better?*

_____

How would you say *I like swimming best?*

_____

How would you say *Monika likes learning German better?*

_____

And if she likes learning German best?

_____

How would you say *Horst likes playing table tennis better?*

_____

And if table tennis were his favorite sport?

_____

7 What happens when you don't like something or don't like doing something?

Which word do you think you should add to the sentence? _____

That's right! You add **nicht.** And where do you place **nicht?** _____
Correct again! You place the **nicht** in front of **gern.** The opposite of **Er spielt gern Tennis** is **Er spielt nicht gern Tennis.**

__ ÜBUNGEN __

F. Match the English with the correct German sentences. Write the matching letter in the space provided:

1. Der Junge hat Fußball gern. ____

2. Das Mädchen hat Deutsch lieber. ____

3. Die Eltern haben Schach am liebsten. ____

4. Mein Vater hat Fußball am liebsten. ____

5. Was spielst du gern? ____

6. Sie kaufen gern Platten. ____

7. Wir singen nicht gern. ____

8. Was spielst du lieber? ____

a. The girl prefers German.
b. My father likes soccer best.
c. The boy likes soccer.
d. What do you prefer to play?
e. They like to buy records.
f. We don't like to sing.
g. The parents like chess best.
h. What do you like to play?

G. Die Umfrage (*The Opinion Poll*). Complete each statement about your likes and dislikes. Use **gern, nicht gern, lieber** or **am liebsten,** as appropriate.

Sport und Spiel:

1. Ich spiele _____ Fußball.

2. Ich spiele _____ Basketball.

3. Ich spiele _____ Volleyball.

4. Ich laufe _____ Ski.

5. Ich schwimme _____ .

6. Ich turne _____ .

7. Ich habe Wandern _____ .

8. Ich habe Kartenspielen _____ .

9. Ich habe Schach _____ .

Farben:

10. Ich habe rot _____ .

11. Ich habe blau _____ .

12. Ich habe grün _____ .

13. Ich habe gelb _____ .

14. Ich habe lila _____ .

Schule:

15. Ich lerne _____ Mathematik.

16. Ich lerne _____ Deutsch.

17. Ich lerne _____ Englisch.

GESPRÄCH

Wortschatz

gewinnen *to win*	**unter die Nase reiben** *to rub in*
Du hast recht. *You're right.*	**doch** *after all*
gewöhnlich *usually*	**gehen wir** *let's go*
weiß *know*	**etwas** *something*
schon *already*	**naschen** *to snack, have a snack*

PERSÖNLICHE FRAGEN

1. Hast du Deutsch gern?

_____

2. Was spielst du gern?

_____

3. Trinkst du lieber Milch oder Cola?

_____

4. Was haben deine Eltern lieber, das Theater oder das Kino?

_____

5. Was spielst du lieber, Tennis oder Fußball?

_____

6. Was spielst du am liebsten?

_____

_DU_

You are joining a computer dating service. Fill out this **Anmeldeformular** (_application form_):

Name: _____			
Wie alt bist du? _____			
Was hast du gern?			
	nicht gern	**gern**	**lieber**	**am liebsten**
Fußball	☐	☐	☐	☐
Baseball	☐	☐	☐	☐
Karten spielen	☐	☐	☐	☐
Basketball	☐	☐	☐	☐
Reiten	☐	☐	☐	☐
Schach	☐	☐	☐	☐
Schwimmen	☐	☐	☐	☐
Skilaufen	☐	☐	☐	☐
Tennis	☐	☐	☐	☐
Tischtennis	☐	☐	☐	☐
Turnen	☐	☐	☐	☐
Volleyball	☐	☐	☐	☐
Wandern	☐	☐	☐	☐

DIALOG

You are the second person in the dialog. Respond in accordance with the cues:

KULTURECKE

Sport in Deutschland

During their free time, many Germans enjoy participating in and watching sports. The most popular spectator sport is **Fußball** (*soccer*). Some Germans are also familiar with American football (**der amerikanische Fußball**). Here are the pictograms of the Olympic sports that are popular in the German-speaking world:

Basketball	**Bogenschießen**	**Boxen**
Fußball	**Handball**	**Hockey**
Judo	**Leichtathletik/Laufen**	**Radfahren**
Reiten	**Ringen**	**Volleyball**

Which sport do you like to play?

10 *Die Mahlzeiten*

Accusative with Definite Articles; the Verb **essen**

1 Here is something you can really sink your teeth into!

Zum Frühstück (*for breakfast*)

das Ei

der Käse

die Wurst

das Brötchen

Zum Mittagessen (*for lunch*)

das Sandwich

Zum Abendessen (*for dinner*)

die Suppe

der Salat

die Tomate

das Fleisch

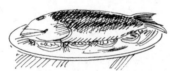
der Fisch

das Huhn

das Brot

die Kartoffel

der Spargel

die Mohrrüben
die Karotten

die Bohnen

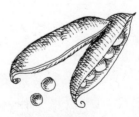
die Erbsen

__ ÜBUNG _____

A. Your mother asks you what you would like to eat for dinner in the coming week.
Tell her:

EXAMPLE: Ich esse gern Wurst.

1. _____

2. _____

3. _____

4. _____

5. _____

6. _____

7. _____

8. _____

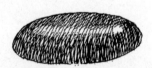

9. _____

10. _____

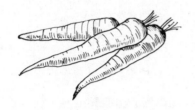

11. _____   12. _____

13. _____   14. _____

 Here's something to fill out the meals:

Zum Nachtisch (*for dessert*)

die Torte   **der Kuchen**   **das Eis**

Zum Naschen (*for snack*)

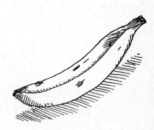

die Trauben   **der Apfel**   **die Banane**

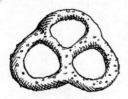

die Brezel

die Kartoffelchips

Zum Trinken (*to drink*)

der Kaffee

der Tee

die Milch

der Orangensaft

der Apfelsaft

der Traubensaft

__ ÜBUNGEN _____

B. Angelika is planning a shopping trip to **die Bäckerei** (*bakery*), **die Konditorei** (*pastry shop*), **die Fleischerei** (*butcher shop*), **das Milchgeschäft** (*dairy store*), and **der Markt** (*open-air market*). Help her organize the following items by placing each one under the store where it is found:

Äpfel	**Erbsen**	**Mohrrüben**
Bananen	**Fleisch**	**Salat**
Bohnen	**Huhn**	**Spargel**
Brot	**Kartoffeln**	**Tomaten**
Brötchen	**Käse**	**Torte**
Eier	**Kuchen**	**Trauben**
Eis	**Milch**	**Wurst**

C. It's the middle of the afternoon and time for a snack. Here is what you find in the refrigerator:

1. _____

2. _____

3. _____

4. _____

5. _____

6. _____

7. _____

8. _____

9. _____

10. _____

11. _____

12. _____

③ Now let's read about the Schmidt's dinner:

Es ist Sonntag, und die ganze Familie ißt das Abendessen. Die Tochter deckt den Tisch. Mutter holt das Essen. Der Vater ißt gern Huhn, Kartoffeln und Spargel. Die kleine Tochter hat Spargel nicht gern. Sie ißt grüne Bohnen statt Spargel. Der Sohn ist wie der Vater. Er ißt auch Huhn, Kartoffeln und Spargel. Schließlich nimmt sich die Mutter etwas Huhn, Kartoffeln und Bohnen. Jetzt essen alle etwas.

decken *to set*
holen *to get*

statt *instead of*

nimmt sich *takes for herself*

Zum Nachtisch essen sie eine Torte. Die Kinder bekommen kleine Portionen, und der Vater und die Mutter bekommen größere Portionen. Es schmeckt sehr gut.

bekommen *to receive*
größere *larger*
   schmecken *to taste*

Nachher räumen Vater und Sohn das Geschirr vom Tisch.

räumen *to clear*
   das Geschirr *the dishes*

__ ÜBUNGEN __

D. **Beantworte die Fragen!**

1. Welcher Tag ist es?

   _____

2. Was macht die Tochter?

   _____

3. Was ißt der Vater gern?

   _____

4. Was ißt die Tochter nicht gern?

   _____

5. Was essen sie zum Nachtisch?

   _____

6. Wer räumt das Geschirr vom Tisch?

   _____

We already know that **trinken** means *to drink*. Let's learn a new verb, but you will notice some irregularities:

essen	*to eat*
ich esse	*I eat, I am eating*
du *ißt*	*you eat, you are eating*
er *ißt*	*he eats, he is eating*
sie *ißt*	*she eats, she is eating*
es *ißt*	*it eats, it is eating*
wir essen	*we eat, we are eating*
ihr eßt	*you eat, you are eating*
sie essen	*they eat, they are eating*
Sie essen	*you eat, you are eating*

Do you see why this verb is irregular? The **du** and **er, sie** (*she*), **es** forms have an **i** as the root vowel instead of an **e**, and **du** uses the same ending as **er, sie** (*she*), **es**. Otherwise, the remaining endings are all regular. The verb **essen** is called an **e → i** stem-changing verb because the root vowel in its stem changes.

__ ÜBUNG _____

E. It's mealtime! Tell what everyone is eating by completing the sentences with the correct forms of **essen**:

1. Die Familie _____ das Abendessen.

2. Vater _____ gern Huhn, Kartoffeln und Spargel.

3. Die kleine Tochter _____ Bohnen statt Spargel.

4. Der Sohn _____ auch Huhn, Kartoffeln und Spargel.

5. Jetzt _____ alle etwas.

 Now let's see if you can figure out how to use the accusative. Look carefully at the following pairs of sentences:

I	II
Der Spargel schmeckt gut.	Der Sohn ißt gern *den Spargel.*
Die Torte schmeckt auch gut.	Das Kind ißt gern *die Torte.*
Das Huhn schmeckt am besten.	Der Vater ißt gern *das Huhn.*
Die Kartoffeln schmecken nicht gut.	Die Tochter ißt *die Kartoffeln* am liebsten.

Underline the verb in each sentence. Now draw an arrow from the verb to the other word in the sentence that tells you which form of the verb to use. The word that the arrow points to is the SUBJECT of the sentence. In which group

are **Spargel, Torte, Huhn,** and **Kartoffeln** the subject? _____ That's right! The nouns in Group I are the subject of the sentence because they "do" the action of the verb and determine the form of the verb.

Now look at the sentences in Group II again. Which nouns are the subject of

each sentence? _____

If you wrote **Sohn, Kind, Vater,** and **Tochter,** you are correct because these nouns "do" the action of the verb. In Group II, **Spargel, Torte, Huhn,** and **Kartoffeln** are the DIRECT OBJECT of the sentences because they receive the action of the verb and in no way determine the form of the verb, **ißt.**

In German, we call the subject the NOMINATIVE (CASE), and we call the direct object the ACCUSATIVE (CASE). "Case" means the form of a noun, article, or adjective that indicates its relationship to other words.

⑥ Let's take a closer look at the noun phrases in the pairs of sentences. Underline all the words that mean "the." Then fill in the rule:

der, die, das in Group I are in the _____ .

den, die, das in Group II are in the _____ .

The accusative form of **der** is _____ .

The accusative form of **die** is _____ .

The accusative form of **das** is _____ .

How many ways are there to say "the" in German? There are _____ .

When do you use **der?** _____

        den? _____

        die? 1. _____

              2. _____

              3. _____

                  _____

das? 1. _____

2. _____

ÜBUNGEN

F. Answer the question with nouns of your choice:

Was ißt du?   Ich esse . . .

1. den _____   7. das _____

2. das _____   8. den _____

3. den _____   9. die _____

4. den _____   10. das _____

5. das _____   11. die _____

6. die _____   12. den _____

G. Was möchtest du essen? Ich möchte . . . *(What would you like to eat? I would like . . .)* Complete each response with the correct definite article:

1. Ich möchte _____ Apfel.

2. Ich möchte _____ Trauben.

3. Ich möchte _____ Sandwich.

4. Ich möchte _____ Banane.

5. Ich möchte _____ Spargel.

6. Ich möchte _____ Kuchen.

7. Ich möchte _____ Eis.

8. Ich möchte _____ Salat.

9. Ich möchte _____ Bohnen.

10. Ich möchte _____ Brezel.

H. Charles the Cook (**Karl der Koch**) has prepared the three meals for today. Can you tell in German what they consist of? Choose from the list of foods on the right:

zum Frühstück

_____

_____

_____

_____

der Fisch

das Ei

das Brot

die Suppe

die Erbsen

der Kaffee

zum Mittagessen

das Sandwich

_____

die Milch

_____

der Apfel

_____

der Orangesaft

das Eis

_____

_____

zum Abendessen

_____

_____

_____

_____

GESPRÄCH

Wortschatz

selbstverständlich *of course*
dazu *with it*
möchten Sie *would you like*

Pommes frites *french fries*
Kleingeld *small change*
Zehnmarkschein *10-mark bill*

——————— PERSÖNLICHE FRAGEN ———————

1. Was ißt du gern?

_____

2. Was trinkst du gern?

_____

3. Was ißt du zum Abendessen?

_____

4. Was ißt deine Mutter zum Nachtisch?

_____

5. Was ißt dein Vater gern?

_____

——————————— DU ———————————

You are shopping for your family. Make a shopping list of the things you would buy:

1. _____   **6.** _____

2. _____   **7.** _____

3. _____   **8.** _____

4. _____   **9.** _____

5. _____   **10.** _____

DIALOG

You are the second person in the dialog. Write an original response to each dialog line:

KULTURECKE

Einkaufen (Shopping)

Besides the large, American-style supermarkets, the small shop still plays a role in Germany, particularly in the smaller towns and villages. The Germans prefer the small, individualized neighborhood stores, where they can be sure of the quality and freshness of the products they buy. In the course of a day, a German person might visit these stores:

Supermarkt

Fleischerei

Bäckerei

Konditorei

Lebensmittelgeschäft

Obst- und Gemüseladen

Feinkostgeschäft

What would you buy in each of these stores?

Also, on market days (once or twice a week, year-round), the open-air market is held all over Germany. One can buy all sorts of foods here: eggs, salami, cheese, fruits and vegetables, fish and meat.

The Germans use the metric system when they go shopping.

WHEN YOU WEIGH FOODS

1 Kilogram (Kg) (1000 Gramm)	=	2.2 pounds (1 lbs)
1 Pfund (Pf)	=	500 Gramm
½ Pfund	=	250 Gramm
¼ Pfund	=	125 Gramm

A German pound is slightly heavier than its American counterpart. The American pound is approximately 454 grams. '

WHEN YOU MEASURE LIQUIDS

1 Liter (L)	=	1.06 quarts
1000 Milliliter (ML)	=	1 Liter

How many milliliters are in a pint?

11 Das Picknick

Accusative with Indefinite Articles; Accusative Prepositions

1 Wortschatz

das Besteck

der Löffel   die Gabel   das Messer

der Teller   die Tasse   das Glas

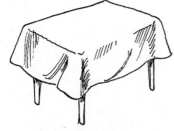  

die Tischdecke   die Serviette   die Thermosflasche

die Butter   das Salz und der Pfeffer   die Limonade/das Cola

187

die Gurken   **der Ketchup**   **der Senf**

___ ÜBUNGEN _____

A. Supply the appropriate definite article. Sometimes the noun is in the nominative and sometimes it is in the accusative:

1. _____ Serviette ist weiß.

2. _____ Lehrer bringt _____ Ketchup.

3. _____ Lehrerin bringt _____ Löffel.

4. _____ Tasse ist groß.

5. _____ Tischdecke ist blau und weiß.

6. Er bringt _____ Senf, _____ Salz und _____ Pfeffer.

B. Deck den Tisch und identifiziere die Dinge! (*Set the table and identify the objects in German.*)

_____   _____

_____   _____

_____   _____

_____   _____

_____   _____

_____   _____

C. You are going on a picnic. What are you taking along?

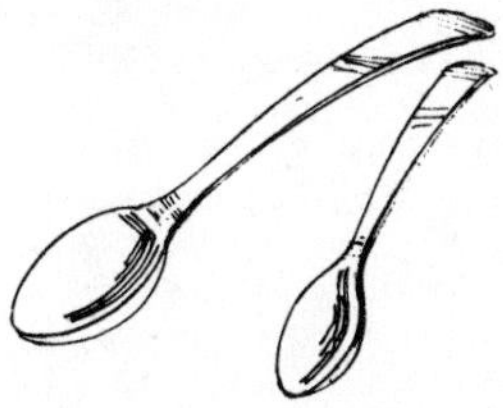

1.  _____   2. _____

3.  _____   4. _____

5.  _____   6. _____

7. _____   8. _____

9. _____   10. _____

 Now see if you can read this story and do the exercises about it. All of the phrases in bold type begin with indefinite articles in the accusative:

Die Deutschklasse macht heute **ein Picknick**. Die Schüler wollen deutsche Spezialitäten vorbereiten. Dann gehen sie durch **einen schönen** Park und bringen die Spezialitäten für die Klassenkameraden zum Picknick. Emil bringt **einen Korb** mit Kartoffelsalat. Der Kartoffelsalat ist sehr gut. Susanne kommt nicht ohne **eine Bratwurst**. Die Bratwurst ist ausgezeichnet. Hans bringt **ein Brot**. Er hat nichts gegen Pumpernickel, aber er bringt zwei Roggenbrote. Heidi bringt **einen Nachtisch**. Sie bringt **einen Apfelkuchen**. Der Apfelkuchen hat viele Äpfel. Marianne bringt die Trauben. Die Trauben sind süß. Alles schmeckt sehr gut!

wollen *want to*
   vorbereiten *to prepare*
durch *through*
   schön *beautiful*
Klassenkameraden
   classmates
   zum *to the*
der Korb *the basket*
ohne *without*
   die Bratwurst *the fried
   sausage*
das Roggenbrot *the rye
   bread*
süß *sweet*

Und was trinken sie alle? Um die Ecke kommt die Lehrerin. Sie hat **eine Erdbeerbowle**. Alle Schüler trinken gern Bowle.

um *around*
   die Ecke *the corner*
die Erdbeerbowle
   strawberry punch

Das Picknick macht viel Spaß. Die Gäste amüsieren sich alle gut.

Spaß machen *to be fun*
   die Gäste *the guests*
   sich amüsieren *to enjoy
   oneself*

__ ÜBUNGEN __

D. **Ergänze die Sätze!**

1. Die Schüler wollen _____ vorbereiten.

2. Emil bringt _____ .

3. Susanne bringt _____ .

4. Hans bringt _____ .

5. Heidi bringt _____ .

6. Der Apfelkuchen hat viele _____ .

7. Die Trauben sind _____ .

8. Alles schmeckt sehr _____ .

9. Die Schüler trinken gern _____ .

10. Das Picknick macht _____ .

E. **Beanworte die Fragen!**

1. Was macht die Deutschklasse?

   _____

2. Was wollen die Schüler vorbereiten?

   _____

3. Was bringt Emil?

   _____

4. Was hat Susanne besonders gern?

   _____

5. Welches Brot hat Hans am liebsten?

   _____

3 Let's see what you remember about the nominative and accusative. Circle the correct choice to complete the rules:

The nominative/accusative is the subject of the sentence.

The nominative/accusative is the direct object of the sentence.

The subject/direct object does the action of the verb and affects the verb form.

The subject/direct object receives the action of the verb and does not affect the verb form.

4 Let's summarize the nominative and accusative with the indefinite article:

MASC.	FEM.	NEUT.	PL.
ein	eine	ein	meine
einen	eine	ein	meine

are in the _____ .

are in the _____ .

The accusative of **ein** is _____ when **ein** is masculine.

The accusative of **ein** is _____ when **ein** is neuter.

The accusative of **eine** is _____ .

IMPORTANT NOTE: The possessives **mein, dein, sein, ihr, unser, euer, Ihr,** and **kein** all follow the same pattern as **ein**.

___ ÜBUNGEN _____

F. Fill in the correct form of *a* or *an* in the accusative:

1. _____ Cola   6. _____ Limonade

2. _____ Gabel   7. _____ Glas

3. _____ Löffel   8. _____ Tasse

4. _____ Messer   9. _____ Bratwurst

5. _____ Nachtisch   10. _____ Platz

G. Complete the following expressions in the accusative:

EXAMPLE: (my) _____ meine _____ Tasse

1. (my) _____ Gabel   2. (his) _____ Glas

3. (our) _____ Picknick **7.** (my) _____ Roggenbrot

4. (your) _____ Limonade **8.** (her) _____ Kartoffelsalat

5. (their) _____ Löffel **9.** (our) _____ Besteck

6. (no) _____ Platz **10.** (your) _____ Erdbeerbowle

H. Complete these statements with the correct forms in German of the words in parentheses:

    1. (my) _____ Vater ißt (no) _____ Kartoffelsalat.

    2. (her) _____ Mutter hat (a) _____ Limonade.

    3. (your) _____ Bruder bringt (a) _____ Bowle.

    4. (our) _____ Schwester ißt heute (a) _____ Bratwurst.

    5. (the) _____ Kind trinkt (his) _____ Milch.

    6. (my) _____ Mann möchte (a) _____ Tasse Kaffee.

    7. (his) _____ Frau bringt (a) _____ Freundin.

    8. (the) _____ Schüler kauft (a) _____ Stück Käse.

    9. (their) _____ Lehrerin hat (a) _____ Brot.

    10. (the) _____ Lehrer bringt (a) _____ Tischdecke.

5 Let's look at the prepositional phrases that appeared in the reading selection:

> durch *einen Park*
> für *die Klassenkameraden*
> gegen *den Pumpernickel*
> ohne die *Bratwurst*
> um *die Ecke*

The objects of all of these prepositions are in the same case. What case is it?

_____ You guessed correctly if you said that they are in the accusative. That is because, when these prepositions introduce the prepositional phrase, their objects must be in the accusative. The noun phrase may be introduced by a definite article, indefinite article, possessive, or **kein**.

If you wanted to use possessives, the phrases above would look like these:

> durch *ihren Park*
> für *seine Klassenkameraden*
> gegen *meinen Pumpernickel*
> ohne *deine Bratwurst*
> um *unsere Ecke*

It's best to memorize the accusative prepositions with their meanings:

durch	*through*	**ohne**	*without*
für	*for*	**um**	*around*
gegen	*against*		

___ ÜBUNGEN _____

I. Complete each sentence with the German equivalent of the preposition in parentheses:

1. (through) Die Familie geht _____ den Park.

2. (for) Ist diese Bratwurst _____ deine Freundin?

3. (without) Ich gehe _____ meinen Freund.

4. (against) Ich habe nichts _____ seinen Bruder.

5. (around) Es gibt schönes Gras _____ das Haus.

J. Complete each sentence with the appropriate German equivalent for the English word in parentheses:

1. (his) Er kauft eine Bluse für _____ Frau.

2. (the) Er geht durch _____ Schule.

3. (my) Er hat nichts gegen _____ Freund.

4. (his) Wir fahren ohne _____ Bruder.

5. (the) Sie gehen schnell um _____ Park.

6. (our) Ich gehe durch _____ Haus.

7. (my) Ist das für _____ Schwester?

8. (her) Was hast du gegen _____ Mann?

GESPRÄCH

Wortschatz

mehr *more*	**gleich** *immediately*
dir *you*	**reichen** *pass*
genug *enough*	**allein** *alone*

DIALOG

It's your first picnic with a special friend. How would you respond?

_____ PERSÖNLICHE FRAGEN _____

1. Wann machst du ein Picknick?

_____

2. Wer kommt zum Picknick?

_____

3. Was bringen die Gäste zum Picknick?

_____

4. Was spielst du beim Picknick?

_____

5. Wer räumt alles vom Tisch?

_____

_____ DU _____

You are in charge of planning the menu for a class picnic. **Wer bringt was?** (*Who is bringing what?*)

WER?	WAS?
_____	_____
_____	_____
_____	_____
_____	_____
_____	_____
_____	_____
_____	_____

KULTURECKE

Ein deutsches Picknick

If you were going on a picnic in a German-speaking country, you would pack a different basket than you would for an American picnic. Compare the scenes below and point out the differences you see:

12 *Die Verkehrsmittel*

Stem-Changing Verbs: a→ä; au→äu

1 How do you get from here to there?

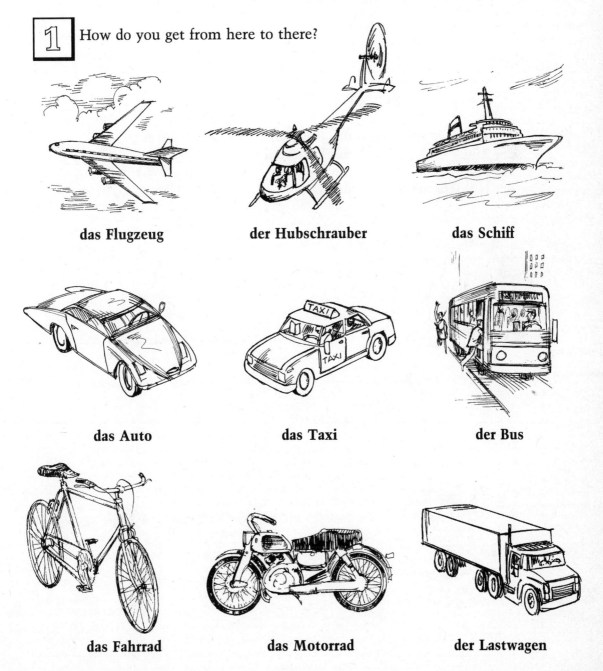

das Flugzeug

der Hubschrauber

das Schiff

das Auto

das Taxi

der Bus

das Fahrrad

das Motorrad

der Lastwagen

der Zug

die Straßenbahn

die U-Bahn

__ ÜBUNG _____

A. Match the words with the corresponding pictures:

das Auto	das Fahrrad	das Flugzeug
der Zug	das Motorrad	das Schiff
der Bus	die U-Bahn	die Straßenbahn
der Hubschrauber	das Taxi	der Lastwagen

1. _____

2. _____

3. _____

4. _____

5. _____

6. _____

7. _____

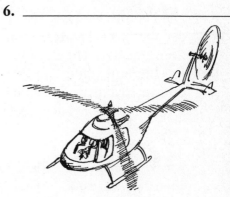

8. _____

9. _____

10. _____

11. _____

12. _____

Can you understand this story? See if you can spot all the forms of the verb **fahren** (*to go, travel*):

In New York gibt es viel zu tun. Es gibt viele Museen und Geschäfte. Die Familie Schmidt aus Hamburg besucht New York. Herr Schmidt macht eine Geschäftsreise. Frau Schmidt und **die Kinder fahren** gern mit. Für sie ist diese Reise wie Ferien.

Die Familie bleibt bei Verwandten in der Stadt. Jeden Morgen **fährt Herr Schmidt** mit der U-Bahn zum Zentrum. Die U-Bahn fährt schnell. Frau Schmidt möchte einkaufen. **Sie fährt** mit dem Bus hin und mit dem Taxi zurück, denn sie hat viele Pakete. Die Kinder bleiben bei den Verwandten. **Sie fahren** nicht mit.

Am Wochenende hat die ganze Familie frei. Sie machen eine Tagestour. „**Fährst du** lieber mit dem Zug, oder soll ich ein Auto mieten?" fragt Herr Schmidt. Frau Schmidt antwortet: „**Ich fahre** lieber mit dem Auto." „Dann **fahren wir** mit dem Auto", sagt Herr Schmidt.

Herr und Frau Schmidt laden die Verwandten ein: „**Fahrt ihr mit?**" „Natürlich!" sagen die Verwandten. „Und morgen **fahren wir** mit dem Fahrrad durch den Park!"

viel a lot
zu tun to do
die Museen the museums
das Geschäft the store
aus from
die Geschäftsreise *business trip*
fahren . . . mit go along
die Reise the trip
wie like
die Ferien the vacation
bleiben to stay
bei at
die Verwandten the *relatives*
in der Stadt in the city
jeden Morgen every *morning*
mit der U-Bahn by subway
zum Zentrum downtown
schnell fast
hin there
zurück back
das Paket the package
das Wochenende the *weekend*
ganze entire
frei free
die Tagestour the day trip
soll should
mieten rent
laden . . . ein invite
natürlich of course

ÜBUNG

B. Richtig oder falsch? If the sentence is incorrect, change it to make it correct:

1. In New York gibt es nicht so viel zu tun.

_____

2. Die Familie Schmidt kommt aus New York.

_____

3. Die Schmidts haben in New York Ferien.

_____

4. Die Schmidts bleiben in einem Hotel.

_____

5. Herr Schmidt fährt mit dem Motorrad zum Stadtzentrum.

_____

6. Frau Schmidt fährt mit dem Bus zum Einkaufen.

_____

7. Die Kinder gehen mit der Mutter einkaufen.

_____

8. Herr Schmidt arbeitet am Samstag und Sonntag.

_____

9. Die Schmidts machen am Wochenende eine Tagestour.

_____

10. Die Schmidts mieten ein Auto.

_____

3 Can you find the forms of the stem-changing verb **fahren** in the story? **Fahren** means _to go_ or _travel_ by some means of transportation. Fill in the proper verb forms for all subjects. MEMORIZE THEM!

ich	_____	**wir**	_____
du	_____	**ihr**	_____
er **sie** **es**	_____	**sie**	_____
		Sie	_____

How is **fahren** different from the regular verbs you know?

_____

That's correct! The **du** and the **er, sie** (_she_), **es** forms add an umlaut (**ä**) over the **a** in the stem. Otherwise, **fahren** is pretty easy.

NOTE: Other stem-changing verbs that change by adding an umlaut over the **a** in the stem are **laufen** (_to run_), **fallen** (_to fall_), **schlafen** (_to sleep_), and **tragen** (_to carry; to wear_).

4   Now that you know that **laufen, fallen, schlafen,** and **tragen** follow the same
pattern as **fahren,** can you complete the following verb charts?

laufen

ich _____   wir _____

du _____   ihr _____

er
sie } _____   sie _____
es

Sie _____

fallen

ich _____   wir _____

du _____   ihr _____

er
sie } _____   sie _____
es

Sie _____

schlafen

ich _____   wir _____

du _____   ihr _____

er
sie } _____   sie _____
es

Sie _____

tragen

ich _____   wir _____

du _____   ihr _____

er ⎫
sie ⎬ _____   sie _____
es ⎭

Sie _____

__ ÜBUNGEN _____

C. Complete each sentence with the correct subject pronoun. Where more than one pronoun is correct, write all possible pronouns in the blank:

1. _____ schlafe bis zehn Uhr.

2. _____ fährst mit dem Auto.

3. _____ fallt vom Baum.

4. _____ laufen schnell.

5. _____ trägt einen Hut.

6. _____ fällt vom Tisch.

7. _____ tragt kurze Hosen.

8. _____ läuft einen Kilometer.

9. _____ fahren mit dem Zug.

10. _____ schläft.

D. Complete each sentence with the correct form of the verb in parentheses:

1. (fallen) Das Papier _____ .

2. (tragen) Meine Mutter _____ ein schönes Kleid.

3. (fahren) Wir _____ mit dem Bus.

4. (schlafen) Ihr _____ zu spät.

5. (laufen) Die Männer _____ sehr schnell.

6. (tragen) _____ du eine Bluse?

7. (laufen) Ich _____ gern.

8. (fallen) Die Bücher _____ auf den Stuhl.

9. (schlafen) Wir _____ jede Nacht.

10. (fahren) Sein Bruder _____ schnell.

E. Here are some sentences in which a stem-changing verb form is used. Can you match these sentences with the pictures they describe?

Er fährt mit dem Zug.
Die Kinder laufen schnell.
Der Apfel fällt nicht vom Baum.
Sie läuft gern.
Er schläft in der Schule.

Der Pilot trägt eine Uniform.
Schläfst du noch?
Ich trage einen Badeanzug.
Wir fahren mit dem Bus.
Der Junge fällt vom Fahrrad.

1. _____

2. _____

3. _____

4. _____

5. _____   6. _____

7. _____   8. _____

9. _____   10. _____

5 Look at the story one more time. How do you say *by subway*?

_____ *by bus*? _____

by bicycle? _____ In German, when you want to say
you are going by a specific means of transportation, use **mit.** Means of transportation that are masculine or neuter are preceded by **dem;** feminine means of
transportation are preceded by **der:**

> **mit dem Bus** *by bus*
> **mit der U-Bahn** *by subway*
> **mit dem Fahrrad** *by bicycle*

___ ÜBUNG _____

F. Each incomplete sentence needs the German equivalent of one of the phrases in
the right column. Match the sentence with the most logical phrase and complete
the sentence with the German equivalent of that phrase. Use each phrase only
once:

	by train
1. Er fliegt _____ von Frankfurt nach New York.	by plane
	by helicopter
2. Er fährt jeden Tag _____ zur Arbeit.	by ship
	by car

1. Er fliegt _____ von Frankfurt nach New York.

2. Er fährt jeden Tag _____ zur Arbeit.

3. Er fliegt _____ von New York nach Chicago.

4. Er fährt jeden Tag _____ zum Zentrum.

5. Er segelt einmal im Jahr _____ .

_____ *PERSÖNLICHE FRAGEN* _____

1. Wie fährst du in die Stadt?

_____

2. Läufst du schnell?

_____

3. Wie lange schläfst du am Morgen?

_____

4. Fliegst du oft mit dem Hubschrauber?

_____

5. Segeln deine Eltern mit dem Schiff nach Europa?

_____

GESPRÄCH

Wortschatz

Karte *ticket*	**nächste** *next*
einfach *one-way*	**Eilzug** *express train*
hin und zurück *round trip*	**Gleis** *track*
Rückfahrkarte *round-trip ticket*	**fährt . . . ab** *departs*
erste *first*	**Tagesrückfahrkarte** *one-day round-trip ticket*
zweite *second*	**Reise** *trip*

DIALOG

You are at your local railroad station and a German tourist approaches you for help. How would you respond?

DU

Here is a picture. Complete it in with pictures of the different means of transportation you know. Label the pictures:

KULTURECKE

Reisen in Deutschland (Traveling in Germany)

The Germans like to travel within their country and abroad. They are as likely to travel by train or plane as by car, since all three means of transportation are equally convenient.

When traveling long distances by car, the Germans use the well-designed **Autobahn** (*expressway*). There is no federally mandated speed limit on this network of limited access highways. Other highways and local roads have speed limits and other controls. Here are some signs you might see on German roads. Can you guess what they mean?

Halt!	Parkverbot	Keine Durchfahrt
Fußgängerüberweg	Vorsicht!	Bushaltestelle
Schleudergefahr	Verbot für Autos und Motorräder	Engstelle
Bauarbeiten	Kühe auf Straße	Ufer
Seitenwind	Sackgasse	

Given the compact size of the country, travel by train or by plane is equally practical. Both forms of mass transit operate a schedule of frequent departures. Here are signs you may see in either **a Bahnhof** (*railroad station*) or **Flughafen** (*airport*):

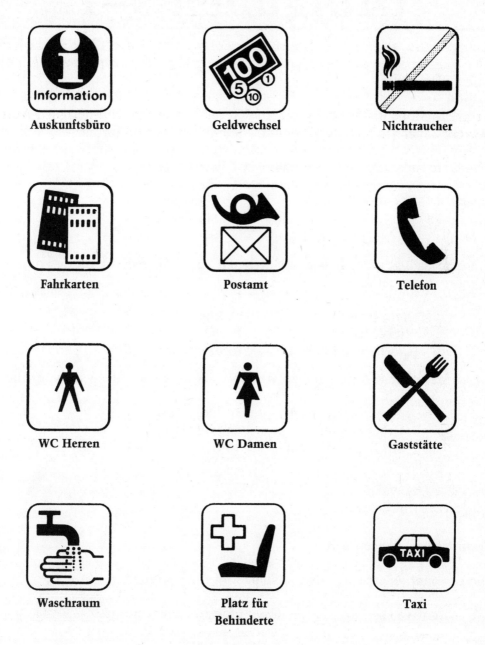

Auskunftsbüro   Geldwechsel   Nichtraucher

Fahrkarten   Postamt   Telefon

WC Herren   WC Damen   Gaststätte

Waschraum   Platz für   Taxi
Behinderte

Wiederholung III (Aufgaben 9–12)

Aufgabe 9

a. The verb **haben** (*to have*) is irregular. Memorize all of its forms:

ich habe	wir haben
du hast	ihr habt
er ⎫	sie haben
sie ⎬ hat	Sie haben
es ⎭	

b. The expressions **gern, lieber, am liebsten** show degrees of liking something or liking to do something:

gern haben	*to like*
lieber haben	*to prefer*
am liebsten haben	*to like best* (*of all*)

Substitute other verbs for **haben** when you want to specify what you like doing:

gern schwimmen	*to like to swim*
lieber spielen	*to prefer to play*
am liebsten essen	*to like to eat best* (*of all*)

Aufgabe 10

a. Nominative and accusative:

The nominative case signals the subject of the sentence.

The accusative case signals the direct object of the sentence.

DEFINITE ARTICLE

	masculine	feminine	neuter	plural
NOMINATIVE	der	die	das	die
ACCUSATIVE	den	die	das	die

b. The verb **essen** (*to eat*) is a stem-changing verb (**e→i**). Memorize all of its forms:

ich esse	wir essen
du ißt	ihr eßt
er ⎫	sie essen
sie ⎬ ißt	Sie essen
es ⎭	

Aufgabe 11

a. Indefinite articles in the nominative and accusative:

	masculine	feminine	neuter	plural
NOMINATIVE	ein	eine	ein	keine
ACCUSATIVE	einen	eine	ein	keine

Endings of possessives (**mein, dein, sein, ihr, unser, euer, Ihr**) and **kein** follow the pattern of **ein**.

b. Accusative prepositions: **durch   für   gegen   ohne   um**

The objects of these prepositions are in the accusative.

Aufgabe 12

The verbs **fahren** (*to travel*), **fallen** (*to fall*), **schlafen** (*to sleep*), and **tragen** (*to carry; to wear*) are **a→ä** stem-changing verbs; **laufen** (*to run*) is an **au→äu** stem-changing verb. Memorize the forms of all of these verbs.

fahren (*to travel*)

ich	fahre	wir fahren
du	fährst	ihr fahrt
er ⎫		
sie ⎬	fährt	sie fahren
es ⎭		
		Sie fahren

fallen (*to fall*)

ich	falle	wir fallen
du	fällst	ihr fallt
er ⎫		
sie ⎬	fällt	sie fallen
es ⎭		
		Sie fallen

schlafen (*to sleep*)

ich	schlafe	wir schlafen
du	schläfst	ihr schlaft
er		
sie }	schläft	sie schlafen
es		
		Sie schlafen

tragen (*to wear*)

ich	trage	wir tragen
du	trägst	ihr tragt
er		
sie }	trägt	sie tragen
es		
		Sie tragen

laufen (*to run*)

ich	laufe	wir laufen
du	läufst	ihr lauft
er		
sie }	läuft	sie laufen
es		
		Sie laufen

___ ÜBUNGEN _____

A. Kreuzworträtsel:

WAAGERECHT

1.    7.   15.

4.    10.   17.

6.    11.    19.

SENKRECHT

2.

8.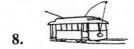

13.

3.

9.

14.

5.

11.

16.

6.

12. ◯

18.

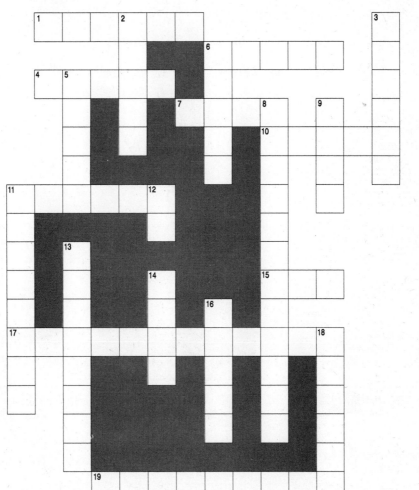

B. Identify the following pictures. Then circle the German words in the puzzle. The words may be read from left to right, right to left, up or down, and diagonally across:

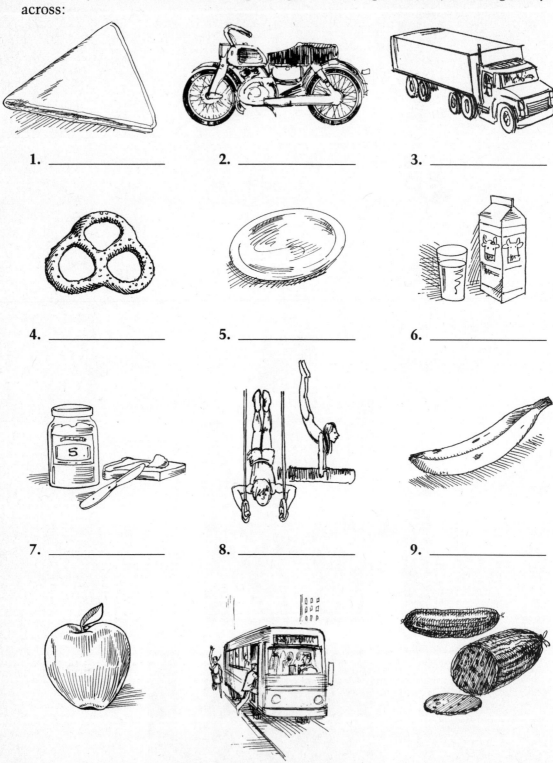

1. _____

2. _____

3. _____

4. _____

5. _____

6. _____

7. _____

8. _____

9. _____

10. _____

11. _____

12. _____

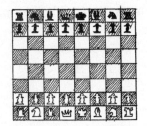

13. _____   14. _____   15. _____

16. _____   17. _____   18. _____

19. _____   20. _____   21. _____

```
S R A T E N N I S S W S
E U B E S S A T E P L T
T S B H R R A S N A E O
T M U C E O U M F R Z E
E O F L A S T W A G E N
I T N I T C Ä P F E R A
V O R M E H L K N L B N
R R E L L A B S S U F A
E R D I L C L E F P A B
S A N M E H C S I E L F
E D A R R H A F E Z O K
T R W A N E N R U T S E
```

C. Jumble: Unscramble the food words. Then unscramble the circled letters to find out the message:

C H I S L E F ☐☐☐☐⊙☐☐

T R U W S ☐⊙☐☐⊙

A N E B N A ⊙☐☐☐☐☐

A M O T E T ☐☐☐☐⊙☐

W A H N D I S C ⊙☐☐⊙☐⊙☐☐

L E F R A F T O K ⊙⊙⊙☐☐☐☐☐☐

Solution: ☐☐ ☐☐☐☐ ☐☐☐☐☐.

D. After filling in all the letters, look at the vertical box to find out Ulrike's favorite sport:

1.  — — — — — —

2.  — — — — —

3.  — — — — — —

4.  — — — — —

5.  — — — — —

6.  — — — — — — — —

Solution: _____

E. Picture Story. Can you read this story? Much of it is in picture form. Whenever you come to a picture, read it as if it were a German word:

Jeden Donnerstag gehen Marianne und ihre ⟨picture⟩ in den ⟨picture⟩

und kaufen die Lebensmittel (*foods*). Heute brauchen sie ⟨picture⟩ für die

⟨picture⟩ zum Mittagessen. Dazu kaufen sie auch ⟨picture⟩ und ⟨picture⟩ zum

Nachtisch. Zum Abendessen brauchen sie ⟨picture⟩ und ⟨picture⟩

⟨picture⟩ kauft auch ⟨picture⟩ und ⟨picture⟩. Dann gehen sie in die ⟨picture⟩ und

kaufen ⟨picture⟩ und ⟨picture⟩. In der ⟨picture⟩ kaufen sie einen ⟨picture⟩. Die

⟨picture⟩ ißt ⟨picture⟩ gern. Bevor sie nach Hause gehen, kauft Mutti auch

⟨picture⟩ im ⟨picture⟩. ⟨picture⟩ hat Marianne am liebsten.

Vierter Teil

13 *Der Körper*

Expressions with **weh tun**

1 DAS MONSTER

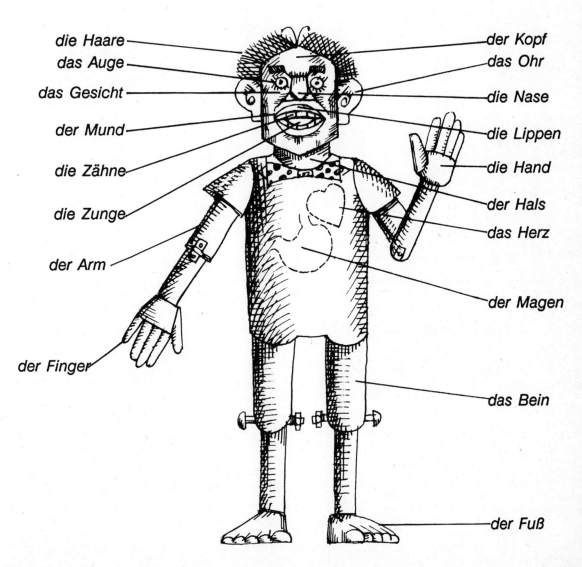

die Haare — der Kopf
das Auge — das Ohr
das Gesicht — die Nase
der Mund — die Lippen
die Zähne — die Hand
die Zunge — der Hals
der Arm — das Herz
der Finger — der Magen
das Bein
der Fuß

___ ÜBUNGEN _____

A. This monster may look weird, but the parts of his body are the same as yours and mine. Study the German names and match the words with the correct pictures:

das Gesicht	**das Ohr**	**die Zunge**
die Haare	**der Mund**	**die Zähne**
die Augen	**die Lippen**	**der Kopf**
die Nase		

1. _____

2. _____

3. _____

4. _____

5. _____

6. _____

7. _____

8. _____

9. _____

10. _____

B. Label these parts of the head:

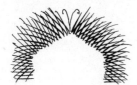

1. _____

2. _____

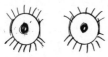

3. _____

4. _____

5. _____

6. _____

7. _____

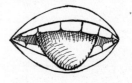

8. _____

9. _____

10. _____

C. Now label some other parts of the body:

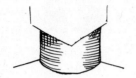

1. _____

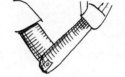

2. _____

3. _____

4. _____

5. _____

6. _____

7. _____

8. _____

D. Every part of the body can do something. Match the part of the body with the action it can perform. Sometimes more than one part of the body will be appropriate. Write the matching part(s) in the space provided:

1. sagen _____   die Füße
                                             die Zähne
2. tanzen _____   die Hände
                                             der Mund
3. singen _____   die Lippen
                                             die Ohren
4. lernen _____   die Zunge
                                             die Beine
5. sehen _____   die Arme
                                             die Augen
6. fallen _____   die Finger

7. verstehen _____

8. schmecken _____

9. laufen _____

10. hören _____

11. antworten _____

12. spielen _____

2 Now that you are an expert on the parts of the body, you are ready to read the amazing story of the mad scientist, Dr. Franz Frankenstein, and the horrible monster he created:

ORT: Labor des verrückten Wissenschaftlers Doktor Franz Frankenstein.

DARSTELLER: Doktor Frankenstein;
    Igor, sein Assistent;
        das Monster, eine Mischung von verschiedenen Körperteilen.

DOKTOR FRANKENSTEIN: Ich habe eine ausgezeichnete Idee. Ich möchte ein Ungeheuer machen.

IGOR: Jawohl, Herr Doktor.

DR. F.: Zuerst ein Körper. Haben wir einen Körper, Igor?

IGOR: Wir haben hier einen Körper, Herr Doktor. Er ist alt und häßlich.

verrückt *crazy*
der Wissenschaftler *the scientist*
die Darsteller *the characters*

die Mischung *the mixture*
der Körperteil *the body part*

das Ungeheuer *the monster*
jawohl *yes, indeed*

DR. F.: Sehr gut. Wir brauchen auch zwei Arme, Igor.

IGOR: Hier sind zwei Arme. Und sie sind sehr haarig.

haarig *hairy*

DR. F.: Gut. Und die Hände?

IGOR: Zwei Hände. Eine Hand von einem Mann und eine Hand von einem Gorilla.

DR. F.: Wie viele Finger haben die Hände?

IGOR: Zehn Finger, Herr Doktor.

DR. F.: Perfekt.

IGOR: Eine Hand hat sieben Finger und die andere Hand hat drei.

DR. F.: Gut. Und die Füße. Haben wir Füße?

IGOR: Gewiß, Herr Doktor. Ein Fuß ist riesig und der andere Fuß ist winzig.

gewiß *certainly*
riesig *tremendous*
winzig *tiny*
fehlt *is missing*

DR. F.: Ausgezeichnet! Aber es fehlt noch ein Kopf.

IGOR: Hier ist ein Kopf. Ein kleiner Kopf mit einem dummen Gesicht.

DR. F.: Toll! Etwas Elektrizität macht das Ungeheuer lebendig.

toll *great*
lebendig *alive*

BZZZZZZZZZZZ

IGOR: Schauen Sie doch! Das Ungeheuer will sprechen.

Schauen Sie doch! *Look!*

DR. F.: Du lebst! Sprich! Sprich!

sprechen *to speak*

DAS MONSTER: Der Kopf tut mir weh. Die Arme tun mir weh . . .

leben *to live*
Sprich! *Speak!*
tut . . . weh *hurts*

DR. F.: Was für ein schreckliches Ungeheuer! Es ist ein Deutschlehrer. Es ist (*Fill in someone's name, someone who won't get too angry with you.*)

mir *me*
tun . . . weh *hurt*
schrecklich *awful*

_____

__ ÜBUNGEN _____

E. **Richtig oder falsch?** If the sentence is incorrect, change it to make it correct:

1. Doktor Frankenstein ist verrückt.

_____

2. Der Körper des Monsters ist jung.

_____

3. Das Monster hat keine Arme.

_____

4. Beide Hände haben fünf Finger.

_____

5. Das Monster tanzt gut.

_____

6. Das Gesicht des Monsters ist intelligent.

_____

7. Der Doktor benutzt Elektrizität, und das Monster lebt dann.

_____

8. Das Monster spricht italienisch.

_____

F. Fill in the names of the labeled parts of the body:

3   What did the monster say when it came to life?

_____ (*My head aches.*)

_____ (*My arms hurt.*)

How would you say the following?

My nose hurts. _____

My foot hurts. _____

My legs hurt. _____

My eyes hurt. _____

Very good! If what hurts is singular, then the verb is **tut;** if what hurts is plural, then the verb is **tun.** Now let's see what happens if it's someone else's eyes that hurt:

Die Augen tun *mir* weh.	*My eyes hurt.*
Die Augen tun *dir* weh.	*Your eyes hurt.* (familiar singular)
Die Augen tun *ihm* weh.	*His eyes hurt.*
Die Augen tun *ihr* weh.	*Her eyes hurt.*
Die Augen tun *ihm* weh.	*Its eyes hurt.*
Die Augen tun *uns* weh.	*Our eyes hurt.*
Die Augen tun *euch* weh.	*Your eyes hurt.* (familiar plural)
Die Augen tun *ihnen* weh.	*Their eyes hurt.*
Die Augen tun *Ihnen* weh.	*Your eyes hurt.* (formal)

Mir, dir, ihm, ihr, uns, euch, ihnen, and **Ihnen** are pronouns. You must memorize them.

___ ÜBUNGEN _____

G. Complete the second sentence with the pronoun that corresponds to the words in heavy type in the first sentence. You may use a pronoun more than once:

mir   dir   ihm   ihr   uns   euch   ihnen   Ihnen

1. Der Hals tut **Bernd** weh. Der Hals tut _____ weh.

2. Der Fuß tut **Inge** weh. Der Fuß tut _____ weh.

3. Die Beine tun **Heinz und mir** weh. Die Beine tun _____ weh.

4. Meine Nase tut weh. Die Nase tut _____ weh.

5. Deine Finger tun weh. Die Finger tun _____ weh.

6. Der Magen tut **Heinz und Inge** weh. Der Magen tut _____ weh.

7. Ihr Kopf tut weh. Der Kopf tut _____ weh.

8. Die Augen tun **Marianne und dir** weh. Die Augen tun _____ weh.

H. Complete each sentence with the pronoun that corresponds to the words in parentheses:

    EXAMPLE: (ich) Das Bein tut _____ mir _____ weh.

1. (ich) Die Füße tun _____ weh.

2. (er) Der Magen tut _____ weh.

3. (Mutti und ich) Die Arme tun _____ weh.

4. (wir) Die Hände tun _____ auch weh.

5. (du) Was tut _____ weh?

6. (Sie) Was tut _____ weh?

7. (ihr) Tut _____ der Kopf weh?

8. (er und du) Tun _____ die Finger weh?

I. Match the German expressions with the English meanings. Write the matching letter in the space provided:

1. Was tut dir weh? _____

2. Der Hals tut ihm weh. _____

3. Der Magen tut ihr weh. _____

4. Die Augen tun uns weh. _____

5. Die Ohren tun uns weh. _____

6. Tut ihm das Bein weh? _____

7. Die Augen tun euch weh. _____

8. Der Kopf tut dir weh. _____

a. Our eyes hurt.
b. What hurts you?
c. Your eyes hurt.
d. Our ears hurt.
e. Your head hurts.
f. His throat hurts.
g. Does his leg hurt?
h. Her stomach hurts.

J.   Match the sentences with the pictures they describe:

Ich habe zwei starke Arme.   Die Finger tun uns weh.
Sein Herz ist groß.   Sie hat große Augen.
Der Hals tut ihm weh.   Hans hat einen langen Hals.
Das Bein tut mir weh.   Die Zähne tun ihr weh.
Sie haben lange Haare.   Der Fuß tut mir weh.

1. _____

2. _____

3. _____

4. _____

5. _____

6. _____

7.

8.

9. _____

10. _____

K. Write in German:

1. His head hurts.

_____

2. Our legs hurt.

_____

3. Their eyes hurt.

_____

4. My head hurts.

_____

5. Her nose hurts.

_____

GESPRÄCH

Wortschatz

arm *poor*
Was ist los? *What's wrong!*
kann *can*
die Grippe *the flu*

das Medikament *the medicine*
muß *must*
ruh dich aus! *rest!*

___ PERSÖNLICHE FRAGEN ___

1. Wie viele Augen hast du?

_____

2. Wie viele Köpfe hast du?

_____

3. Wie geht's?

_____

4. Was tut dir weh?

_____

5. Tun dir die Beine weh?

_____

___ DU ___

Describe yourself:

EXAMPLE: Haare   Ich habe kurze (*short*) Haare.

1. Nase _____

2. Augen _____

3. Mund _____

4. Hände _____

5. Ohren _____

6. Arme _____

DIALOG

You are at the doctor's office. Respond to his questions:

KULTURECKE

Eine „Drogerie" ist kein „drugstore"

If you have the misfortune of becoming ill during your stay in a German-speaking country and your doctor gives you a prescription, the corner **Drogerie** may turn out to be a disappointment.

A German **Drogerie** is not quite the same as an American drugstore. A **Drogerie** sells toiletries and some over-the-counter medications, as well as camera supplies and other goods. It does not deal in prescription medicines.

An **Apotheke** (*pharmacy*) sells medicine with and without prescriptions and also some toiletries.

A third health-related store, the **Reformhaus,** is comparable to an American health-food store. It sells special foods, teas, and vitamins.

And, by the way, **Gute Genesung!** (*Speedy Recovery!*)

14 *Mein Haus*

Stem-Changing Verbs e→ie; Accusative Pronouns

1 | Look at the pictures and try to guess the meanings of the new words:

das Haus

die Wohnung

die Treppe

die Küche

das Eßzimmer

das Wohnzimmer

das Schlafzimmer

das Badezimmer

der Tisch

das Sofa   der Sessel   die Lampe

das Bett   der Schrank   der Kühlschrank

das Radio   der Fernseher

ÜBUNGEN

A. Was ist das? Identify the objects. Use indefinite articles:

1. _____   2. _____

3. _____

4. _____

5. _____

6. _____

7. _____

8. _____

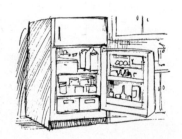

9. _____

10. _____

11. _____   12. _____

B. You are writing a composition about your house. Complete these sentences:

1. Vater sitzt auf dem Sofa im _____ .

2. Der Kühlschrank steht in der _____ .

3. Ich esse im _____ .

4. Der Fernseher ist im _____ .

5. Ich schlafe im _____ .

2 Now read the following story:

Hier ist mein Haus. Siehst du es? Es ist ein Einfamilienhaus. Es hat zwei Stockwerke und einen Keller. Im Keller ist viel Kram. Im Erdgeschoß sind die Küche, das Wohnzimmer und das Eßzimmer. Mein Vater liest die Zeitung gern im Wohnzimmer. Er liest gerade jetzt die Zeitung. Siehst du ihn?

Mutti kocht das Abendessen in der Küche. Siehst du sie?

Im ersten Stock sind die Schlafzimmer und das Badezimmer. Die Kinder schlafen jetzt im Schlafzimmer. Siehst du sie? Über dem zweiten Stock ist der Dachboden und noch mehr Kram.

Wir wohnen schon seit zehn Jahren in diesem schönen Haus!

siehst du? *do you see*
das Einfamilienhaus *the one-family-house*
  das Stockwerk *floor, story*
  der Keller *the basement*
der Kram *the junk*
liest *reads*
gerade *just*
  ihn *him*
kochen *to cook*

über *above*
der Dachboden *the attic*
  noch mehr *still more*

___ ÜBUNG _____

C. Answer the following questions in German:

1. Was für ein Haus ist das?

   _____

2. Wie viele Stockwerke hat es?

   _____

3. Was gibt es im Keller?

   _____

4. Welche Zimmer sind im Erdgeschoß?

   _____

5. Warum ist der Vater im Wohnzimmer?

   _____

6. Was macht die Mutter in der Küche?

   _____

7. Was tun die Kinder im Schlafzimmer?

   _____

8. Was ist über dem zweiten Stock?

   _____

9. Was gibt es im Dachboden?

   _____

10. Wie lange wohnt die Familie in diesem Haus?

   _____

3 Let's see if you can find the words in the story that mean *do you see?*

_____ That's right: **siehst du? siehst** is the **du**-form of **sehen. Sehen** is also a stem-changing verb. The stem change is **e** to **ie** in the **du** and **er, sie, es** forms. The remaining forms of **sehen** are regular. Can you complete the table for **sehen?**

ich _____   wir _____

du _____   ihr _____

er
sie } _____   sie _____

es

                                          Sie _____

Another verb similar to **sehen** is **lesen** (*to read*). Can you complete the table for **lesen?**

ich _____   wir _____

du _____   ihr _____

er
sie } _____   sie _____

es

                                          Sie _____

__ ÜBUNG _____

D. Make logical sentences by completing them with the appropriate form of **lesen** or **sehen**:

1. (lesen) Mein Vater _____ die Zeitung.

2. (sehen) Wir _____ das Haus.

3. (sehen) Die Kinder _____ den Film.

4. (lesen) Ich _____ gern Bücher.

5. (lesen) _____ du gern?

6. (sehen) Ihr _____ die Treppe.

4 Now let's go back to the story. How would you say:

Do you see him? _____

Do you see her? _____

Do you see them? _____

In our examples, the pronouns **ihn** and **sie** are direct object pronouns in the accusative case. The accusative pronouns are:

mich	*me*	**uns**	*us*
dich	*you*	**euch**	*you*
ihn	*him*		
sie	*her*	**sie**	*them*
es	*it*		
		Sie	*you*

Memorize these accusative pronouns.

__ ÜBUNG _____

E. Complete the second sentence in each pair with the accusative pronoun that corresponds to the bold-type segment of the first sentence:

1. Ich sehe **meine Eltern**. Ich sehe _____ .

2. Der Vater fragt **meine Mutter und mich.** Der Vater fragt _____ .

3. Er sieht **seinen Bruder.** Er sieht _____ .

4. Jürgen besucht **dich und deine Mutter.** Jürgen besucht _____ .

5. **Du** hast Besuch (*visitors*). Deine Freunde besuchen _____ .

6. **Ich** habe auch Besuch. Meine Freunde besuchen _____ .

7. Mein Vater liest gern **die Zeitung.** Mein Vater liest _____ gern.

8. Meine Schwester liest **ihr Buch.** Meine Schwester liest _____ .

F. These sentences are all jumbled. Reorder the words so that they make sense:

1. Vater / seine / mein / liest / Zeitung

   _____

2. du / Kuchen / siehst / den / Eßzimmer / im?

   _____

3. sie / in der Küche / ihr / seht?

   _____

4. Sie / Krawatte / gern / haben / meine?

_____

5. er / den / sieht / im Keller / den Kram

_____

_____

G. Make a sentence out of each group of words. Change the verb forms and add extra words wherever necessary to complete the meaning:

1. ich / sehen / Buch

_____

2. er / tragen / Hut

_____

3. wir / essen / Salat

_____

4. sie / lesen / Aufsatz

_____

5. ihr / trinken / Limonade

_____

6. du / schreiben / Brief

_____

_____

H. Rewrite each sentence in Exercise G, replacing each accusative noun phrase with the accusative pronoun closest to it in meaning:

1. _____

2. _____

3. _____

4. _____

5. _____

6. _____

Now read the following questions:

Wer liest die Zeitung?

Wen siehst du?

Circle the verb in each question. You should have circled **liest** and **siehst.** Now draw an arrow from the verb to its subject. What is the subject of **liest?**

_____ That's right! **Wer** is the subject of the question. When you answer the question, the noun phrase that will replace **wer** will be the subject in the NOMINATIVE case.

What is the subject of **siehst?** _____ Right again! **Du** determines the verb form in the second question. Then what does **wen** mean? **Wen** means *whom.* When you answer a question beginning with **wen,** the noun phrase that replaces **wen** is the direct object in the ACCUSATIVE case.

Let's assume that **Vater** is in the answer to both questions. Answer these questions:

Wer liest die Zeitung? _____

Wen siehst du? _____

Add **wen** to the rest of the question words that you learned in Lesson 4 (page 65). Review the question words before you do the next exercise.

___ **ÜBUNG** _____

I.   Complete the question by supplying the question word that is appropriate to the answer:

1. _____ schreibt einen Brief? — Onkel Karl schreibt einen Brief.

2. _____ bringst du? — Ich bringe Tante Emma.

3. _____ schreibst du? — Ich schreibe einen Aufsatz.

4. _____ geht's? — Danke, gut. Und dir?

5. _____ ist die Milch? — Die Milch ist im Kühlschrank.

6. _____ ist das? — Das ist meine Mutter.

7. _____ ist das? — Das ist ein Hut.

GESPRÄCH

Wortschatz

neben *beside*
(der) Liebling *darling*
(der) Schatz *treasure*

(der) Engel *angel*
Bis später! *See you later!*

DIALOG

You are the second person in the dialog. Answer the questions in German:

_____
(Say it's on the sofa.)

_____
(Say it's next to the belt.)

_____
(Say that you see them under the TV.)

_____
(Say it's on the speaker's head.)

_____ *PERSÖNLICHE FRAGEN* _____

1. Wie viele Stockwerke hat dein Haus?

_____

2. Was ist dein Lieblingszimmer?

_____

3. Wie lange wohnst du in deinem Haus?

_____

4. Wo ißt du das Frühstück?

_____

5. In welchem Zimmer siehst du fern?

_____

_____ *DU* _____

Draw your house and especially your room. Label the rooms in your house and the objects in your room.

KULTURECKE

Zu Hause (At home)

Most German families dream of owning their own homes. In fact, many do own their own homes. The Germans' home is indeed their private castle.

German homes are constantly being modernized to keep pace with the times. The German kitchen has undergone the greatest change. It is up to date with sophisticated decor and modern equipment. Today's German kitchen contains all the necessary appliances: a refrigerator, a dishwasher (**der Geschirrspüler**), and a microwave oven (**der Mikrowellenherd**).

There are different styles of housing to reflect the variety of tastes. Typical housing includes:

Einfamilienhaus

Reihenhaus

Mietshaus

Hochhaus

In the larger cities, housing may look ultramodern from the outside as well as the inside. In the smaller towns, however, the exteriors of houses are designed to blend in with the character of the village.

Note how the floors in a German building are designated:

Dritter (3.) Stock

Zweiter (2.) Stock

Erster (1.) Stock

Erdgeschoß

15 Die Tage und die Monate

How to Express Dates in German

1 Die Tage

(der) Montag	(der) Donnerstag	(der) Samstag
(der) Dienstag	(der) Freitag	(der) Sonntag
(der) Mittwoch		

NOTE: German has a second word for *Saturday*: **(der) Sonnabend. Samstag** is generally favored in Southern Germany and **Sonnabend** in Northern Germany.

ÜBUNGEN

A. Fill in the name of the day of the week:

1. M _ _ t _ _   4. S _ _ _ _ a _   6. M _ _ _ w _ _ _

2. D i _ _ _ _ a _   5. S _ n _ _ _ _   7. D _ _ n _ _ _ t _ _

3. F _ _ i _ _ g

B. Complete with the correct information:

1. Es gibt _____ Tage in einer Woche.

2. Die Tage der Woche sind _____

_____

3. Es gibt keine Schule am _____ und am _____ .

C. Fill in the days before and after the day given:

1. _____ Montag _____

2. _____ Mittwoch _____

3. _____ Freitag _____

4. _____ Sonntag _____

2 Now you can read this story about the days of the week:

Was ist dein Lieblingstag? Warum?

ROLF: Samstag und Sonntag. Es gibt keine Schule.
FRANZ: Montag. Ich gehe gern in die Schule.
SUSI: Montag, Dienstag, Mittwoch, Donnerstag und Freitag. Ich telefoniere mit Paul. Paul ist ein Schüler in der Deutschklasse.
KARL: Sonntag. Gabi und ich sehen gern Sport im Fernsehen.
HANS: Samstag. Ich habe jeden Samstag eine Verabredung mit einem hübschen Mädchen.
ANNA: Mittwoch. Dann habe ich Jugendgruppe.

die Verabredung *the date*
hübsch *pretty*
die Jugendgruppe *the youth group*

ÜBUNGEN

D. Match the person with his/her favorite day. Write the number and matching letter in the space provided.

1. Anna _____   4. Hans _____

2. Susi _____   5. Franz _____

3. Rolf _____   6. Karl _____

a. Samstag
b. Montag
c. Mittwoch
d. Samstag und Sonntag
e. Sonntag
f. Montag, Dienstag, Mittwoch, Donnerstag, Freitag

E. Give the reason in German why each person prefers his/her favorite day:

1. Karl und Gabi _____

2. Anna _____

3. Rolf _____

4. Franz _____

5. Hans _____

6. Susi _____

③ Die Monate

(der) Januar

(der) Februar

(der) März

(der) April

(der) Mai

(der) Juni

(der) Juli

(der) August

(der) September

(der) Oktober

(der) November

(der) Dezember

F. Complete the names of the months:

1. J _ n _ _ r

2. O _ t _ _ _ _

3. N o _ e _ _ _ _

4. F _ _ r _ _ r

5. M _ _

6. J _ l _

7. M _ _ z

8. A _ _ _ _ _ t

9. J _ n _

10. A _ _ _ l

11. D _ _ e _ b _ _

12. S e _ _ _ _ b _ _

G. Fill in the months before and after the month given:

1. _____ Februar _____

2. _____ Mai _____

3. _____ April _____

4. _____ November _____

5. _____ Januar _____

6. _____ August _____

7. _____ Juli _____

8. _____ Oktober _____

4 Now you can read this story about the months of the year:

Was ist dein Lieblingsmonat? Warum?

HEIDI: Januar. Ich gehe gern Skilaufen.
GRETEL: Juli. Ich gehe gern schwimmen.
MATTHIAS: Oktober. Ich spiele gern Fußball.
ANTON: April. Ich spiele gern draußen.
KARL: September. Ich gehe gern in die Schule.
PAUL: August. Ich habe die Sommerferien gern.
ERICH: Dezember. Ich habe Weihnachten am
    liebsten.
ELKE: Mai. Ich habe die schönen Blumen gern.

die Sommerferien *the
summer vacation*
Weihnachten *Christmas*

___ ÜBUNGEN _____

H. Match the person with his/her favorite month. Write the number and matching letter in the space provided:

1. Paul _____   5. Heidi _____   **a.** Mai
                                                   b. Januar
2. Anton _____   6. Erich _____   **c.** Dezember
                                                   d. April
3. Elke _____   7. Gretel _____   **e.** Juli
                                                   f. Oktober
4. Matthias _____   8. Karl _____   **g.** August
                                                   h. September

I. Give the reason in German why each person prefers his/her month:

1. Paul _____

2. Anton _____

3. Elke _____

4. Matthias _____

5. Heidi _____

6. Erich _____

7. Gretel _____

8. Karl _____

Was ist das Datum heute? (*What is today's date?*)

Let's see how the date is expressed in German. Look at the dates circled in the calendar (**der Kalender**):

1992

	JANUAR	FEBRUAR	MÄRZ	APRIL
MONTAG	6 13 20 27	3 10 17 24	2 9 16 23 30	6 13 20 27
DIENSTAG	7 14 21 28	④ 11 18 25	3 10 17 24 31	7 14 21 28
MITTWOCH	1 8 15 22 29	5 12 19 26	4 ⑪ 18 25	1 8 15 22 29
DONNERSTAG	2 9 16 23 30	6 13 20 27	5 12 19 26	2 9 16 23 30
FREITAG	3 10 17 24 31	7 14 21 28	6 13 20 27	3 10 17 24
SAMSTAG	4 11 18 25	1 8 15 22 29	7 14 21 28	4 11 18 25
SONNTAG	5 12 19 26	2 9 16 23	1 8 15 22 29	5 12 19 26

	MAI	JUNI	JULI	AUGUST
MONTAG	4 11 18 25	1 8 15 22 29	6 13 20 27	3 10 17 24 31
DIENSTAG	5 12 19 26	2 9 16 23 30	7 14 ㉑ 28	4 11 18 25
MITTWOCH	6 13 20 27	3 10 17 24	1 8 15 22 29	5 12 19 26
DONNERSTAG	7 14 21 28	4 11 18 25	2 9 16 23 30	6 13 20 27
FREITAG	1 8 ⑮ 22 29	5 12 19 26	3 10 17 24 31	7 14 21 28
SAMSTAG	2 9 16 23 30	6 13 20 27	4 11 18 25	1 8 15 22 29
SONNTAG	3 10 17 24 31	7 14 21 28	5 12 19 26	2 9 16 23 20

	SEPTEMBER	OKTOBER	NOVEMBER	DEZEMBER
MONTAG	7 14 21 28	5 12 19 26	2 9 16 23 30	⑦ 14 21 28
DIENSTAG	① 8 15 22 29	6 13 20 27	3 10 17 24	1 8 15 22 29
MITTWOCH	2 9 16 23 30	7 14 21 28	4 11 18 25	2 9 16 23 30
DONNERSTAG	3 10 17 24	1 8 15 22 29	5 12 19 26	3 10 17 24 31
FREITAG	4 11 18 25	2 9 16 23 30	6 13 20 27	4 11 18 25
SAMSTAG	5 12 19 26	③ 10 17 24 31	7 14 21 28	5 12 19 26
SONNTAG	6 13 20 27	4 11 18 25	1 8 15 22 29	6 13 20 27

FEBRUAR			
3	10	17	24
④	11	18	25
5	12	19	26
6	13	20	27
7	14	21	28
1 8	15	22	29
2 9	16	23	

MÄRZ				
2 19	16	23	30	
3	10	17	24	31
4	⑪	18	25	
5	12	19	26	
6	13	20	27	
7	14	21	28	
1 8	15	22	29	

Heute ist der 4. (vierte) Februar.
Heute ist Dienstag, der 4. Februar.

Heute ist der 11. (elfte) März.
Heute ist Mittwoch, der 11. März.

```
              MAI                              JULI
        4   11   18   25                6   13   20   27
        5   12   19   26                7   14  (21)  28
        6   13   20   27           1    8   15   22   29
        7   14   21   28           2    9   16   23   30
  1     8  (15)  22   29           3   10   17   24   31
  2     9   16   23   30           4   11   18   25
  3    10   17   24   31           5   12   19   26
```

Heute ist der 15. (fünfzehnte) Mai.   **Heute ist der 21. (einundzwanzigste) Juli.**
Heute ist Freitag, der 15. Mai.   **Heute ist Dienstag, der 21. Juli.**

Can you fill the blanks? To express the date, use:

Heute ist der + _____ **(s)te +** _____.

Use **-te** for the numbers **zwei** to **neunzehn** and **-ste** for the numbers **zwanzig** and higher. Note that dates are customarily written in German by figures followed by a period.

There are three exceptions:

```
         SEPTEMBER                           OKTOBER
        7   14   21   28                5   12   19   26
 (1)    8   15   22   29                6   13   20   27
  2     9   16   23   30                7   14   21   28
  3    10   17   24            1        8   15   22   29
  4    11   18   25            2        9   16   23   30
  5    12   19   26           (3)      10   17   24   31
  6    13   20   27            4       11   18   25
```

Heute ist der 1. (erste) September.   **Heute ist der 3. (dritte) Oktober.**
Heute ist Dienstag, der 1. September.   **Heute ist Samstag, der 3. Oktober.**

```
            DEZEMBER
          (7)  14   21   28
    1      8   15   22   29
    2      9   16   23   30
    3     10   17   24   31
    4     11   18   25
    5     12   19   26
    6     13   20   27
```

Heute ist der 7. (siebte) Dezember.
Heute ist Montag, der 7. Dezember.

The first of the month is expressed by **der erste.**

The third of the month is expressed by **der dritte.**

The seventh of the month is expressed by **der siebte.**

If you want to include the day of the week, use:

Heute ist _____ , **der** + _____ +

_____ .

__ ÜBUNGEN _____

J. These are your friends' birthdays. Express them in German:

  1. April 22 _____

  2. August 7 _____

  3. February 1 _____

  4. July 29 _____

  5. January 12 _____

  6. Monday, March 30 _____

  7. Saturday, December 4 _____

  8. Wednesday, June 15 _____

  9. Sunday, September 14 _____

  10. Thursday, November 16 _____

  11. Tuesday, May 13 _____

  12. Friday, October 21 _____

K. Give the dates in German for these important events:

  1. Your birthday

  _____

2. Christmas

_____

3. New Year's Day

_____

4. American Independence Day

_____

5. Thanksgiving

_____

6. Your favorite day of the year

_____

6 Did you notice that, in German, the day always precedes the month? Express in German:

April 5 _____

Now note how we write dates in numbers and how the Germans write them:

	ENGLISH	GERMAN
July 11, 1947	7/11/47	11. 7. 47
May 3, 1974	5/3/74	3. 5. 74
September 27, 1992	9/27/92	27. 9. 92

In German, the _____ comes first, then the

_____ , and finally the _____ .

__ ÜBUNG _____

L. For your German pen pal, express the dates in Übung K in numbers, German style:

1. _____   **4.** _____

2. _____   **5.** _____

3. _____   **6.** _____

7 Now read this conversation about dates:

Was ist dein Lieblingsdatum? Warum?

ROLF: Der fünfundzwanzigste Dezember. Ich liebe den Weihnachtsbaum und die Verzierungen.
FRANZ: Der vierte Juli. Ich sehe gern Feuerwerk.
SUSI: Der fünfzehnte April. Das ist mein Geburtstag. Ich habe Geschenke gern.
ROGER: Der erste Januar. Ich esse ein großes Mittagessen in einem eleganten Restaurant.
ANNA: Der erste Juli. Die Sommerferien beginnen.

der Weihnachtsbaum *the Christmas tree*
die Verzierungen *the decorations*
das Feuerwerk *the fireworks*
der Geburtstag *the birthday*
das Geschenk *the present*

__ ÜBUNGEN __

M. Match the person with his/her favorite date. Write the matching letter in the space provided:

1. Anna _____
2. Susi _____
3. Rolf _____
4. Franz _____
5. Roger _____

a. der 25. Dezember
b. der 1. Januar
c. der 4. Juli
d. der 15. April
e. der 1. Juli

N. Give the reason in German why each person prefers his/her favorite day:

1. Roger _____
2. Anna _____
3. Rolf _____
4. Franz _____
5. Susi _____

GESPRÄCH

Wortschatz

ich muß *I have to*   ich würde *I would*
ich weiß nicht *I don't know*

_____ PERSÖNLICHE FRAGEN _____

1. Was ist das Datum heute?

_____

2. Was ist das Datum von deinem Geburtstag?

_____

3. Was sind deine Ferienmonate?

_____

4. Was ist dein Lieblingstag? Warum?

_____

5. Was ist dein Lieblingsmonat? Warum?

_____

_____ DU _____

Draw a picture of yourself in the space provided on this **Steckbrief** (*"Wanted" poster*). Then complete the rest of the poster with the requested information:

STECKBRIEF

Name: _____

Kosename: _____

Geburtstag: _____

Lieblingsmonat _____

Lieblingsjahreszeit: _____

Haarfarbe: _____

Augenfarbe: _____

DIALOG

Now let's reverse the roles. She is asking him for a date. How does he respond?

KULTURECKE

Deutsche Feiertage

Here are some of the important German holidays:

Karneval, called **Fasching** or **Fastnacht** in Southern Germany and **Fasnet** in the Black Forest, is celebrated mainly in Catholic areas. The major carnival cities are Köln, Mainz, and München, where people dress in costumes, parade about the city, and party. The climax of **Karneval** comes on the last few days before Ash Wednesday, the beginning of the solemn season of Lent.

Ostern (*Easter*) falls on the first Sunday after the first full moon of spring. Easter customs include coloring Easter eggs, Easter rides, and Easter bonfires.

Der Tag der Arbeit (der 1. Mai), Labor Day, is celebrated with parades and festive maypole dances in the smaller towns. In the cities, this holiday is celebrated mostly by not working.

Pfingsten (*Pentecost*) occurs seven weeks after Easter. It is a traditional time for family outings. Green twigs are its most popular symbol.

Das Oktoberfest, an annual Bavarian folk festival in Munich, actually begins in September. In addition, there is a **Trachtenfest** (*folk-costume festival*) parade during the event.

On **Sankt Nikolaustag (der 6. Dezember),** Saint Nicholas comes on a sled drawn by a donkey. German children place one of their shoes on the window sill, and the next morning the shoes are filled with goodies.

Weihnachten begins with **Heiliger Abend (der 24. Dezember),** which is the main event. Germans celebrate **Weihnachten** by exchanging gifts and cards. Each home has a **Weihnachtsbaum** (*Christmas tree*).

Other major holidays are:

Neujahr (der 1. Januar) — New Year's Day
Christi Himmelfahrt (40 days after Easter) — Ascension Day
Tag der deutschen Einheit (der 3. Oktober) — German Unification Day
Silvester (der 31. Dezember) — New Year's Eve

16 *Wie ist das Wetter?*

Weather Expressions; Seasons; Word Order

 A great conversation starter is the weather:

Es ist Frühling.
Das Wetter ist schön.
Es ist windig.

Es ist Sommer.
Es ist heiß.
Die Sonne scheint.

Es ist Herbst.
Das Wetter ist schlecht.
Es regnet.

Es ist Winter.
Es ist kalt.
Es schneit.

__ ÜBUNGEN __

A. Match the following weather expressions with the correct pictures:

Es ist windig.	**Es schneit.**
Die Sonne scheint.	**Es regnet.**
Es ist kalt.	**Es ist schön.**
Es ist heiß.	**Es ist schlecht.**

1. _____

2. _____

3. _____

4. _____

5. _____

6. _____

7. _____   8. _____

B. Do you know which months belong to which season?

der Frühling	der Sommer	der Herbst	der Winter
_____	_____	_____	_____
_____	_____	_____	_____
_____	_____	_____	_____

2 In the story that follows, sometimes the word order seems a little different. Can you figure it out?

Wenn **das Wetter** schön **ist, mache ich** nicht meine Aufgaben. Dann **machen meine Freunde und ich** einen Ausflug. Wenn **wir** in den Park **kommen, spielen die Jungen** Fußball. **Spielen die Mädchen** auch Fußball? Nein, **die Mädchen spielen** lieber Tennis. Nachher **machen alle** ein Picknick.

der Ausflug *the excursion*

nachher *afterwards*

Am nächsten Tag **fragt der Lehrer,** warum **wir** die Aufgabe in der Schule **schreiben. Ich antworte,** daß **wir** die Aufgabe nicht **machen,** wenn **das Wetter** schön **ist. Der Lehrer sagt** uns, daß **er** uns eine Strafarbeit **gibt.**

am nächsten Tag *on the next day*

die Strafarbeit *the punishment assignment*

___ ÜBUNG _____

C. Complete the sentences:

1. Wenn das Wetter schön ist, macht der Schüler nicht _____ .

2. Er macht _____ mit seinen Freunden.

3. Im Park _____ die Jungen Fußball.

4. Die Mädchen spielen lieber _____ .

5. Nachher _____ . .

6. Am nächsten Tag fragt der Lehrer, warum _____ .

7. Der Schüler antwortet, daß _____ .

8. Der Lehrer sagt, daß _____ .

③ What did you notice about the word order in the longer sentences? That's right! The subject and verb were not always where you would expect them to be. Now, go back to the story and underline all of the subjects and circle the verbs. All subjects and verbs are in heavy type. Then draw an arrow from each verb to its subject. Remember, there is a subject for every verb.

You should have come up with three patterns:

SUBJECT ◄─ (VERB)　　(VERB) ─► SUBJECT　　SUBJECT . . . (VERB)

What seems to affect word order? _____
That's right! What comes before the subject affects where the verb stands.

SUBJECT ◄─ (VERB) is NORMAL WORD ORDER. The subject comes first and the verb comes second, and nothing separates the subject from the verb. Write the three clauses, beginning or ending with the nearest comma or period, that show normal word order:

_____

_____

_____

Use normal word order when the subject is the first element in the sentence or when it follows **aber** (*but*), **denn** (*because*), **oder** (*or*), **und** (*and*), **ja,** or **nein.**

(VERB)→ SUBJECT is called INVERTED WORD ORDER. The verb comes first and its subject second; nothing separates the subject from the verb. Write the five clauses, from or to the nearest comma or period, which show inverted word order:

_____

_____

_____

_____

_____

Use inverted word order when the first element of the total sentence is not the subject. Sometimes the first element can be an entire clause:

Wenn das Wetter schön ist, mache ich meine Aufgaben.

ELEMENT #1 VERB SUBJECT

If it is a clause, then the clause is separated from the next sentence segment by a comma.

Sometimes the first element is a word or phrase:

Dann machen meine Freunde und ich einen Ausflug.

#1 VERB SUBJECT

Am nächsten Tag fragt der Lehrer . . .

#1 VERB SUBJECT

Here no comma separates the first element from the rest of the sentence.

Of course, you also use inverted word oder when you ask a question:

Spielen die Mädchen . . . ?

VERB SUBJECT

SUBJECT . . . VERB is TRANSPOSED WORD ORDER. The verb is transposed to the final position of the clause and is separated from its subject by the rest of the clause. Write the six clauses, from or to the nearest comma or period, that show transposed word order:

_____

_____

_____

_____

_____

_____

Use transposed word order in clauses that begin with **daß** (*that*), **weil** (*because*), **ob** (*if, whether*), **wenn** (*whenever*), or any question word used as a conjunction (such as **warum**). How do you know that the question word is being used as a

conjunction? _____

That's right! There's no question mark at the end of the sentence:

Wenn das Wetter schön ist, . . .

SUBJECT   VERB

, . . . warum wir die Aufgaben in der Schule schreiben.

SUBJECT   VERB

, daß wir die Aufgaben nicht machen , . . .

SUBJECT   VERB

Word order is what makes German sound special, because sometimes you have to wait a long time before you hear the verb. The word order does not, however, affect the meaning of the words. As you practice your German, you'll get the hang of the word order and be able to use it correctly.

ÜBUNGEN

D. Choose the correct ending for the sentence and write it in the space provided:

1. Der Junge spielt heute Fußball, und _____ .
   a. er spielt morgen Tennis.
   b. spielt er morgen Tennis.
   c. er morgen Tennis spielt.

2. Ich mache meine Aufgaben, wenn _____ .
   a. das Wetter ist schlecht
   b. ist das Wetter schlecht
   c. das Wetter schlecht ist

3. Heute _____ .
   a. ich bringe mein Buch
   b. bringe ich mein Buch
   c. ich mein Buch bringe

4. Mein Lehrer fragt, wann _____ .
   a. ich schreibe die Strafarbeit
   b. schreibe ich die Strafarbeit
   c. ich die Strafarbeit schreibe

5. Seine Mutter sagt, daß _____ .
   a. er ist sehr intelligent
   b. ist er sehr intelligent
   c. er sehr intelligent ist

E. Make each of the sentences in Exercise D negative:

1. _____

2. _____

3. _____

4. _____

5. _____

F. Describe the weather in these pictures:

1. _____

2. _____

3. _____

4. _____

5. _____

6. _____

7. _____

8. _____

G. Es gibt vier Jahreszeiten. In welcher Jahreszeit sind wir?

1. Diese Jahreszeit ist sehr schön. Das Wetter ist herrlich. Im Park gibt es viele Blumen. Alles ist grün. Die Vögel singen. Man trägt leichte Kleidung. Man feiert Ostern in dieser Jahreszeit. Auch feiert man den Muttertag.

   die Jahreszeit *the season*
   herrlich *magnificent*
   die Vögel *the birds*

   Diese Jahreszeit ist _____ .

2. Diese Jahreszeit ist die Lieblingsjahreszeit für Schüler, denn es gibt jetzt Schulferien. Das Wetter ist sehr heiß, und die Sonne scheint oft. Die Schüler gehen zum Strand und schwimmen. Die Tage sind lang und die Nächte kurz. Wichtige Feiertage sind der vierte Juli und der Vatertag.

   oft *often*
   der Strand *the beach*
   lang *long*

   Diese Jahreszeit ist _____ .

3. Während dieser Jahreszeit sind die Schüler traurig, weil das Schuljahr wieder beginnt. Sie müssen wieder in die Schule gehen. Das Wetter ist noch schön, aber etwas kühler. Die Blätter der Bäume werden bunt: sie sind nicht mehr grün, sondern gelb und orange. Dann fallen sie vom Baum.

   wieder *again*

   das Blatt *the leaf*
   bunt *colorful*

   Diese Jahreszeit ist _____ .

4. Hast du es gern, wenn das Wetter kalt ist? Während dieser Jahreszeit schneit es viel, und es ist sehr kalt. Man trägt viele Kleidungsstücke. Die Nächte sind lang und die Tage kurz. Viele Leute glauben, daß diese Jahreszeit sehr traurig ist. Es gibt jedoch schöne Feiertage wie Weihnachten, Neujahr und den Valentinstag.

   das Kleidungsstück *the
   article of clothing*

   jedoch *however*

   Diese Jahreszeit ist _____ .

GESPRÄCH

Wortschatz

schrecklich *awfully*
nicht wahr? *isn't that true!*

Welch ein Zufall! *What a coincidence!*
leider *unfortunately*

PERSÖNLICHE FRAGEN

1. Wie ist das Wetter heute?

_____

2. In welcher Jahreszeit machst du ein Picknick?

_____

3. Wann machst du deine Aufgaben?

_____

4. Was machst du, wenn es heiß ist?

_____

5. Was machst du im Winter?

_____

DU

Pick your favorite season and write a short paragraph in German about it, using the following cues: the season you like; the weather during that season; the holidays during that season; two things you do during the season:

_____

_____

_____

_____

_____

_____

DIALOG

You are the second person in the dialog. Respond in complete German sentences:

KULTURECKE

Die Temperatur

If you want to talk about the weather with German neighbors, you should know about the temperature scale they use. Although our Fahrenheit scale was developed by a German physicist, Germans, like most Europeans, use the Celsius scale:

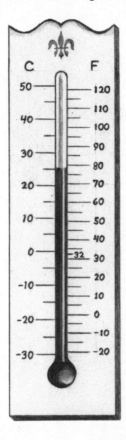

To convert Fahrenheit to Celsius or vice versa, use the following formulas:

$$\text{CELSIUS} = \text{C} \qquad\qquad \text{FAHRENHEIT} = \text{F}$$
$$\text{C} = \tfrac{5}{9}\,(\text{F} - 32) \qquad \text{F} = \tfrac{9}{5}\,\text{C} + 32$$

To change Fahrenheit to Celsius, subtract 32 from the Fahrenheit reading, multiply by 5, and divide by 9. To change Celsius to Fahrenheit, multiply the Celsius reading by 9, divide by 5, and add 32.

Wiederholung IV (Aufgaben 13–16)

Aufgabe 13

weh tun *to hurt*

Der Kopf tut *mir* weh.	*My head hurts.*
Der Kopf tut *dir* weh.	*Your head hurts.*
Der Kopf tut *ihm* weh.	*His head hurts.*
Der Kopf tut *ihr* weh.	*Her head hurts.*
Der Kopf tut *ihm* weh.	*Its head hurts.*
Die Köpfe tun *uns* weh.	*Our heads hurt.*
Die Köpfe tun *euch* weh.	*Your heads hurt.*
Die Köpfe tun *ihnen* weh.	*Their heads hurt.*
Der Kopf tut *Ihnen* weh.	*Your head hurts.*
Die Köpfe tun *Ihnen* weh.	*Your heads hurt.*

Aufgabe 14

a. Stem-changing verbs e→ie

sehen		lesen	
ich sehe	wir sehen	ich lese	wir lesen
du *siehst*	ihr seht	du *liest*	ihr lest
er		er	
sie } *sieht*	sie sehen	sie } *liest*	sie lesen
es		es	
	Sie sehen		Sie lesen

b. Accusative pronouns:

mich	uns
dich	euch
ihn	
sie }	sie
es	
	Sie

282

c. *Who* in the nominative and *whom* in accusative:

NOMINATIVE: **wer?**
ACCUSATIVE: **wen?**

Aufgabe 15

DIE TAGE	DIE MONATE
(der) **Montag**	(der) **Januar**
(der) **Dienstag**	(der) **Februar**
(der) **Mittwoch**	(der) **März**
(der) **Donnerstag**	(der) **April**
(der) **Freitag**	(der) **Mai**
(der) **Samstag**	(der) **Juni**
(der) **Sonnabend**	(der) **Juli**
(der) **Sonntag**	(der) **August**
	(der) **September**
	(der) **Oktober**
	(der) **November**
	(der) **Dezember**

Aufgabe 16

a. Normal word order:

SUBJECT + VERB + REST OF SENTENCE
Der Vater liest die Zeitung.

Use normal word order with simple sentences where the subject is the first element of the sentence, or where the subject follows **und, oder, aber, denn, ja, nein,** or any other element that could stand by itself as a complete thought.

b. Inverted word order:

. . . VERB + SUBJECT + REST OF SENTENCE
Dann *liest die Mutter* die Zeitung.

Use inverted word order when the sentence begins not with the subject but with something else that cannot stand by itself as a complete thought.

c. Transposed word order:

. . . SUBJECT + REST OF SENTENCE + VERB
Er sagt, daß *der Vater* die Zeitung *liest.*

Use transposed word order after **daß, ob, weil, wenn,** or any question word used to connect two clauses.

— ÜBUNGEN ———————————————————

A. Write the German word under the picture you see. Then find the German word in the puzzle on page 285.

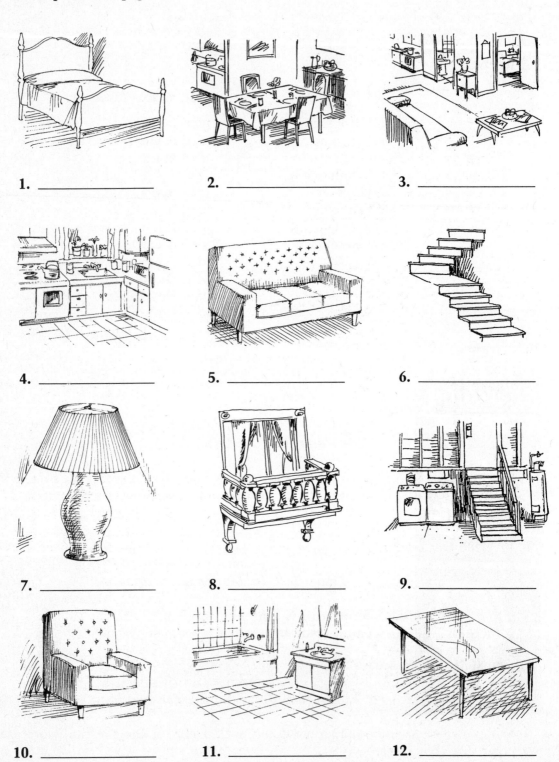

1. _____

2. _____

3. _____

4. _____

5. _____

6. _____

7. _____

8. _____

9. _____

10. _____

11. _____

12. _____

 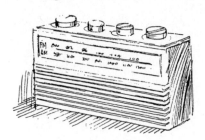 

13. _____   14. _____   15. _____

16. _____   17. _____   18. _____

B	A	L	K	O	N	H	A	N	S	K
A	R	T	T	E	B	A	O	E	N	G
D	U	R	H	P	F	U	S	A	S	N
E	S	E	C	M	S	S	R	S	O	U
Z	E	P	S	A	E	H	T	I	F	N
I	M	P	I	L	C	U	D	L	A	H
M	I	E	T	S	H	A	U	S	R	O
M	A	R	K	L	R	Ü	L	L	E	W
E	H	C	Ü	K	E	L	L	E	R	H
R	E	M	M	I	Z	S	S	E	Ü	C

B. Kreuzworträtsel:

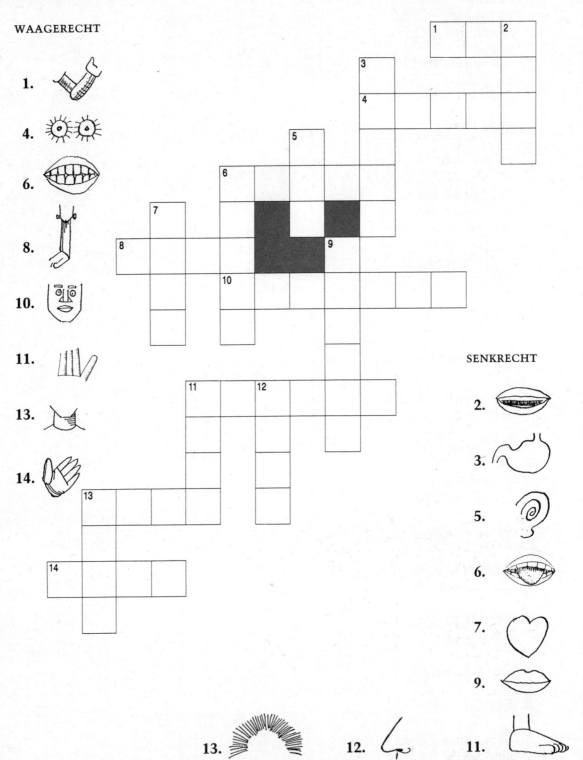

WAAGERECHT

1.

4.

6.

8.

10.

11.

13.

14.

SENKRECHT

2.

3.

5.

6.

7.

9.

13. 12. 11.

C. Monika has just received a letter from a friend. But the letter is hard to read because the writing is not clear. Can you help her figure out what the missing words are? (Clue: The missing words are all conjunctions like **und, oder, aber, denn, daß, ob, weil, wenn**):

Liebe Monika!

Es tut mir leid, _____ ich erst (*only*) heute schreibe. Ich möchte

jede Woche schreiben, _____ ich habe keine Zeit.

Wie geht's? Es geht hier prima, _____ das Wetter sehr gut ist.

Ich gehe heute schwimmen, _____ morgen gehe ich einkaufen.

Ich schwimme jeden Tag, _____ die Sonne scheint.

Ich muß jetzt schließen (*close*), _____ wir essen bald Abend-essen.

Deine Marianne

D. After filling in all the horizontal boxes, look at the vertical box. You will find something that many Germans wear:

1. Der Vater _____ die Zeitung.

2. Wir essen im _____ .

3. Ich schwimme gern im Sommer, _____ das Wetter ist schön.

4. Wir feiern Weihnachten im _____ .

5. Ich kann nicht laufen. Der Fuß tut _____ weh.

6. Die Milch ist im _____ in der Küche.

7. Der Sofa ist im _____ .

8. Der _____ Januar ist Neujahr.

9. September, Oktober und November sind im _____ .

10. Wir _____ jeden Freitag einen Film.

E. Picture Story. Can you read this story? Much of it is in picture form. Whenever you come to a picture, read it as if it were a German word:

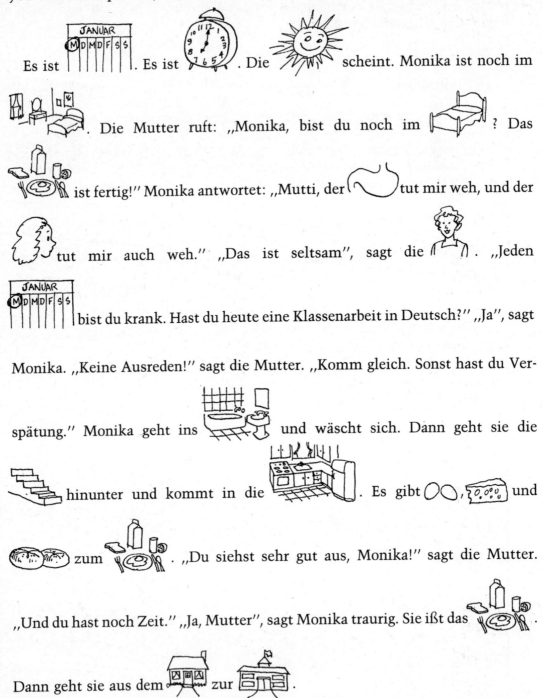

Es ist [Montag]. Es ist [sieben Uhr]. Die [Sonne] scheint. Monika ist noch im [Schlafzimmer]. Die Mutter ruft: "Monika, bist du noch im [Bett]? Das [Frühstück] ist fertig!" Monika antwortet: "Mutti, der [Magen] tut mir weh, und der [Kopf] tut mir auch weh." "Das ist seltsam", sagt die [Mutter]. "Jeden [Montag] bist du krank. Hast du heute eine Klassenarbeit in Deutsch?" "Ja", sagt Monika. "Keine Ausreden!" sagt die Mutter. "Komm gleich. Sonst hast du Verspätung." Monika geht ins [Badezimmer] und wäscht sich. Dann geht sie die [Treppe] hinunter und kommt in die [Küche]. Es gibt [Eier], [Käse] und [Brötchen] zum [Frühstück]. "Du siehst sehr gut aus, Monika!" sagt die Mutter. "Und du hast noch Zeit." "Ja, Mutter", sagt Monika traurig. Sie ißt das [Frühstück].

Dann geht sie aus dem [Haus] zur [Schule].

Wortschatz

seltsam *strange*	**gleich** *immediately*	**hinunter** *down*
die Ausrede *the excuse*	**sonst** *otherwise*	**traurig** *unhappy*
die Klassenarbeit *the test*	**wäscht sich** *gets washed*	

Fünfter Teil

17 *Die Schulfächer*

Imperative

 Can you guess the names of these subjects?

Deutsch

Englisch

Latein

Spanisch

Französisch

Italienisch

Mathematik

Geometrie

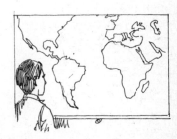

Erdkunde/Geographie

Biologie   Chemie   Physik

Geschichte   Turnen   Musik

Kunst   Hauswirtschaft   Handwerk

__ ÜBUNG _____

A. You've just received your class schedule for next year. What subjects are you studying?

EXAMPLE: Ich lerne Englisch.

1. _____

2. _____

3. _____

4. _____

5. _____

6. _____

7. _____

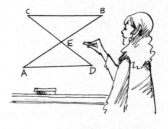

8. _____

9. _____

10. _____

2 The imperative is important because it helps get things done. Read this page from Karl's assignment book and try to figure out how the imperative helps Karl to accomplish this goal:

Karls Aufgaben

DEUTSCH: **Schreib** einen Aufsatz über deine Sommerferien!

ENGLISCH: **Lern** die Vokabeln für die Klassenarbeit!

GESCHICHTE: **Lies** Seiten 206–217 im Textbuch!

MUSIK: **Übe** 30 Minuten lang Klavier!

BIOLOGIE: **Beantworte** die Fragen 1–6 auf Seite 317 im Textbuch!

KUNST: **Zeichne** ein Landschaftsbild!

FRANZÖSISCH: **Lies** das Gedicht auf Seite 42! **Schreib** einen Brief!

TURNEN: **Lauf** einen Kilometer!

über *about*

die Vokabeln *the vocabulary*
die Seite *the page*
das Klavier *the piano*

zeichnen *to draw*
  das Landschaftsbild *the landscape picture*
das Gedicht *the poem*
der Brief *the letter*

__ ÜBUNG _____

B. Karl lost his assignment book. Help him remember his assignments:

1. _____   2. _____

3. _____   4. _____

5. _____

6. _____

7. _____

8. _____

3 Have you figured out the purpose of the imperative? It is a verb that commands one or more people to do something. What were the imperatives in Karl's assignments?

_____   _____   _____

_____   _____   _____

_____   _____

Very good! You found them all! How are imperatives punctuated?

_____

That's right, too. In German, imperatives are punctuated with an exclamation point.

In German, there are as many ways of telling someone to do something as there are ways of saying *you* — three. There is a command form for **du,** one for **ihr,** and one for **Sie.**

Karl's assignments used the **du**-command. You would use this command when talking to someone you would normally address with **du.** Let's see how the **du**-command works:

INFINITIVE	er-FORM	du-COMMAND
schreiben	er schreibt	Schreib!
lernen	er lernt	Lern!
lesen	er liest	Lies!
üben	er übt	Übe!
beantworten	er beantwortet	Beantworte!
zeichnen	er zeichnet	Zeichne!
laufen	er läuft	Lauf!

The **du**-command is the same as the **er**-form of the verb without the **t** ending (and without umlaut, if one was added, as in **laufen**). Some **du**-commands have an **e** ending to make them easier to pronounce.

Notice that, in addition to the verb **antworten,** we used the verb **beantworten.** Both mean *to answer.* Use **beantworten** with a direct object. Use **antworten** when there is no object. Compare:

Antworte auf deutsch!	Answer in German.
Beantworte die Frage!	Answer the question.

___ ÜBUNG _____

C. You're the teacher. Tell one student to do the following:

1. (setzen) _____ dich!

2. (stehen) _____ auf!

3. (schreiben) _____ einen Aufsatz!

4. (lernen) _____ gut! Morgen ist die Klassenarbeit.

5. (gehen) _____ an die Tafel!

6. (holen) _____ das Papier!

7. (heben) _____ die Hand!

8. (warten) _____ !

9. (beginnen) _____ !

10. (halten) _____ !

5 You don't always tell one person to do something. Sometimes you give two or more people the same instructions at the same time. If you would normally address this group with **ihr,** you use the **ihr**-command. The **ihr**-command is the same as the **ihr**-form of the verb. What are the **ihr**-commands for these **du**-commands?

Schreib **einen Aufsatz!** _____

Lern **die Vokabeln!** _____

Lies **das Buch!** _____

Übe **Klavier!** _____

Beantworte **die Frage!** _____

Zeichne **ein Bild!** _____

Lauf **einen Kilometer!** _____

Mach **eine Reise!** _____

Sehr gut! The **ihr**-commands are:

Schreibt **einen Aufsatz!**
Lernt **die Vokabeln!**
Lest **das Buch!**
Übt **Klavier!**
Beantwortet **die Frage!**
Lauft **einen Kilometer!**
Macht **eine Reise!**

___ ÜBUNG _____

D. You're still the teacher. This time, tell the entire class to do these things:

1. (setzen) _____ euch!

2. (lesen) _____ das Buch!

3. (schreiben) _____ einen Brief!

4. (lernen) _____ gut! Morgen ist die Klassenarbeit.

5. (gehen) _____ an die Tafel!

6. (stehen) _____ auf!

7. (heben) _____ die Hände!

8. (warten) _____ !

9. (beginnen) _____ !

10. (halten) _____ !

6 | Then there are times when it is necessary to give instructions to a person or people whom you would address with **Sie.** The **Sie**-command is the **Sie**-form of the verb followed by the pronoun **Sie.** What are the **Sie**-commands for these **ihr**-commands?

Schreibt einen Aufsatz! _____

Lernt die Vokabeln! _____

Lest ein Buch! _____

Übt Klavier! _____

Beantwortet die Frage! _____

Zeichnet ein Bild! _____

Lauft einen Kilometer! _____

Macht eine Reise! _____

You're correct if your list looks like this:

Schreiben Sie einen Aufsatz!
Lernen Sie die Vokabeln!
Lesen Sie ein Buch!
Üben Sie Klavier!
Beantworten Sie die Frage!
Zeichnen Sie ein Bild!
Laufen Sie einen Kilometer!
Machen Sie eine Reise!

__ ÜBUNG _____

E. Here's the chance you've been waiting for! Tell your teacher to do these things:

1. (setzen) _____ sich!

2. (lesen) _____ das Heft!

3. (schreiben) _____ einen Aufsatz!

4. (lernen) _____ gut!

5. (gehen) _____ an die Tafel!

6. (holen) _____ das Papier!

7. (heben) _____ die Hand!

8. (warten) _____ !

9. (beginnen) _____ !

10. (stehen) _____ auf!

---

7 **Sein** and **haben** do not follow the rules. Here are their command forms:

	sein	haben
(du)	**Sei!** (*Be.*)	**Hab!** (*Have.*)
(ihr)	**Seid!** (*Be.*)	**Habt!** (*Have.*)
(Sie)	**Seien Sie!** (*Be.*)	**Haben Sie!** (*Have.*)

Common commands with **sein** and **haben** are:

Sei vorsichtig!
Seid vorsichtig!   } *Be careful.*
Seien Sie vorsichtig!

Hab keine Angst!
Habt keine Angst!   } *Don't be afraid.*
Haben Sie keine Angst!

__ ÜBUNG _____

F. Tell these people what to do (or not to do). Use the **du, ihr,** or **Sie** command, as appropriate:

1. (laufen) _____ nicht so schnell, Michael!

2. (sein) _____ vorsichtig, Herr Braun!

3. (gehen) _____ zur Schule, Kinder!

4. (schlafen) _____ gut, Frau Weiß!

5. (essen) _____ ein Eis, Martina!

6. (schreiben) _____ einen Brief, Fräulein Halm!

7. (haben) _____ keine Angst, Kinder!

8. (lesen) _____ diesen Aufsatz, Herr Schmidt!

9. (antworten) _____ doch auf deutsch, Petra!

10. (machen) _____ schnell, Jungen!

8 | Sometimes it's more effective to include yourself in the command:

***Gehen wir* schwimmen!**	*Let's go swimming.*
***Seien wir* vorsichtig!**	*Let's be careful.*
***Haben wir* keine Angst!**	*Let's not be afraid.*

An inclusive command in English starts with *Let's.* To form an inclusive command in German, use the **wir**-form of the verb followed by **wir.**

___ ÜBUNG _____

G. Wie sagt man das auf deutsch? How do you say these sentences in German?

1. Let's read the newspaper.

   _____

2. Let's hike.

   _____

3. Let's write a letter.

   _____

4. Let's play cards.

   _____

5. Let's eat.

   _____

GESPRÄCH

Wortschatz

sicher *sure*	**sieht . . . aus** *looks like*
weiter *further*	**das Rezept** *the recipe*
holen *to get*	**kennen** *to know*
die Scheibe *the slice*	**Genau!** *Exactly!*
legen *to put*	

DIALOG

You are the first person in the dialog, the one giving most of the directions:

_____ *PERSÖNLICHE FRAGEN* _____

1. Welche Fächer lernst du in der Schule?

_____

2. Welches Schulfach hast du am liebsten? Warum?

_____

3. Welches Schulfach hast du nicht gern? Warum?

_____

4. Um wieviel Uhr beginnt der Schultag?

_____

5. Um wieviel Uhr endet der Schultag?

_____

6. Was machst du nach der Schule?

_____

_____ *DU* _____

Complete this **Stundenplan** (*class schedule*):

Klasse: _____   **Name:** _____

ZEIT	MONTAG	DIENSTAG	MITTWOCH	DONNERSTAG	FREITAG

KULTURECKE

Stundenpläne und Zeugnisse

You can tell a lot about German school life by looking at a student's **Stundenplan**. Look at this **Stundenplan**:

SCHULE: LESSING GYMNASIUM			NAME: HEIKE SCHULZ 7A		
ZEIT	MONTAG	DIENSTAG	MITTWOCH	DONNERSTAG	FREITAG	SAMSTAG
8.00–8.45	Deutsch	Mathe	Französisch	Geschichte	Französisch	Französisch
8.45–9.30	Englisch	Deutsch	Mathe	Geographie	Chemie	Musik
9.30–10.15	Latein	Englisch	Deutsch	Latein	Kunst	Biologie
10.40–11.25	Geographie	Biologie	Physik	Deutsch	Mathe	Latein
11.25–12.10	Chemie	Kunst	Geschichte	Englisch	Deutsch	
12.20–13.05	Sport	Geschichte	Sport	Mathe	Englisch	

Pauses between classes are unnecessary because the students normally stay in the same room. The teachers go from room to room. The **Große Pause** (*long recess*) at this school is from 10:15 to 10:40. During this time students may socialize and eat their mid-morning snack. The **Kleine Pause,** from 12:10 to 12:20, is a shorter stretch of free time.

Periodically, students are issued **Zeugnisse** (*report cards*), which they bring home to their parents. Grades range from 1 to 6. Most students want "eine Eins" (1), which is the highest grade. A grade of 5 or 6 is unsatisfactory.

What other differences do you notice between the German and American school day?

18 *Elektronische Apparate*

Dative with the Definite Article; the Verb **geben**

1 Can you figure out the meanings of these modern-day electronic marvels?

der Computer

der Mikrowellenherd

das schnurlose Telefon

das Telefaxgerät

die elektrische Schreibmaschine

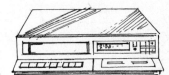

der Videorecorder/der VCR

die Videokamera

der Minifernseher

der Großbild(farb)fernseher

der CD-Spieler

der Solarrechner

__ ÜBUNGEN _____

A. Herr und Frau Kühl are shopping for a birthday present for their teenager. Tell what they are looking for:

EXAMPLE: Sie suchen ein Telefaxgerät.

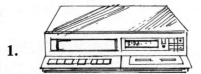

1. _____

2. _____

3. _____

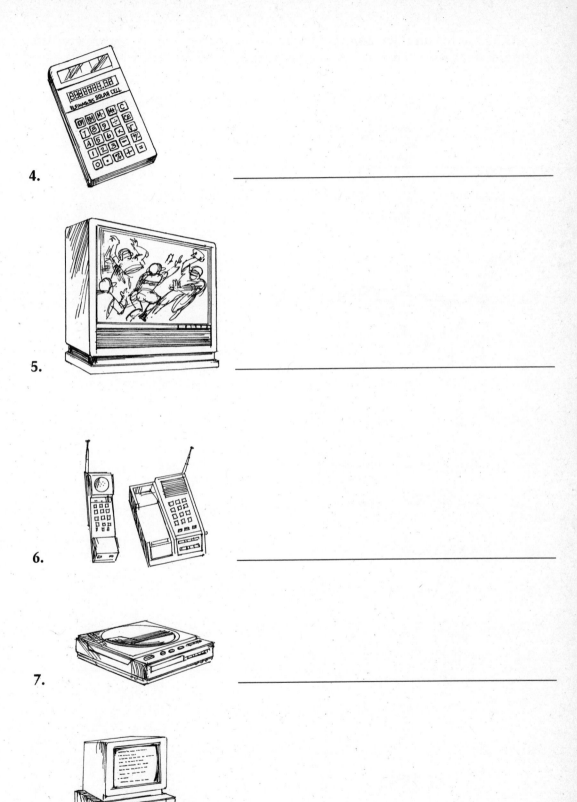

4. _____

5. _____

6. _____

7. _____

8. _____

B. Alois wanted all the comforts of home when he went away to college. Tell what modern-day conveniences Alois has with him:

EXAMPLE:  Er hat einen Solarrechner.

1.  _____

2. 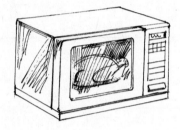 _____

3.  _____

4.  _____

5. _____

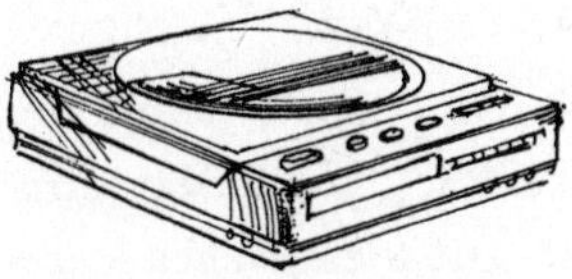

6. _____

7. _____

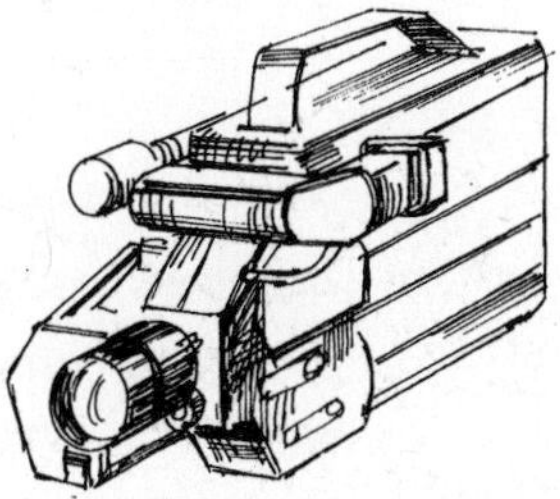

8. _____

C. List five electronic items you would like to have in your room:

1. _____

2. _____

3. _____

4. _____

5. _____

Read this story about an overeager young woman. The noun phrases in heavy type are all in the dative case. Try to figure out how the dative works:

Elke beendet ihr Studium an der Universität. Sie findet eine Stelle als Redakteurin in einer großen, angesehenen Firma. Damit sie für ihre Arbeit gut vorbereitet ist, gibt sie eine große Summe Geld in einem Elektronikladen aus, wo sie alle nötigen Geräte kauft, die eine moderne Geschäftsfrau haben sollte. Sie erklärt **der Freundin Gabi,** daß der Computer, das Telefax, die elektrische Schreibmaschine, der Rechner und das Telefon nützlich sind, wenn sie zu Hause arbeitet. Elke denkt, das ist sehr intelligent.

das Studium *the studies*
die Redakteurin *the editor*
angesehen *respected*
  die Firma *the firm*
  damit *so that*
gibt ... aus *spends*
der Elektronikladen *the electronics store*
  nötig *necessary*
die Geschäftsfrau *the businesswoman*
sollte *should*
nützlich *useful*

Der erste Arbeitstag kommt. Elke geht ins Büro und sagt **dem Chef:**

das Büro *the office*
der Chef *the boss*

ELKE: Verzeihung. Wo ist mein Computer?

CHEF: Wir benutzen die Maschinen nicht. Wir haben vor dem Computer Angst, denn er hat Ausstrahlungen, die sehr gefährlich sind.

ELKE: Das stimmt. Aber wo ist denn mein Textautomat?

CHEF: Die Maschine ist zu teuer. Unser Schlagwort ist: „Spare in der Zeit, so hast du in der Not."*

ELKE: Aber sicher steht **dem Büro** ein Telefax zur Verfügung.

CHEF: Leider nicht. Diese Geräte sind noch nicht perfekt genug.

ELKE: Sie geben mir doch mindestens eine elektrische Schreibmaschine?

CHEF: Es tut mir leid. Die elektrische Schreibmaschine ist kaputt, und der Reparateur ist drei Monate auf Urlaub.

ELKE: Ach, diese Firma ist hoch angesehen, aber sie ist gar nicht modern. Mutter hatte recht, als sie sagte: „Man soll den Tag nicht vor dem Abend loben."**

Verzeihung *Excuse me*

benutzen *to use*
die Austrahlung *the ray*
gefährlich *dangerous*
stimmen *to be true*
der Textautomat *the word processor*
teuer *expensive*
  das Schlagwort *the slogan*
zur Verfügung stehen *to be available*

leider *unfortunately*

mindestens *at least*

kaputt *broken*
  der Reparateur *the repairman*
auf Urlaub *on vacation*
hoch *highly*
sagte *said*

* "Waste not, want not." (Literally, "Save when you can so that you have in time of need.")
** "Don't count your chickens before they hatch." (Literally, "One should not praise the day before the evening.")

__ ÜBUNG _____

C. **Ergänze die Sätze!**

1. Elke beendet _____ .

2. Sie findet eine Stelle als _____ .

3. Die Firma ist _____ .

4. Im Elektronikladen kauft sie _____ .

5. Sie denkt, diese Geräte _____ .

6. Elke denkt, sie ist _____ .

7. Die Firma benutzt den Computer nicht, denn _____

_____ .

8. Die Firma benutzt Textautomaten nicht, denn _____

_____ .

9. Das Schlagwort der Firma ist: _____

_____ .

10. Die Firma gebraucht das Telefax nicht, denn _____

_____ .

11. Die elektronische Schreibmaschine ist _____ .

12. Der Reparateur ist _____ .

13. Die Firma ist hoch angesehen, aber _____ .

14. Elkes Mutter sagte: _____

_____ .

3 Now look at these groups of sentences. Pay special attention to the noun that appears in all three sentences in each group.

Der Mann ist intelligent.
Ich sehe *den Mann*.
Ich gebe *dem Mann* den Computer.

Die Frau ist intelligent
Ich sehe *die Frau*.
Ich gebe *der Frau* den Videorecorder.

Das Mädchen ist intelligent.
Ich sehe *das Mädchen*.
Ich gebe *dem Mädchen* das Telefaxgerät.

Die Kinder sind intelligent.
Ich sehe *die Kinder*.
Ich gebe *den Kindern* den Minifernseher.

How do **Mann, Frau, Mädchen,** and **Kinder** function in the first sentence of

each group? _____ Yes, they're the subject; they're in the NOMINATIVE CASE. And in the second sentence of each group, how do

they function? _____ That's right, too. They're in the ACCUSATIVE CASE, so they're the direct object. What's the direct object in

the third sentence of each group? _____

Sehr gut! Computer, Videorecorder, Telefaxgerät, and **Minifernseher** are the direct objects of their respective sentences because they are in the accusative and there is no accusative preposition in the sentence.

Now, here is the new part! How do **Mann, Frau, Mädchen, Kindern** function in

the third sentence of each group? Can you guess? _____ .
They are the indirect object. In German, we say they are in the DATIVE CASE:

Ich gebe *dem Mann den Computer*.
I give the man the computer.

What's being given? _____ = Accusative

To whom is it being given? _____ = Dative

Ich gebe *der Frau den Videorecorder*.
I give the woman the VCR.

What's being given? _____ = Accusative

To whom is it being given?_____ = Dative

Ich gebe *dem Mädchen das Telefaxgerät*.
I give the girl the fax machine.

What's being given? _____ = Accusative

To whom is it being given? _____ = Dative

Ich gebe *den Kindern den Minifernseher*.
I give the children the mini-TV.

What's being given? _____ = Accusative

To whom is it being given? _____ = Dative

How do you say *the* in the dative?

_____   _____   _____

When do you use **dem?** _____

When do you use **der?** _____

When do you use **den?** _____

What else do you do if you use **den** in the dative?

_____

Richtig! Add an **n** to the plural noun form if it does not already end in **n**.

IMPORTANT EXCEPTION: Do not add **n** to a plural noun that ends in **s**.

4 Summary:

	MASCULINE	FEMININE	NEUTER	PLURAL
NOMINATIVE	der	die	das	die
ACCUSATIVE	den	die	das	die
DATIVE	dem	der	dem	den (+n on noun)

___ ÜBUNGEN ___

D. Change the following nominative noun phrases to the dative:

1. die Frau _____

2. der Vater _____

3. das Kind _____

4. die Tochter _____

5. der Onkel _____

6. das Mädchen _____

7. die Töchter _____

8. der Bruder _____

9. die Katze _____

10. die Jungen _____

E. Change the following accusative noun phrases to the dative:

1. den Vetter _____

2. den Vater _____

3. die Frau _____

4. die Mädchen _____

5. den Onkel _____

6. die Kinder _____

7. das Fräulein _____

8. den Bruder _____

9. die Frauen _____

10. den Hund _____

F. Complete each sentence with the appropriate definite article in the dative:

1. Er gibt _____ Klasse eine Strafarbeit.

2. Sie bringt _____ Familie eine Torte.

3. Ich gebe _____ Mutter das Eis.

4. Wir kaufen _____ Mädchen (singular) Blumen.

5. Ich lese _____ Vater die Zeitung vor.

6. Sie bestellen _____ Kindern die Bratwurst.

7. Du kaufst _____ Bruder einen Kuli.

8. Ihr bringt _____ Eltern das Salz.

9. Ich kaufe _____ Tante eine Bluse.

10. Du gibst _____ Kindern die Kreide.

G. Complete each sentence with the appropriate definite articles in the nominative, accusative, and dative:

1. _____ Mann kauft _____ Frau _____ Buch.

2. _____ Frau bringt _____ Söhnen _____ Kaffee.

3. _____ Sohn gibt _____ Schwester _____ Heft.

4. _____ Schwester bringt _____ Mutter _____ Nachtisch.

5. _____ Mutter kauft _____ Vater _____ Krawatte.

6. _____ Vater gibt _____ Onkel _____ Hemd.

7. _____ Onkel bringt _____ Tante _____ Lebensmittel.

8. _____ Tante kauft _____ Nichten _____ Kleider.

5 │ Now look at these questions and answers:

Wer liest die Zeitung?   *Der Vater* liest die Zeitung.
Wen siehst du?   Ich sehe *meine Mutter.*
Wem gibst du die Torte?   Ich gebe *dem Bruder* die Torte.

What does **wer** mean? _____

What does **wen** mean? _____

What does **wem** mean? _____

The answer to **wer** (*who*) is in the nominative. The answer to **wen** (*whom*) is in the accusative. The answer to **wem** ([*to, for*]) *whom* is in the dative.

___ ÜBUNG _____

H. Complete each question with **wer, wen,** or **wem:**

1. _____ sagt das? — Mein Vater sagt das.

2. _____ besuchst du? — Ich besuche meinen Onkel.

2. _____ gibst du einen Apfel. — Ich gebe dem Lehrer einen Apfel.

3. _____ sieht der Mann? — Der Mann sieht die Frau.

4. _____ kaufst du eine Platte? — Ich kaufe der Schwester eine Platte.

6 In our story, there's another stem-changing verb similar to **essen**. What is it?

_____ You're correct if you wrote **geben** (*to give*). Now complete the table for **geben:**

ich _____   wir _____

du _____   ihr _____

er
sie } _____   sie _____
es

                            Sie _____

The **e** of the stem changes to **i** in the **du, er, sie, es** forms of **geben**. Otherwise, it's a regular verb. Now complete the table for the imperative:

(du)   _____ !

(Sie)   _____ !

(ihr)   _____ !

(wir)   _____ !

ÜBUNG

I. Complete each sentence with the correct form of **geben:**

1. Ich _____ der Mutter Blumen.

2. Wir _____ den Eltern Apfelsaft.

3. Du _____ dem Mann einen Hut.

4. Ihr _____ dem Kind einen Ball.

5. Er _____ der Frau eine Bluse.

4. _____ deinem Bruder ein Stück Käse, Ernst!

5. _____ Sie Ihrer Frau einen Computer zum Geburtstag?

6. Susi _____ ihrer Schwester einen Videorecorder.

7. _____ wir dem Mädchen eine Torte!

8. _____ Sie dem Mädchen ein Eis!

_____ PERSÖNLICHE FRAGEN _____

1. Wie viele Fernseher hat deine Familie?

   _____

2. Wie viele Telefone hat deine Familie?

   _____

3. Welche Farbe hat dein Telefon?

   _____

4. Welcher Computer ist der beste?

   _____

5. Hast du Angst vor dem Computer? Warum (nicht)?

   _____

_____ DU _____

Write five sentences about what you do with your favorite electronic gadget. If you haven't learned the German term for your choice of appliance, consult a dictionary or your teacher:

1. _____

2. _____

3. _____

4. _____

5. _____

GESPRÄCH

Wortschatz

mir gefällt *I like*   besitzen *to own*
Gar nicht *Not at all.*

KULTURECKE

Deutsches Fernsehen

German TV networks are "public corporations." They are supervised by civic authorities made up of representatives of the political parties represented in the state parliaments and of the major professional and social groups, such as the trade unions, churches, educational institutions, and youth organizations.

No commercials interrupt German TV programs. Advertising is nevertheless an important source of income for German TV. Commercials are packaged into several short broadcasts at the beginning of the evening's programs (before 8 p.m. and never on Sundays).

German TV's major source of income is the **Gebühr** (*fee*) that each set owner pays the **Bundespost** (German federal postal system) every month. The **Bundespost** keeps a portion of this fee to maintain the towers, transmitters, cables, and other equipment needed to broadcast the programs. The remainder of the money goes to the networks.

Here is a sample listing from a day's programming of one of the major German networks:

> **13.45 Wirtschafts-Telegramm**
> **14.00 Sesamstraße**
> **14.30 „. . . und das Leben geht weiter"**
> **15.30 Tagesschau**
> **15.35 Wer hat Angst vorm kleinen Mann?**
> **15.50 Flieg, Vogel, flieg**
> **17.15 Tagesschau**
> **Regionalprogramme**
> **BR**: 17.35 Forstinspektor Buchholz 18.45 Zwei alte Damen geben Gas 19.20 Pleiten, Pech und Pannen **HR**: 17.25 Villa Brockelstein 17.35 Friedrichstadtpalast 18.05 Von A–Z 18.45 Büro. Büro **NDR**: 17.35 Karussell der Puppen 18.45 Spielergeschichten **RB**: 17.35 Sommersprossen 17.40 Liebesgeschichten **SFB**: 17.25 Wer Haß hat . . . 18.50 Drei Damen vom Grill **SR**: 17.35 Einfach klassisch 18.25 Büro. Büro 18.55 Polizeiinspektion 1 **SDR, SWF**: 17.35 Einfach klassisch 18.45 Büro. Büro 19.15 Mich laust der Affe **WDR**: 17.35 Hart aber herzlich 18.30 Hier und heute 18.25 Sekt oder Selters
> **19.58 Heute im Ersten**
> **20.00 Tagesschau**
> **20.15 Ein Klassemädchen**
> **21.45 Plusminus**
> Das ARD-Wirtschaftsmagazin
> **22.30 Tagesthemen**
> mit Bericht aus Bonn
> **23.00 Golden girls**
> Die Damen der Nacht
> **22.35 Sportschau**
> **23.50 ARD-Gruselkabinett**
> **Die vier Schädel des Jonathan Drake**
> **1.00 Tagesschau**

What differences do you notice between German and American TV?

_____ **DIALOG** _____

You are at someone's house admiring some things you see. Fill in the blanks in the dialog to complete it:

19 *Die Stadt*

Dative with Indefinite Articles and Possessives; the Verb **nehmen**

1 Can you guess the meanings of these interesting places in the city? Some of the words you have already learned. Do you remember them?

der Bahnhof

der Flughafen
der Flugplatz

die Bibliothek

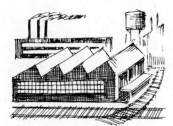

die Fabrik

die Tankstelle

die Kirche

das Schwimmbad

das Kaufhaus

die Universität

das Museum

das Gymnasium

das Hotel

der Garten

das Theater

das Kino

das Restaurant

das Schloß

das Café

__ ÜBUNGEN _____

A. You have a lot of places to visit. Can you identify them?

1. _____

2. _____

3. _____

4. _____

5. _____

6. _____

7. _____

8. _____

9. _____

10. _____

11. _____

12. _____

B. Where would you do the following things in the city?

1. Ich sehe „Cats" und „Les Misérables" im _____ .

2. Ich lese Bücher in der _____ .

3. Ich schwimme im _____ .

4. Ich sehe Filme im _____ .

5. Ich fahre mit dem Flugzeug vom _____ .

6. Ich fahre mit dem Zug vom _____ .

7. Ich esse im _____ .

8. Ich sehe van Goghs und da Vincis im _____ .

9. Ich kaufe schöne Kleider im _____ .

10. Ich kaufe Benzin für das Auto an der _____ .

2 Elise is working in New York. She writes this letter to her mother in Germany:

New York, den 11.7.

Liebe Mutti!

Ich liebe New York! Diese Stadt ist so groß und aufregend. Heute zeige ich einer Gruppe von Touristen
die schönsten Sehenswürdigkeiten New Yorks: den
Flughafen, den Central Park mit den großen Bäumen
und schönen Blumen, das Empire State Building und
die Freiheitsstatue.

lieben *to love*
aufregend *exciting*
   zeigen *to show*
      die Gruppe *the group*
die Sehenswürdigkeit *the sight*

Heute abend zeige ich einem Freund die Kunst-
werke im Museum. Morgen zeige ich meinen
Kollegen das Broadway Theater. Wir sehen „Cats".
Nachher nehmen wir ein Taxi zum Seehafen an der
Südstraße. Dann gehen wir zu Fuß ins Restaurant.

das Kunstwerk *work of art*
der Kollege *the colleague*

nachher *afterwards*
   nehmen *to take*
      der Seehafen *the seaport*
zu Fuß *by foot*
die Reiseführerin *the tour
   guide*
verdienen *to earn*
   deshalb *therefore*

Es freut mich sehr, daß ich als Reiseführerin genug
Geld verdiene. Ich wohne deshalb in einer schönen
Wohnung.

Viele Grüße!

Deine Simone

___ ÜBUNG _____

C. Beantworte die Fragen!

1. Wo ist Simone?

_____

2. Was liebt sie?

_____

3. Welches Datum hat der Brief?

_____

4. Was denkt Simone über New York?

_____

5. Wem zeigt sie den Flughafen?

_____

6. Wem zeigt sie die Kunstwerke?

_____

7. Wem zeigt sie das Broadway Theater?

_____

8. Was sehen sie im Theater?

_____

9. Wie verdient Simone Geld?

_____

10. Wo wohnt sie?

_____

_____

3 Now let's learn more about the dative. Look at these sentences:

> Ich zeige *meinem Bruder* den Park.
> Ich zeige *meiner Schwester* die Bibliothek.
> Ich zeige *meinem Kind* das Museum.
> Ich zeige *meinen Eltern* die Kirche.

Underline the dative object in these sentences; **meinem Bruder, meiner Schwester, meinem Kind, meinem Eltern** are the masculine, feminine, neuter, and plural forms, respectively, of the dative.

The possessives **mein, dein, sein, ihr, unser, euer, Ihr,** the indefinite article **ein,** and **kein** form the dative by adding **em** in the masculine and neuter singular forms, **er** in the feminine singular form, and **en** in the plural. The plural noun itself has an **n** ending if the plural form does not already end in **n.** Of course, there is no dative plural for **ein.**

4

In summary, the endings for **ein, kein,** and the possessives are:

	MASCULINE	FEMININE	NEUTER	PLURAL
NOMINATIVE	—	-e	—	-e
ACCUSATIVE	-en	-e	—	-e
DATIVE	-em	-er	-em	-en

Here is how the endings look on a model possessive:

	MASCULINE	FEMININE	NEUTER	PLURAL
NOMINATIVE	mein	meine	mein	meine
ACCUSATIVE	meinen	meine	mein	meine
DATIVE	meinem	meiner	meinem	meinen

ÜBUNGEN

D. Alois Forster is a tour guide. Tell him to show the pictured objects to the people indicated:

EXAMPLE: (ein Freund) Zeig einem Freund das Gymnasium!

1.   (eine Frau)   _____

_____

2.   (ein Vater)   _____

_____

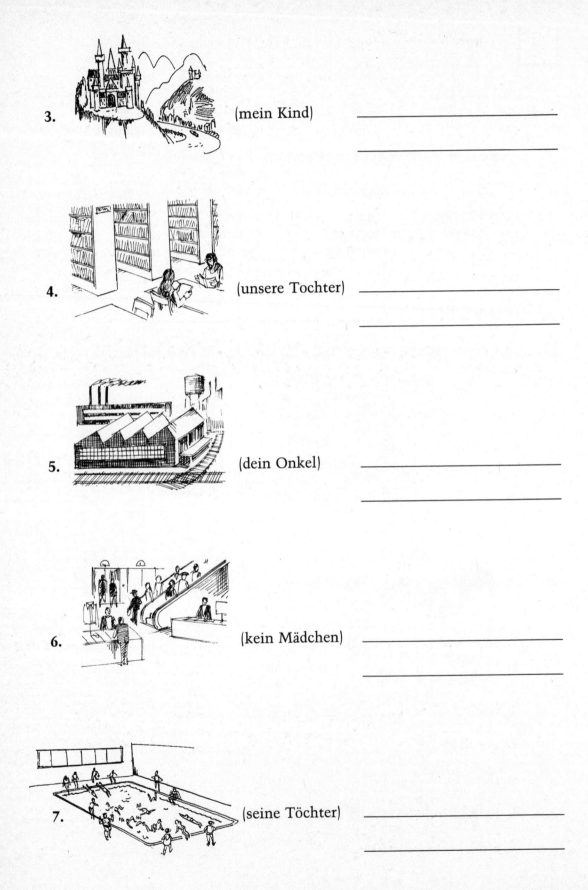

3. (mein Kind) _____

    _____

4. (unsere Tochter) _____

    _____

5. (dein Onkel) _____

    _____

6. (kein Mädchen) _____

    _____

7. (seine Töchter) _____

    _____

8. (ihr Bruder) _____

9. (eine Lehrerin) _____

10. (keine Jungen) _____

E. Change the following accusative phrases to the dative:

1. seinen Vetter _____

2. meinen Vater _____

3. deine Frau _____

4. ein Mädchen _____

5. ihren Onkel _____

6. keine Kinder _____

7. ein Theater _____

8. deinen Bruder _____

9. keine Frauen _____

10. unseren Hund _____

F. Complete each sentence with the appropriate indefinite article in the dative:

1. Er zeigt _____ Freund den Park.

2. Ich zeige _____ Vetter das Theater.

3. Er zeigt _____ Lehrerin das Gymnasium.

4. Wir zeigen _____ Gruppe das Museum.

5. Du zeigst _____ Frau das Hotel.

6. Sie zeigen _____ Mann das Dorf.

7. Luise zeigt _____ Fräulein den Garten.

8. Rolf zeigt _____ Kind den Bahnhof.

9. Susanne zeigt _____ Mädchen einen Apfel.

10. Der Lehrer zeigt _____ Klasse einen Film.

G. Complete each sentence by supplying the correct ending, if needed, on the indefinite articles in the nominative, accusative, or dative, as appropriate:

1. Mein_____ Mutter gibt ihr_____ Bruder ein_____ Buch.

2. Ein_____ Lehrer bringt sein_____ Klasse ein_____ Kuli.

3. Sein_____ Frau kauft sein_____ Sohn ein_____ Lederhose.

4. Unser_____ Schwester schreibt mein_____ Lehrer ein_____ Karte.

5. Dein_____ Reiseführer zeigt ein_____ Mann ein_____ Bahnhof.

6. Ein_____ Mann gibt sein_____ Freund unser_____ Fußball.

7. Euer_____ Lehrerin bringt unser_____ Klasse dein_____ Aufsatz.

8. Mein_____ Bruder kauft dein_____ Schwester ein_____ Buch.

5 Another stem-changing verb similar to **essen** and **geben** is **nehmen** (*to take*). Note carefully how the **du** and **er, sie, es** forms differ:

ich nehme	wir nehmen
du *nimmst*	ihr nehmt
er	
sie} *nimmt*	sie nehmen
es	
	Sie nehmen

What kind of stem-changing verb is **nehmen**? _____

What other spelling change happens with **nehmen**? _____

Can you give the imperative forms?

(du) _____ !

(Sie) _____ !

(ihr) _____ !

(wir) _____ !

__ ÜBUNG _____

H. Complete each sentence with the correct form of **nehmen**:

1. Heute abend _____ wir den Bus.

2. Ich _____ lieber das Taxi als den Bus.

3. _____ einen Apfel, Hans!

4. _____ einen Bleistift, Herr Weiß!

5. _____ du ein Telefon oder einen Rechner?

6. Das Kind _____ nicht gern Aspirin.

7. Das Mädchen _____ eine Tasse aus dem Schrank.

GESPRÄCH

Wortschatz

verbringen *to spend* (time)	**eigen** *own*
empfehlen *to recommend*	**lebendig** *lively*
die Ostküste *the East Coast*	**der Flug** *the flight*

_____ PERSÖNLICHE FRAGEN _____

1. Welches Restaurant hast du gern?

_____

2. Welches Museum besuchst du gern?

_____

3. Wo ißt du das Mittagessen?

_____

4. Gehst du oft ins Kino?

_____

5. Was ist deine Lieblingssehenswürdigkeit?

_____

6. Wo ist sie?

_____

_____ DU _____

Name five places that you show your friends when they visit:

Ich zeige meinen Freunden . . .

1. _____

2. _____

3. _____

4. _____

5. _____

DIALOG

You are a customer at the **Reisebüro** (*travel agency*). Respond with expressions that you have learned:

Naschen unterwegs (Eating on the run)

During a long day touring the city, you can certainly develop an appetite. German cities have a large variety of places where you can eat:

A **Café** is a coffee shop, where you can also order pastries, snacks, and drinks. Sometimes a **Konditorei** has a small café. In Austria, the café is called a **Kaffeehaus,** and in Switzerland it's sometimes called a **Tea-Room.**

A **Milchbar** serves plain and flavored milk drinks with pastries.

A **Schnellimbiß** is a snack bar. The **Schnellimbiß** usually has a limited menu. For example, at a **Bratwurststand,** one would find mainly **Bratwurst** and french fries.

For lunch, go to the **Restaurant** in the **Kaufhaus.** Many department stores have a restaurant that serves hearty and inexpensive meals.

Finally, if you miss American-style snacks, many fast-food chains have outlets in Germany, too! Among them are McDonald's, Wendy's, and Wienerwald.

Guten Appetit!

20 *Wohin gehen wir heute?*

Dative Prepositions

1 Can you figure out the meanings of these places?

die Post/das Postamt   **die Bank**   **der Supermarkt**

das Geschäft/der Laden   **die Bäckerei**   **die Fleischerei**

das Lebensmittelgeschäft   **die Apotheke**   **die Buchhandlung**

der Strand   **das Stadion**   **der Zoo**

A. **Wohin gehst du?** Where would you go in the right column to do the things in the left column? Write the matching letter in the space provided:

1. Fleisch kaufen   _____

2. schwimmen   _____

3. Tiere sehen   _____

4. Lebensmittel kaufen   _____

5. ein Fußballspiel sehen   _____

6. Kuchen kaufen   _____

7. ein Buch kaufen   _____

8. einen Brief senden   _____

9. Aspirin kaufen   _____

10. Bäume und Blumen sehen   _____

a. zum Zoo
b. zum Supermarkt
c. zum Postamt
d. zur Buchhandlung
e. zur Bäckerei
f. zum Park
g. zur Apotheke
h. zum Stadion
i. zur Fleischerei
j. zum Strand

2 In the letter that follows are some dative prepositions. See if you can find them:

Kiel, den 7. August

Liebe Marianne!

Wie geht's? Mir geht's gut. Ich freue mich, daß ich jeden Tag an den Strand gehen kann. Ich gehe mit meiner Freundin Andrea. Wir wohnen jetzt **bei** ihrem Onkel. Er wohnt **seit** einem Jahr da.

bei ihrem Onkel *at her uncle's house*

Jeden Morgen **nach** dem Frühstück gehen wir an den Strand. Wir schwimmen viel, aber das Wasser ist eiskalt! Dann kommen wir **aus** dem Wasser. **Vom** Strand gehen wir wieder **zu** dem Onkel. Den Nachmittag verbringen wir in der Stadt. Manchmal holen wir dem Onkel eine Torte **beim** Bäcker, oder wir gehen **zum** Supermarkt. Wir holen auch Fleisch **beim** Fleischer. Oft gehen wir einfach einkaufen — ins Kaufhaus oder in ein Geschäft. Die Kleider sind so hübsch.

eiskalt *ice-cold*
zu dem Onkel *to the uncle's house*
der Nachmittag *the afternoon*
manchmal *sometimes*
der Fleischer *the butcher*
einfach *simply*

Marianne, kommst du bald **mit** Deiner Familie nach Deutschland? Hoffentlich sehen wir uns dann wieder.

wieder *again*

Mit freundlichen Grüßen,

Deine Ursula

ÜBUNG

B. Beantworte die Fragen!

1. Wo verbringt Ursula die Ferien?

2. Wie geht es Ursula?

3. Wohin geht sie nach dem Frühstück?

4. Mit wem geht sie?

5. Was machen sie nachmittags (*in the afternoon*)?

6. Was machen sie da manchmal?

7. Wohin gehen sie oft?

8. Warum gehen sie dorthin?

_____

9. Wohin kommt Marianne bald?

_____

10. Mit wem kommt sie vielleicht?

_____

3 Did you find all the dative prepositions? They are the little words in heavy type followed by the noun in the dative:

> *aus* dem Wasser
> *bei* ihrem (*beim*) Onkel
> *mit* meiner Freundin
> *nach* dem Frühstück
> *seit* einem Jahr
> *von* dem (*vom*) Strand
> *zu* dem (*zum*) Supermarkt

What do these dative prepositions mean?

aus	*out of*
bei	*by, at*
mit	*with*
nach	*after, to (a country, city)*
seit	*since*
von	*from, of*
zu	*to*

Memorize the prepositions and their meanings!

___ ÜBUNGEN _____

C. Complete each sentence with the dative preposition corresponding to the English meaning in parentheses:

1. (to) Jetzt gehen wir _____ dem Fleischer.

2. (from) Ich habe einen Brief _____ meinem Vetter.

3. (out of) Um fünf Uhr kommt er _____ der Fabrik.

4. (to) Nächste Woche fliege ich _____ Deutschland.

5. (since) Sie singen _____ vielen Jahren.

6. (at) Ich wohne _____ meiner Mutter.

7. (with) Er geht oft _____ seinen Eltern ins Kino.

8. (after) Ich mache die Aufgabe _____ der Schule.

D. Complete each sentence with the dative form of the word of your choice to complete the sentence. You may use definite articles, indefinite articles, or possessives:

1. Jeden Morgen um acht Uhr komme ich aus _____ Haus.

2. Marianne wohnt jetzt bei _____ Onkel.

3. Nach _____ Mittagessen mache ich einen Ausflug.

4. Morgen laufe ich mit _____ Freundin.

5. Sie wohnt seit _____ Jahr hier.

6. Er ist ein Freund von _____ Tante.

4 Take another look at the letter:

How do you say "to the supermarket"? _____

How do you say "from the baker"? _____

How do you say "at the butcher's"? _____

What does **zum** mean? _____

What does **vom** mean? _____

What does **beim** mean? _____

The prepositions **bei, von,** and **zu** plus **dem** combine to form commonly used contractions:

bei dem = beim   **von dem = vom**   **zu dem = zum**

In addition, **zu** plus **der** also forms a contraction:

zu der = zur

How do you say "at her uncle's house"? _____

How do you say "to the uncle's house"? _____

What's missing in the German version of "at her uncle's house" and "to the uncle's house"? _____

When you talk about staying at or going to someone's house, do not use **Haus:**

bei meiner Mutter   *at my mother's (house)*
zu meiner Mutter   *to my mother's (house)*

___ ÜBUNGEN _____

E. Express in German. Use contractions whenever possible:

1. I live at my parents' house.

_____

2. They go to the supermarket.

_____

3. He goes to his uncle's house.

_____

4. Do you have a letter from the teacher?

_____

5. Sometimes I go with my friends.

_____

6. I get meat at the butcher's.

_____

7. I go to the bakery.

_____

F. You have to run a number of errands for your mother. Which places do you go to?

EXAMPLE: Ich gehe zum Supermarkt.

1. _____

2. _____

3. _____

4. _____

5. _____

6. _____

7. _____

8. _____

9. _____

10. _____

11. _____

12. _____

 Read these questions:

Wo sind deine Eltern?	Sie sind hier.
Wohin gehen deine Eltern?	Sie gehen zum Park.
Woher kommen deine Eltern?	Sie kommen aus der Fabrik.

What do the questions mean?

_____

_____

_____

What does **wo** mean? _____

What does **wohin** mean? _____

What does **woher** mean? _____

How do you determine whether to use **wo, wohin,** or **woher?** Look at the verb. If the verb expresses motion toward another location (like **gehen, fahren, laufen**), use **wohin,** because **wohin** means *to where.* If the verb expresses motion from someplace (like **kommen**), use **woher,** because **woher** means *from where.* If the verb shows no movement in either direction (like **stehen** or **sein**), use **wo** (*where*).

Add **wohin** and **woher** to your list of question words.

__ ÜBUNG _____

G. Complete each question with **wo, wohin,** or **woher,** as appropriate:

1. _____ ist der Supermarkt?

2. _____ gehst du jetzt?

3. _____ fahren deine Freunde?

4. _____ ist dein Lehrer?

5. _____ verbringst du die Sommerferien?

6. _____ kommt diese Frau?

7. _____ läuft er?

8. _____ steht die Milch?

9. _____ ist das Buch?

10. _____ hole ich Fleisch?

GESPRÄCH

Wortschatz

die Verabredung *the date*
Beruhige dich! *Calm down!*

die Gitarre *the guitar*
beschäftigt *busy*

_____ PERSÖNLICHE FRAGEN _____

1. Warum gehst du in die Schule?

   _____

2. Mit wem gehst du ins Kino?

   _____

3. Wohin gehst du nach der Schule?

   _____

4. Wann gehst du an den Strand?

   _____

5. Bei wem wohnst du?

   _____

6. Wohin gehst du, wenn du eine Torte kaufst?

   _____

_____ DU _____

Name five places (in German) where you go frequently:

1. _____

2. _____

3. _____

4. _____

5. _____

DIALOG

You are a member of the Schulz family. Your parents are asking the whereabouts of your brothers and sisters. Respond with answers of your own choice:

KULTURECKE

Andere Länder, andere Sitten (Other countries, other customs)

How is life in the German-speaking world different from life in the United States?

UNITED STATES	DEUTSCHLAND
American buildings number the floors from the ground level.	Germans call the ground floor **Erdgeschoß.** The floor above is called **Erster Stock** (first floor).
Americans pay their telephone bills to the local telephone company.	German phone service is administered by the post office.
American department stores have frequent sales.	Typically, German department stores run two sales a year, one at the end of winter and one at the end of summer. Each **Ausverkauf** (*sale*) runs for two weeks. Sometimes there are **Sonderangebote** (*special offers*) outside of these sales.
Shopkeepers set their own hours and are usually open Saturdays and sometimes Sundays, too.	Most stores in Germany close at 6:30 p.m. weekdays and at 2 p.m. on Saturdays. On the first Saturday of the month and on the four Saturdays before Christmas, stores may stay open until 6 p.m.
When Americans give a bouquet of flowers, they hand the wrapped package to the recipient. He or she then proceeds to open the gift.	Germans bring flowers wrapped and unwrap them before handing them to the recipient. Five or seven flowers make up the typical bouquet.
Public notices are posted in a variety of places, including store windows and roadside billboards.	Public notices are posted on columns called **Anschlagsäulen** (*advertising pillars*) or **Litfaßsäulen** (after Ernst Litfaß, the Berlin printer who created the first one in 1855). These columns are everywhere on German streets.

Wiederholung V
(Aufgaben 17–20)

Aufgabe 17

a. Imperatives express commands. There are three commands: **du, ihr,** and **Sie.** The **du** command is the **er-**form of the verb less the **t** ending. The **ihr** command is the same as the **ihr** form of the verb. The **Sie** command is the same as the **Sie** form of the verb followed by the pronoun **Sie.** Use the command that is appropriate to the circumstances: the **du**-command with someone you address with **du**, the **ihr**-command with a group you address with **ihr**, and the **Sie**-command with someone you address formally. Examples:

	spielen	essen
(du)	Spiel!	Iß!
(ihr)	Spielt!	Eßt!
(sie)	Spielen Sie!	Essen Sie!

b. The inclusive command includes the speaker in the command. It says "Let's . . ." The inclusive command is the **wir**-form of the verb followed by **wir:**

Gehen wir!   *Let's go.*

c. The irregular verbs **sein** and **haben** have irregular command forms:

	sein	haben
(du)	Sei!	Hab!
(ihr)	Seid!	Habt!
(Sie)	Seien Sie!	Haben Sie!
(Inclusive)	Seien wir!	Haben wir!

d. All imperatives are punctuated with an exclamation point.

Aufgabe 18

a. The dative expresses the indirect object: The definite articles in the dative are:

MASCULINE	FEMININE	NEUTER	PLURAL
dem	der	dem	den

In addition, in the dative plural, an **n** is added to the end of plural nouns not already ending in **n** or **s.**

Summary: Definite Articles

	MASCULINE	FEMININE	NEUTER	PLURAL
NOMINATIVE	der	die	das	die
ACCUSATIVE	den	die	das	die
DATIVE	dem	der	dem	den (=n or noun)

b. **Wer, wen,** and **wem** are question words. **Wer** means *who*, **wen** means *whom*, and **wem** means *to whom* or *for whom*. The answer to **wer** is in the nominative. The answer to **wen** is in the accusative. The answer to **wem** is in the dative.

c. The verb **geben** (*to give*) is an **e→i** stem-changing verb. Memorize all of its forms:

ich gebe   wir geben
du gibst   ihr gebt
er ⎫
sie ⎬ gibt   sie geben
es ⎭
                Sie geben

Aufgabe 19

a. The endings on indefinite articles and possessives in the dative are as follows:

MASCULINE	FEMININE	NEUTER	PLURAL
-em	-er	-em	-en (+n or noun)

The table summarizes the endings on indefinite articles and possessives in the nominative, accusative, and dative:

	MASCULINE	FEMININE	NEUTER	PLURAL
NOMINATIVE	—	-e	—	-e
ACCUSATIVE	-en	-e	—	-e
DATIVE	-em	-er	-em	-en

These endings may be attached to **ein, kein, mein, dein, sein, ihr, unser, euer, Ihr.**

b. The verb **nehmen** (*to take*) is a stem-changing **e→i** verb. In addition to the vowel change, the **h** is replaced by **m** in the **du** and **er, sie, es** forms. Memorize the forms of **nehmen:**

ich nehme   wir nehmen
du nimmst   ihr nehmt
er ⎫
sie ⎬ nimmt   sie nehmen
es ⎭
                Sie nehmen

Aufgabe 20

a. The dative prepositions are followed by objects in the dative. Memorize the dative prepositions and their meanings:

aus	*out, out of*
bei	*by, at*
mit	*with*
nach	*after, to*
seit	*since*
von	*from, of*
zu	*to*

b. The prepositions **bei** and **zu** plus **dem** or **der** form contractions:

bei dem = beim	**zu dem = zum**
von dem = vom	**zu der = zur**

c. When the object of a prepositional phrase beginning with **bei** or **zu** is a person, that phrase can take on the meaning of *at* or *to* that person's house or place of business:

bei meinem Vater	*at my father's house*
zu meinem Vater	*to my father's house*
beim Bäcker	*at the baker's (bakery)*
zum Bäcker	*to the baker's (bakery)*

___ ÜBUNGEN ___

A. Write the German word under the picture. Then circle the German word in the puzzle on page 355. The words may be read from left right, right to left, up or down, or diagonally:

1. _____   2. _____   3. _____

4. _____

5. _____

6. _____

7. _____

8. _____

9. _____

10. _____

11. _____

12. _____

13. _____ 14. _____ 15. _____

16. _____ 17. _____ 18. _____

19. _____ 20. _____ 21. _____

22. _____   23. _____   24. _____

25. _____   26. _____   27. _____

```
B O H S U A H F U A K R B O L
K L P A B I N O R O M E Ä F D
E C O P O S E M T É F A C L A
H R S O S T T B Ü R O Ü K U B
T E T T S T R A N D H E E G M
O S A H S T A D I O N H R H M
I T M E R L G N Ä H H C E A I
L A T K N K I N O N A R I F W
B U R E O O Z T U A B I M E H
I R D R S A E R P A R K U N C
B A S K H L O N N B E Q E P S
L N F A B R I K O R Ü M S A O
E T T K R A M R E P U S U K P
G N U L D N A H H C U B M L Ü
M R A B E L L E T S K N A T B
```

B. Kreuzworträtsel:

WAAGERECHT

1. Er _____ seine Freunde jeden Tag.
3. Ich gehe _____ meinem Freund Skilaufen.
4. _____ deinen Eltern die Freiheitsstatue!
6. Im September gehen wir _____ Schule.
8. _____ das Buch, Hans!
10. Wieviel Uhr ist _____?
11. _____ keine Angst, Kinder!
13. Ich wohne _____ vier Jahren in Deutschland.
14. Guten Tag. _____ geht's?
16. Ich habe _____ Musik nicht gern.
17. _____ antwortet die Frage?
18. Ich kaufe einen Kuchen _____ Bäcker.
20. _____ Schreibmaschine ist kaputt.
21. Fahren wir mit dem Bus, _____ gehen wir zu Fuß?
22. Sie zeigt _____ Vater das Zeugnis.
24. Was machst du _____ der Schule?
26. Die Frau gibt _____ Mann einen Computer.
27. Nimm _____ Aufsatz!

SENKRECHT

2. Wen _____ du lieber?

3. Ich gebe _____ Mutter eine Bluse.

4. Gehen wir _____ Postamt!

5. _____ kauft seiner Frau Blumen.

7. New York und Boston sind an der _____küste.

9. Von allen _____ habe ich Berlin am liebsten.

10. Wir geben _____ Kind eine Videokassette.

12. Er wohnt _____ seinen Eltern.

14. _____ gibst du das Geschenk?

15. _____ Sie Ihrem Bruder das Buch!

16. _____ Sie vorsichtig!

17. *Again*, auf deutsch.

19. _____ fährst du diesen Sommer?

20. Ich habe _____ Stunden Pause.

23. Ich habe zwei Bücher, und er hat drei Bücher. Er hat _____ Bücher.

25. Ich gebe _____ Freunden viele Geschenke.

C. **Silbenrätsel** (*Syllable puzzle*). Karl has a busy day ahead of him. Find out what he has planned by combining the following syllables into the words that complete the paragraph below:

AB COR DE DE DER DUNG ERD FRAN GE GIE HAUS
HERD KUN KRO KAS LEN LO MA MI MU NE NO O
RE RE SCHAFT SCHI SCHICH SCHREIB SET SIK SISCH TE
TECH TEN VER VI WEL WIRT ZÖ

Karl hat heute viel vor. In _____ lernt er „Bonjour" und „Au

revoir" sagen. Dann hat er eine Aufgabe in _____ ; er schreibt

einen Aufsatz über Deutschland im Jahre 1890. Er lernt ein neues Rezept in

_____ , und er lernt etwas über den Computer in

_____ . Nachher lernt er die Geographie Deutschlands

in _____ . Er spielt Klavier in der _____stunde. Schließlich

schreibt er eine Aufgabe mit der elektronischen _____ .

Nach der Schule hat er eine _____ mit einem netten Mäd-

chen. Sie sehen einen Film im _____ , und er kocht ihr

Abendessen im _____ .

D. This is what the well-equipped office should look like, or is it? In the spaces provided, write the names of the machines that belong in an office. Then draw a line to connect each word to the machine it describes. At the bottom of the page, write the names of the machines that do not belong:

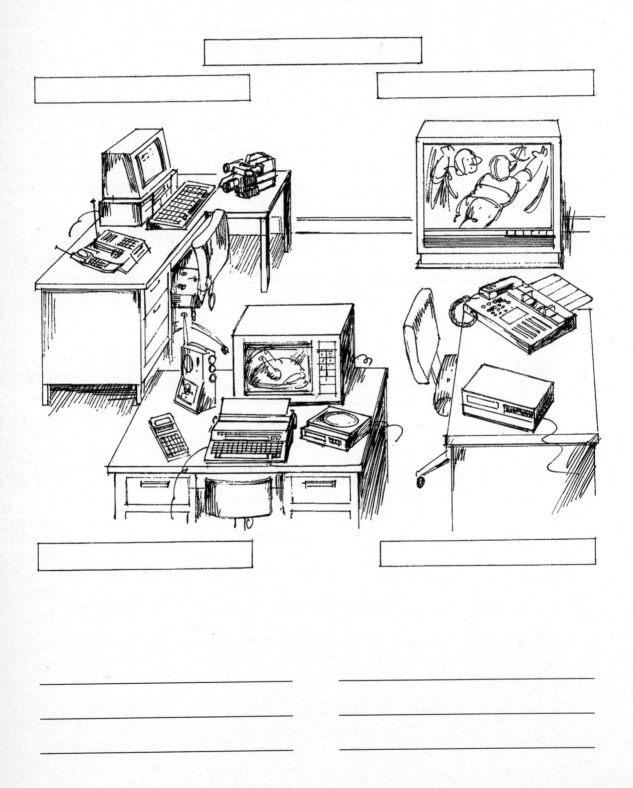

E. Picture Story. Can you read this story? Much of it is in picture form. Whenever you come to a picture, read it as if it were a German word:

In Amerika gibt es viele große [Städte]. Zwei von diesen

[Städte] heißen New York und Minneapolis.

New York ist der „große [Apfel]". In New York gibt es viel zu sehen: die [Freiheitsstatue],

viele [Häuser] und schöne [Parks]. Bei kaltem Wetter spielen

hier die Leute [Hockey]. Viele Studenten kommen nach New York und

studieren an vielen ausgezeichneten [Universitäten].

Minneapolis ist der „Mini [Apfel]". Minneapolis ist nicht so groß wie New

York. Minneapolis ist modern. Es gibt gute [Häuser], elegante

[Restaurants] und schöne [Geschäfte] hier. Im Sommer spielen hier die „Twins" Baseball im großen . Viele Studenten besuchen hier

auch die ▨▨▨ .

Beide ▨▨ haben gute Verkehrsmittel. Man nimmt ein 🚗

oder fährt mit dem 🚌. Natürlich sieht man mehr, wenn man zu

🚶 geht oder mit dem 🚲 fährt.

Besuch New York und Minneapolis! Beide 🍎🍎 schmecken sehr gut!

Sechster Teil

21 *Die Welt ist klein*

Nationalities, Countries, Languages; the Verb **sprechen**

1 Wortschatz

LÄNDER	MÄNNER	FRAUEN	SPRACHEN
die Vereinigten Staaten	der Amerikaner	die Amerikanerin	Englisch
Deutschland	der Deutsche ein Deutscher	die Deutsche eine Deutsche	Deutsch
England	der Engländer	die Engländerin	Englisch
Frankreich	der Franzose	die Französin	Französisch
Italien	der Italiener	die Italienerin	Italienisch
Rußland	der Russe	die Russin	Russisch
Spanien	der Spanier	die Spanierin	Spanisch
Österreich	der Österreicher	die Österreicherin	Deutsch
China	der Chinese	die Chinesin	Chinesisch
Japan	der Japaner	die Japanerin	Japanisch
die Schweiz	der Schweizer	die Schweizerin	Deutsch Französisch Italienisch

ÜBUNGEN

A. Give the nationality and the country each person comes from:

1. Pablo _____

2. Mario _____

3. François _____

4. Mary _____

5. Natasha _____

6. Hans _____

7. Han-Ling _____

8. Heidi _____

B. Match the dish with the country it comes from. Write the matching letter in the space provided:

1. Pizza   _____   5. Crepes suzette   _____   **a.** Rußland
                                                                 b. Japan
2. Borscht   _____   6. Paella   _____   **c.** Deutschland
                                                                 d. Österreich
3. Sukiyaki   _____   7. Sauerbraten   _____   **e.** Italien
                                                                 f. Frankreich
4. Wonton soup   _____   8. Wienerschnitzel _____   **g.** China
                                                                 h. Spanien

2 Now look carefully at the following sentences:

I	II
Ich wohne *in* Deutschland.	Ich fliege *nach* Deutschland.
Ich wohne *in* England.	Ich reise *nach* England.
Ich wohne *in* Österreich.	Ich fahre *nach* Österreich.
Ich wohne *in* China.	Ich gehe *nach* China.

In Group I, which word is used to say IN a country? _____

In Group II, which word is used to say TO a country? _____

3 Now compare these sentences:

I	II
Ich wohne *in den* Vereinigten Staaten.	Ich fliege *in die* Vereinigten Staaten.
Ich wohne *in der* Schweiz.	Ich fahre *in die* Schweiz.

In Group I, how do you say IN THE _____

In Group II, how do you say TO THE _____

4 Summary:

To say IN the United States, use _____

To say IN Switzerland, use _____

To say TO the United States, use _____

To say TO Switzerland, use _____

For all other listed countries:

To say IN a country, use _____

To say TO a country, use _____

5 Compare these sentences:

Karl ist *Amerikaner.*	Julia ist *Amerikanerin.*
George ist *Engländer.*	Elizabeth ist *Engländerin.*
Giovanni ist *Italiener.*	Angela ist *Italienerin.*
François ist *Franzose.*	Michele ist *Französin.*
Ivan ist *Russe.*	Natasha ist *Russin.*
Pablo ist *Spanier.*	Anita ist *Spanierin.*
Anton ist *Schweizer.*	Anna ist *Schweizerin.*
Georg ist *Österreicher.*	Marianne ist *Österreicherin.*
Han-Ling ist *Chinese.*	Su-Ling ist *Chinesin.*
Tom ist *Japaner.*	Sun ist *Japanerin.*
Hans ist *Deutscher.*	Susi ist *Deutsche.*

What is the difference between the man and the woman for most of these

nationalities? _____
That's right! The feminine form of most nationalities ends in **in.** What is the

exception? _____ Correct again! It's **Deutscher** and
Deutsche. How would you say "He is an American" in German?

_____
Very good: **Er ist Amerikaner.** What English word is not accounted for in the

German? _____ That's right. Just as with a profession, trade, or occupation (as you learned in Lesson 8), we do not use **ein** or **eine** with a nationality after a form of the verb **sein.**

6 | Look at these sentences:

> **Woher kommt Charles? Er kommt *aus den Vereinigten Staaten*.**
> **Woher kommt Anna? Sie kommt *aus der Schweiz*.**
> **Woher kommt Hans? Er kommt *aus Deutschland*.**
> **Woher kommt Giovanni? Er kommt *aus Italien*.**

If you want to say that someone comes from a country, how do you say FROM?

_____

Which two countries add an extra word? _____

_____

_ ÜBUNG _____

C. Complete the answer to each question with **nach, in, in die, in der, aus, aus den, aus der** before the name of the country:

1. Wohin fliegst du? Ich fliege _____ Japan.

2. Wohin reisen wir? Wir reisen _____ Deutschland.

3. Wo sind sie? Sie sind _____ Spanien.

4. Wohin fährt sie? Sie fährt _____ Vereinigten Staaten.

5. Woher kommst du? Ich komme _____ Frankreich.

6. Wo wohnen sie? Sie wohnen _____ England.

7. Wohin reisen Sie? Ich reise _____ Rußland.

8. Woher kommst du? Ich komme _____ Schweiz.

9. Wohin fahren sie? Sie fahren _____ Österreich.

10. Wohin fliegt er? Er fliegt _____ Italien.

11. Woher kommt ihr? Wir kommen _____ Vereinigten Staaten.

7 Let's read something about our world, its countries, and its languages:

In der Welt gibt es viele Länder und viele Sprachen. Weißt du, daß es heutzutage mehr als tausend Sprachen in der Welt gibt. Im allgemeinen hat jedes Land seine eigene offizielle Sprache. In Frankreich ist es Französisch; in Spanien ist es Spanisch; in Italien ist es Italienisch; in Deutschland und Österreich ist es Deutsch.

> **die Welt** the world
> **die Sprache** the language
> **heutzutage** nowadays
> **tausend** thousand
> **im allgemeinen** in general

Einige Länder haben mehr als eine offizielle Sprache. In der Schweiz, zum Beispiel, spricht man Französisch, Italienisch und Deutsch. In Polen und in der Tschechoslowakei sprechen viele Leute auch Deutsch als zweite Sprache. Weißt du, woher der berühmte Schriftsteller Franz Kafka kam? Er kam aus der Tschechoslowakei, aber er schrieb auf deutsch.

> **einige** several
> **zum Beispiel** for example
> **Polen** Poland
> **die Tschechoslowakei** Czechoslovakia
> **der Schriftsteller** writer
> **kam** came
> **schrieb** wrote

Viele Leute sprechen Deutsch im internationalen Geschäft. Viele deutsche Firmen verkaufen ihre Produkte in den Vereinigten Staaten. Kennst du einige? Wähle sechs deutsche Automobilhersteller von dieser Liste!

> **im Geschäft** in business
> **verkaufen** to sell
> **kennen** to know
> **wählen** to choose
> **der Hersteller** manufacturer

Audi	Porsche
Fiat	Volkswagen
Opel	Renault
Mercedes	BMW

Die Antwort: Die sechs deutschen Firmen sind Audi, Opel, Mercedes, Porsche, Volkswagen und BMW.

Jetzt weißt du, warum es wichtig ist, Deutsch zu können.

> **können** to be able to speak

__ ÜBUNGEN _____

D. **Beantworte die Fragen!**

1. Wie viele Sprachen gibt es in der Welt?

_____

2. Im allgemeinen, wie viele offizielle Sprachen gibt es in jedem Land?

_____

3. Was sind die offiziellen Sprachen in der Schweiz?

_____

4. Was spricht man in Österreich?

_____

5. Wo spricht man Deutsch als zweite Sprache?

_____

6. Woher kam Franz Kafka?

_____

7. Wo sprechen viele Leute Deutsch?

_____

8. Welche Automobilhersteller sind deutsch?

_____

E. Complete the sentences with the correct information:

1. Wir kommen aus _____ .

Dort wohnen die _____ .

Sie sprechen _____ .

2. Wir kommen aus _____ .

Dort wohnen die _____ .

Sie sprechen _____ .

3. Wir kommen aus _____ .

Dort wohnen die _____ .

Sie sprechen _____ .

4. Wir kommen aus _____ .

Dort wohnen die _____ .

Sie sprechen _____ .

5. Wir kommen aus _____ .

Dort wohnen die _____ .

Sie sprechen _____ .

6. Wir kommen aus _____ .

Dort wohnen die _____ .

Sie sprechen _____ .

7. Wir kommen aus _____ .

Dort wohnen die _____ .

Sie sprechen _____ .

8. Wir kommen aus _____ .

Dort wohnen die _____ .

Sie sprechen _____ .

⑧ Another stem-changing verb like **essen, geben, nehmen** is **sprechen** (*to speak*). Can you complete the following table of its forms?

ich _____   wir _____

du _____   ihr _____

er
sie } _____   sie _____
es

Sie_____

Sprechen is an **e→i** stem-changing verb. The **du**-form is **sprichst** and the **er, sie, es** form is **spricht**. Otherwise, the remaining forms are regular. Now give the imperative forms:

(du)   _____ !

(Sie)   _____ !

(ihr)   _____ !

(wir)   _____ !

__ ÜBUNG _____

F. Complete each sentence with the correct form of **sprechen**:

1. Meine Eltern _____ Englisch.

2. Ich _____ Deutsch und Englisch.

3. _____ du Spanisch?

4. Wir _____ Italienisch.

5. _____ Sie Französisch?

6. Er _____ Russisch.

7. _____ Deutsch, Karl!

8. _____ wir Deutsch!

9. _____ Sie Italienisch?

10. _____ Englisch, Kinder!

GESPRÄCH

_____ *DIALOG* _____

You are the first person in the dialog. Ask the questions that correspond to the answers:

_____ PERSÖNLICHE FRAGEN _____

1. Welche Sprachen sprichst du?

_____

2. Was ist deine Nationalität (*nationality*)?

_____

3. Woher kommst du?

_____

_____ DU _____

You have just won a free trip to go anywhere in the world. List in order of your preference the countries you would most like to visit and the language(s) spoken there:

EXAMPLE: Ich möchte Deutschland besuchen. Man spricht Deutsch in Deutschland.

1. _____

2. _____

3. _____

4. _____

5. _____

KULTURECKE

Wie weit ist es nach . . . ? (How far is it to . . . ?)

Technology has contributed greatly to the creation of a much smaller world. Distances around the world are now measured not in days but in the number of hours away from us. Also, the speed at which we are able to convey a message anywhere in the world is measured in seconds.

Physical distance between cities in Germany are measured in **Kilometer. Meter, Zentimeter,** and **Millimeter** measure smaller distances:

1 Kilometer	=	1000 meters (0.36 mile)
1 Meter	=	100 centimeters (39.37 inches)
1 Zentimeter	=	1000 millimeters (0.39 inch)
1 Millimeter	=	0.03 inch

Here is a chart that shows the distance between major cities in Germany. If you were in Berlin, how would you answer the question: **"We weit ist es nach Frankfurt?"**

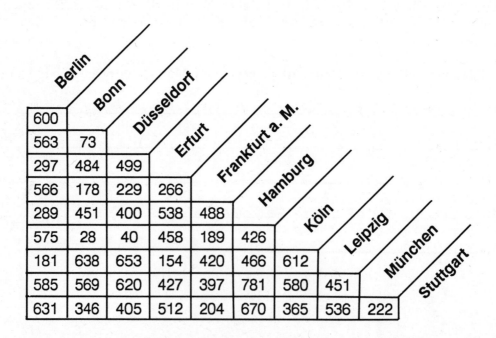

22 *Die Tiere*

Noun Genders

1 Wortschatz

die Katze

der Hund

das Pferd

die Kuh

die Ziege

das Schwein

der Esel

das Schaf

der Hase

| der Löwe | der Elefant | der Tiger |

| der Wolf | der Fuchs | der Affe |

| der Vogel | die Giraffe | das Huhn |

ÜBUNGEN

A. You went to visit the zoo. Here are some of the animals you saw. Label the pictures:

1. _____   2. _____   3. _____

4. _____   5. _____   6. _____

7. _____   8. _____

B. Can you name all the animals on Peter's farm?

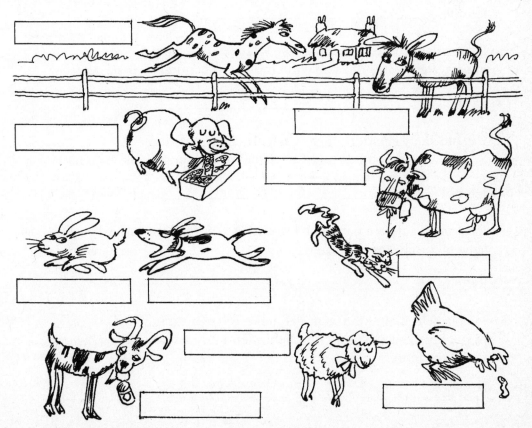

C. **Wer bin ich?** Now that you know the German names of some animals, let's see if you can figure out who they are by their descriptions:

1. Ich wohne auf einem Bauernhof. Ich fresse Gras. Ich bin groß und intelligent. Man reitet auf mir. Ich helfe bei der Arbeit. Ich laufe sehr schnell.

   der Bauernhof *the farm*
   fressen *to eat (for animals)*
   reiten *to ride*
   helfen *to help*

   Ich bin _____ .

2. Ich bin klein. Ich fresse Fleisch. Ich bin des Menschen bester Freund. Mein Herr streichelt mich, wenn ich gut bin. Ich habe Katzen nicht gern.

   des Menschen *the human being's*
   der Herr *the master*
   streicheln *to pet*

   Ich bin _____ .

3. Ich bin groß. Ich wohne auf dem Land. Ich fresse Pflanzen. Ich gebe Milch.

   auf dem Land *in the country*
   die Pflanze *the plant*

   Ich bin _____ .

4. Ich bin ein wildes Tier. Ich bin wie ein Hund. Ich fresse Fleisch. Wenn die Leute mich sehen, laufen sie weg.

   weg *away*

   Ich bin _____ .

5. Ich bin das größte Tier. Ich fresse Pflanzen. Ich habe eine riesige Nase, die ich wie eine Hand benutze.

   riesig *giant*

   Ich bin _____ .

6. Ich bin ein Haustier, aber ich laufe auch auf der Straße. Ich habe Hunde nicht gern. Ich fresse Mäuse.

   die Maus *the mouse*

   Ich bin _____ .

7. Ich wohne auf dem Land. Ich bin eine Art Vogel. Ich gebe Eier. Ich fresse Körner.

   die Art *the kind, type*
   die Körner *(pl.)* *feed*

   Ich bin _____ .

8. Ich bin sehr dick. Man sagt, daß ich sehr schmutzig bin. Ich gebe den Speck, den Schinken und andere Fleischgerichte.

   der Speck *the bacon*
   der Schinken *the ham*

   Ich bin _____ .

9. Ich bin sehr intelligent. Ich wohne in den
Bäumen. Ich helfe Menschen mit wissenschaft-
lichen Forschungen. Man findet mich auch
im Zoo und im Zirkus.

wissenschaftlich *scientific*
die Forschung *the research*

Ich bin _____ .

10. Ich wohne auf dem Land. Man benutzt meine Wolle
für Pullover und andere Kleidung.

die Wolle *the wool*

Ich bin _____ .

D. Put the animals in groups:

Haustiere	Bauernhoftiere	Wilde Tiere
_____	_____	_____
_____	_____	_____
	_____	_____
	_____	_____
	_____	_____
	_____	_____
	_____	

E. There are 10 animals hidden in this picture. Find them and list them below:

1. _____   6. _____

2. _____   7. _____

3. _____   8. _____

4. _____   9. _____

5. _____   10. _____

2 Now that your vocabulary is getting larger, you may have noticed some patterns in the gender of nouns. For example, it's **der Lehrer, der Schüler, der Winter, der Sommer, der Bruder;** BUT **die Butter, das Zimmer, die Mutter, die**

Schwester. What do all of these nouns have in common? _____

If you had to guess the gender of a noun ending with **-er,** what would be a good

guess? _____

Most nouns ending in **-er** are masculine. Memorize the exceptions and their meanings.

Here's another group: It's **die Bluse, die Vase, die Giraffe, die Klasse, die Lampe, die Trompete, die Liste;** BUT **der Junge, der Löwe, der Hase, der Affe.** What do

all of these nouns have in common? _____
If you had to guess the gender of a noun ending in **-e,** what would be a good

guess? _____

Most nouns that end in **-e** are feminine.

IMPORTANT: Some nouns ending in **-e** are masculine. Such nouns add **n** in the accusative and dative and all plural forms:

	SINGULAR	PLURAL
NOMINATIVE	**der Junge**	**die Jungen**
ACCUSATIVE	**den Jungen**	**die Jungen**
DATIVE	**dem Jungen**	**den Jungen**

3 **Elefant** adds **en** to all forms beyond the nominative singular:

	SINGULAR	PLURAL
NOMINATIVE	**der Elefant**	**die Elefanten**
ACCUSATIVE	**den Elefanten**	**die Elefanten**
DATIVE	**dem Elefanten**	**den Elefanten**

Recognizing patterns helps make determining noun gender forms in German easier. As your vocabulary becomes bigger, you will notice other patterns.

__ ÜBUNGEN __

F. Construct carefully a complete sentence for each group of words. Add the determiners (articles, possessives) of your choice before the nouns. In addition, pay special attention to the endings on verbs and nouns, wherever necessary:

1. ich / sehen / Giraffe

_____

2. Mutter / streicheln / Hund

_____

3. Vater / füttern / Vogel

_____

4. Junge / sehen / Elefant / im Tierpark

_____

5. Mädchen / geben / Affe / Banane

_____

6. Hase / laufen / auf dem Land

_____

4 Read these sentences:

> *Es gibt* einen Esel im Bauernhof.
> *Es gibt* eine Giraffe im Zoo.
> *Es gibt* ein Schaf auf dem Land.
> *Gibt es* Pferde in der Stadt?
> *Gibt es* einen Arzt im Haus?

What does **es gibt** mean? _____

What does **gibt es** mean? _____

In what case is the noun phrase that follows **es gibt** or **gibt es**? _____

__ÜBUNG__

G. **Was gibt es im Zoo?**

1. Es gibt _____.

2. _____.

3. _____.

4. _____.

5. _____.

6. _____.

GESPRÄCH

Wortschatz

ruhig *peaceful, calm, quiet*   **leben** *to live*

_____ PERSÖNLICHE FRAGEN _____

1. Was ist dein Lieblingstier?

_____

2. Welches Tier hast du nicht gern?

_____

3. Welches Tier ist dumm?

_____

4. Welches Tier ist intelligent?

_____

5. Welches Tier gibt Milch?

_____
_____

_____ DU _____

You are the animal curator at the zoo. Show where all the animals are in your zoo. Put up signs with the German names of the animals:

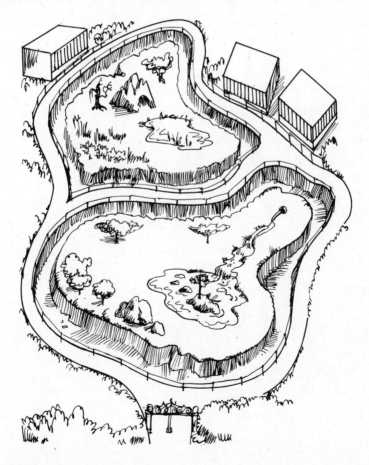

DIALOG

Your country friend is trying to convince you to move to the country. How would you respond?

KULTURECKE

Spaß mit Tieren (Fun with animals)

The noises that animals make have German equivalents. Here is a list of some common German animal noises:

die Biene: summ, summ!

der Hund: wau, wau!

die Ente: quak, quak!

die Katze: miau, miau!

der Esel: iah, iah!

die Kuh: muh, muh!

der Frosch: quak, quak!

das Schaf: mäh, mäh!

der Hahn: kikeriki!

das Schwein: chrrm!

das Huhn: put, put!

die Ziege: mähähähä!

The Germans also like **Zungenbrecher** (*tongue twisters*). Here is one that involves an animal. Do you recognize the animal?

Fischers Fritz fischt frische Fische,
Frische Fische fischt Fischers Fritz.

23 *Die Musik*

Dative Pronouns; the Verbs
wissen, gefallen, treffen

1 **Wortschatz**

die Schallplatte

die Compact Disc

der Plattenspieler

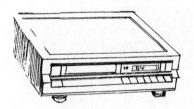

der CD-Spieler

die Kassette

der Kassettenrecorder

das Radio
das Transistorradio

die Stereoanlage

das Konzert
das Orchester

die Kapelle

die klassische Musik

die Volksmusik

die Schlagermusik

die Rockmusik

der Jazz

___ ÜBUNGEN _____

A. You and your friends go to concerts regularly. What kind of music do you like?

1. _____

2. _____

3. _____

4. _____

5. _____

B. You also listen to a lot of things at home. Tell what you listen to:

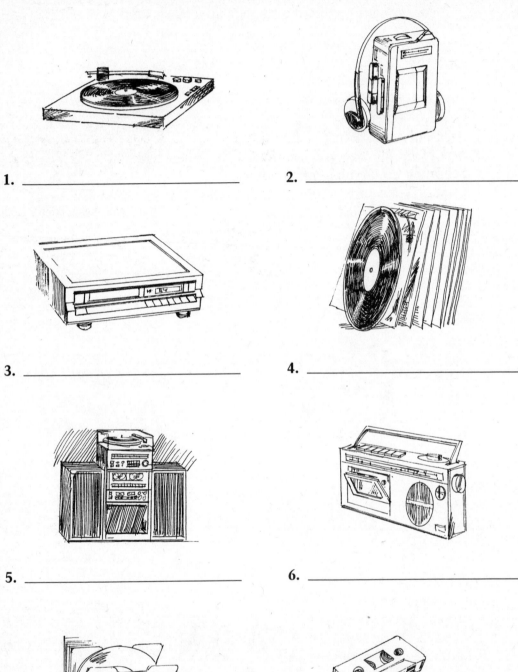

1. _____

2. _____

3. _____

4. _____

5. _____

6. _____

7. _____

8. _____

2 Ulrike's birthday is coming up and her friend Paul doesn't know what kind of gift to give her. Listen in as he discusses the matter with a friend:

PAUL: Ich weiß nicht, was ich tun soll! Ulrike wird fünfzehn, und ihr Geburtstag is am Samstag. Ich habe keine Idee, was für ein Geschenk ich ihr kaufen soll.

tun soll *am supposed to do*
wird *becomes*

RICHARD: Gefällt ihr der Schmuck? Eine Halskette oder eine Brosche vielleicht?

PAUL: Nein, sie hat viel Schmuck. Außerdem ist Schmuck für sie nichts besonderes.

gefallen *to please*
    der Schmuck *the jewelry*
    die Halskette *the necklace*
die Brosche *the brooch, pin*
außerdem *besides*
nichts besonderes *nothing special*

RICHARD: Weiß ihre Freundin Karla etwas? Hat sie eine Idee, was Ulrike gefällt?

PAUL: Karla sagt, Spaß haben gefällt ihr. Materielle Dinge sind ihr nicht wichtig.

RICHARD: Was soll das bedeuten?

PAUL: Ich weiß nicht, aber ihre Eltern sagen auch, daß ihr gute Musik gefällt.

RICHARD: Was für Musik gefällt ihr?

PAUL: Ihren Eltern gefällt klassische Musik, aber sie sagen nicht, was Karla gefällt.

RICHARD: Sie ist immer mit den Freunden im Jazz-klub. Den Freunden gefällt Jazz. Vielleicht gefällt ihr auch Jazz. Kauf ihr eine Jazzschallplatte!

immer *always*

PAUL: Ich weiß nicht, Richard. Sie hat keinen Plat-tenspieler, und außerdem spielen Compact Discs die Musik besser.

RICHARD: Dann kauf ihr eine Compact Disc!

PAUL: Sie hat keinen CD-Spieler.

RICHARD: Kauf ihr lieber einen CD-Spieler!

PAUL: So viel Geld habe ich nicht!

RICHARD: Was wissen ihre Schulfreunde von ihren Vorlieben?

die Vorliebe *the preference*

PAUL: Leider nichts.

RICHARD: Ich habe eine Idee. Ihr zwei seid gute Freunde. Warum gibst du ihr nicht eine Eintritts-karte für ein Konzert?

die Eintrittskarte *the ticket*

PAUL: Das ist eine sehr gute Idee!

RICHARD: Was für Musik gefällt dir?

PAUL: Mir gefällt Rockmusik.

RICHARD: Ausgezeichnet! Die Gruppe Schattenspiel hat am Samstag ein Konzert, und es gibt noch Karten an der Kasse.

an der Kasse *at the box office*

PAUL: Ich gehe gleich und kaufe die Karten. Dann rufe ich Ulrike an. Ich weiß, daß ihr dieses Geschenk sicher gefällt.

RICHARD: Und vielleicht trefft ihr Monika und mich im Konzert. Die Rockmusik gefällt uns auch.   **treffen** *to meet*

__ ÜBUNG _____

C. **Ergänze die Sätze!**

1. Am Samstag ist _____ .

2. Paul weiß nicht, _____ .

3. Ulrike gefällt _____ nicht sehr.

4. Karla sagt, daß _____ .

5. Ulrikes Eltern sagen, daß _____ .

6. Ulrikes Eltern gefällt _____ .

7. Den Freunden gefällt _____ .

8. Richard schlägt vor (*suggests*): „_____

_____ ."

9. Ulrike aber hat keinen _____ .

10. Paul sagt, Compact Discs spielen _____ .

11. Paul kauft ihr keinen CD-Spieler, denn er _____ .

12. Dann hat Richard eine gute _____ .

13. Paul gefällt _____ .

14. Paul kauft _____ .

15. Die Rockmusik _____ Monika und Richard auch.

3   In the story we learn that Paul decides to give Ulrike a concert ticket for her birthday:

Ich gebe *ihr* eine Eintrittskarte.
I give her a concert ticket.

What is the indirect object of the sentence? _____ That's correct! The indirect object is **ihr** [*to*] (*her*); **ihr** is a dative pronoun. The dative pronouns are **mir, dir, ihm, ihr, ihm, uns, euch, ihnen,** and **Ihnen.**

Let's see if you can complete the following sentences with the correct dative pronoun equivalent to the English meaning in parentheses:

Paul gibt (*me*) _____ eine Eintrittskarte.

Paul gibt (*you, familiar*) _____ eine Eintrittskarte.

Paul gibt (*him*) _____ eine Eintrittskarte.

Paul gibt (*her*) _____ eine Eintrittskarte.

Paul gibt (*it*) _____ eine Eintrittskarte.

Paul gibt (*us*) _____ eine Eintrittskarte.

Paul gibt (*you, familiar plural*) _____ eine Eintrittskarte.

Paul gibt (*them*) _____ eine Eintrittskarte.

Paul gibt (*you, formal*) _____ eine Eintrittskarte.

Very good! In summary:

PRONOUNS

NOMINATIVE		ACCUSATIVE		DATIVE	
ich	(*I*)	**mich**	(*me*)	**mir**	([to] *me*)
du	(*you*)	**dich**	(*you*)	**dir**	([to] *you*)
er	(*he*)	**ihn**	(*him*)	**ihm**	([to] him)
sie	(*she*)	**sie**	(*her*)	**ihr**	([to] her)
es	(*it*)	**es**	(*it*)	**ihm**	([to] it)
wir	(*we*)	**und**	(*us*)	**uns**	([to] us)
ihr	(*you*)	**euch**	(*you*)	**euch**	([to] you)
sie	(*they*)	**sie**	(*them*)	**ihnen**	([to] them)
Sie	(*you*)	**Sie**	(*you*)	**Ihnen**	([to] you)

Dative pronouns are used as indirect objects of verbs or as objects of dative prepositions.

__ ÜBUNGEN _____

C. Complete the second sentence with the dative pronoun that corresponds most closely to the meaning conveyed in the first sentence.

1. Ich gebe Marianne eine Party. Ich gebe _____ eine Party.

2. Wir schenken Karl Platten. Wir schenken _____ Platten.

3. Ich bekomme eine Kassette von Karl. Karl schenkt _____ eine Kassette.

4. Hans kauft Marianne und Susi eine Compact Disc. Hans kauft _____ eine Compact Disc.

5. Wir bekommen eine Stereoanlage von Heidi. Heidi gibt _____ eine Stereoanlage.

6. Du bekommst einen CD-Spieler. Deine Eltern schenken _____ einen CD-Spieler zum Geburtstag.

7. Karl bringt dir und deiner Mutter einen Kassettenrecorder. Karl bringt _____ einen Kassettenrecorder.

D. Here's a real challenge! Complete the sentences with the appropriate German pronoun according to the meaning in parentheses. Some pronouns are in the nominative, some in the accusative, and some in the dative:

1. (I) Kaufe _____ die Kassette?

2. (us) Er macht _____ ein Geschenk.

3. (them) Siehst du _____ ?

4. (him) Wir treffen _____ im Konzert.

5. (her) Ich schenke _____ eine Schallplatte zum Geburtstag.

6. (you, fam. sing.) Er holt _____ eine Eintrittskarte.

7. (me) Hört er _____ ?

8. (me) Er schenkt _____ eine Stereoanlage.

9. (him) Ich schenke _____ eine Compact Disc.

10. (him) Ich treffe _____ im Konzert.

 Another special verb introduced in the story is **wissen** (*to know* [*a fact*]):

ich weiß	wir wissen
du weißt	ihr wißt
er	
sie } weiß	sie wissen
es	
	Sie wissen

Memorize all the forms of this irregular verb.

__ ÜBUNG _____

E. Complete each sentence with the correct form of **wissen**:

1. Ich _____ nicht, wie alt er ist.

2. Er _____ , wann das Konzert beginnt.

3. Du _____ , was für Musik Monika gern hat.

4. _____ ihr, wo die Kapelle spielt?

5. Karl und Erika _____ , wer eine Compact Disc hat.

6. Die Eltern _____ , wieviel die Eintrittskarte kostet.

7. Was _____ ich?

 Yet another useful verb is **gefallen** (*to please*). It is conjugated like **fallen** but, because of its meaning, is used in only two forms: **gefällt** and **gefallen.**

If what pleases is singular, use **gefällt**:

Dieses Geschenk *gefällt* mir.   *This gift pleases me.*
                                        I like this gift.

If what pleases is plural, use **gefallen**:

Diese Geschenke *gefallen* mir.   *These gifts please me.*
I like these gifts.

In addition, the person pleased is always in the dative.

__ ÜBUNGEN _____

F. Who likes what? Complete each sentence with the pronoun closest in meaning to the English pronoun in parentheses:

1. Jazzmusik gefällt (me) _____ nicht.

2. Gefällt (you) _____ deine Geburtstagsparty?

3. Das Konzert gefällt (her) _____ sehr.

4. Die Schallplatten gefallen (us) _____ .

5. Gefällt (you) _____ euere Schule?

6. Meine Aufsätze gefallen (them) _____ .

G. Complete each sentence with **gefällt** or **gefallen**:

1. _____ dir Rockmusik?

2. Schöne Blusen _____ mir.

3. Laute Musik _____ ihm nicht.

4. Basketball _____ uns.

5. Die Schule _____ ihnen sehr.

6. Mir _____ dein Kassettenrecorder.

H. Restate these sentences. Use a form of **gefallen**:

1. Ich habe Volksmusik gern.

2. Er hat Tennis gern.

_____

3. Wir haben diesen CD-Spieler gern.

_____

4. Sie haben Skilaufen gern.

_____

5. Ihr habt Geburtstagspartys nicht gern.

_____

6
The verb **treffen** (_to meet_) is an **e→i** stem-changing verb that is similar to other **e→i** stem-changing verbs you have already learned. Complete the following table:

ich _____   **wir** _____

du _____   **ihr** _____

er
sie } _____   **sie** _____
es

Sie _____

What is the rule for **e→i** stem-changing verbs?

_____

What are the **e→i** stem-changing verbs that you have learned so far?

_____

Which other stem-change patterns exist in German? _____

Which verbs fit each of these patterns? _____

_____

_____

— ÜBUNGEN _____

I. All these people have appointments at various times and in various places. Complete each sentence with the correct form of **treffen:**

1. Er _____ seine Freundin um acht Uhr.

2. Wir _____ sie im Theater.

3. Karl und Monika _____ die Kinder in der Bäckerei.

4. Ich _____ meine Mutter im Restaurant.

5. Wann _____ wir dich?

6. _____ du mich später?

7. Wo _____ er seine Freunde?

8. Warum _____ uns die Eltern nicht bei den Großeltern?

J. Complete the sentences with the correct form of **treffen, gefallen,** or **wissen,** whichever is the most logical verb for the sentence:

1. Ich _____ nicht, was er sagt.

2. Diese Kassette _____ mir sehr.

3. Ich _____ seine Eltern nächsten Dienstag.

4. Er _____ nicht, wie alt Ursel ist.

5. Monika und ihre Mutter _____ mich um acht Uhr.

6. Wir _____ , wo er wohnt.

7. Diese Schallplatten _____ ihnen sehr.

8. Wann _____ wir dich?

9. Uschi _____ die Antwort.

10. _____ du, wie er heißt?

GESPRÄCH

Wortschatz

Am Apparat. *Speaking.*

DIALOG

Choose the appropriate responses:

PERSÖNLICHE FRAGEN

1. Wann ist dein Geburtstag?

_____

2. Wie alt bist du?

_____

3. Hast du Geburtstagspartys gern? Warum (nicht)?

_____

4. Was für Geschenke gefallen dir?

_____

5. Weißt du, wie alt deine Mutter ist?

_____

DU

Write five sentences about your preferences in music:

1. _____

2. _____

3. _____

4. _____

5. _____

KULTURECKE

Die Musik

Rock music is very popular in the German-speaking world. German teenagers listen to American and British groups, as well as to their own, such as Kraftwerk. Other popular German recording artists include Bernd Clüver, Udo Jürgens, and James Last.

Germans also like folk music. One of Germany's most popular folksongs is "Die Lorelei." This song is about the legendary Lorelei, a beautiful maiden, who sits high atop a rock on the shore of the Rhine River. The Lorelei sings a beautiful song while combing her long hair. Sailors become enamored with her singing and beauty and forget the perilous waters on which they are sailing. As a result, many are ship-wrecked on the rocks.

The poet Heinrich Heine (1797–1856) wrote the poem, and Friedrich Silcher wrote the melody. Perhaps your teacher can help you learn to sing this beautiful song:

Die Lorelei

Ich weiß nicht, was soll es bedeuten,
Daß ich so traurig bin;
Ein Märchen aus alten Zeiten,
Das kommt mir nicht aus dem Sinn.

was soll es bedeuten *what it's supposed to mean*
das Märchen *the fairy tale, legend*
der Sinn *the mind*
es dunkelt *it's getting dark*

Die Luft ist kühl und es dunkelt,
Und ruhig fließt der Rhein;
Der Gipfel des Berges funkelt
Im Abendsonnenschein.

der Gipfel *the top*
funkelt *sparkles*

Die schönste Jungfrau sitzet
Dort oben wunderbar,
Ihr goldnes Geschmeide blitzet,
Sie kämmt ihr goldenes Haar.

die Jungfrau *the maiden*
das Geschmeide *the jewelry*
blitzet *glistens*
kämmt *is coming*

Sie kämmt es mit goldenem Kamme,
Und singt ein Lied dabei;
Das hat eine wundersame,
Gewaltige Melodei

dabei *while doing so*
gewaltig *powerful*
die Melodei = die Melodie

Den Schiffer im kleinen Schiffe
Ergreift es mit wildem Weh;
Er schaut nicht die Felsenriffe,
Er schaut nur hinauf in die Höh.

der Schiffer *the boatman*
ergreift es *is seized*
das Weh *the woe*
der Felsenriff *the reef*

Ich glaube, die Wellen verschlingen
Am Ende Schiffer und Kahn;
Und das hat mit ihrem Singen
Die Lorelei getan.

die Welle *the wave*
verschlingen *devour*
der Kahn *the boat*

24 *Die Hobbys*

How to Talk About Things in the Past

1 What do you like to do in your spare time? Can you guess the meanings of these leisure activities?

das Basteln

die Handarbeit

die Gartenarbeit

das Reisen

ein Musikinstrument spielen

das Zelten

die Malerei

das Turnen

das Wandern

das Kochen   das Briefmarkensammeln   das Münzensammeln

ÜBUNG

A. Was ist dein Lieblingshobby? Mir gefällt . . .

1. _____ 2. _____

3. _____ 4. _____

5. _____ 6. _____

7. _____   8. _____

9. _____   10. _____

11. _____   12. _____

 Now let's see how well Karl's and Monika's family prepare for summer vacation. Pay special attention to the verbs in heavy type. They are in the past tense:

Karl und Monika haben jetzt Sommerferien. Die ganze Familie macht einen Ausflug.

der Ausflug *the excursion*

MUTTER: Heinz, **wir haben** die Rucksäcke **gepackt. Hast du** die Gartenarbeit **gemacht?**

der Rucksack *the knapsack*

VATER: Ja, Renate. **Ich habe** die Gartengeräte in den Keller **gestellt.** Ich nehme die Rucksäcke jetzt zum Wagen. Wo sind die Kinder?

das Gartengerät *the gardening tool*

MUTTER: **Karls Münzensammlung ist** auf den Boden im Schlafzimmer **gefallen.** Er räumt jetzt auf. **Monika hat** gestern **vergessen,** die Zelte bei Meyers abzuholen. Sie kommt bald zurück.

MONIKA: Vati, kannst du mir helfen? Die Zelte sind sehr schwer.

VATER: Ja, sicher, Monika. Ich komme sofort.

MUTTER: Karl, bist du fertig?

KARL: Ja, Mutti! Darf ich auch meine Kamera mitnehmen?

MUTTER: Ja, das ist eine gute Idee.

die Münzensammlung *the coin collection*
räumt ... auf *straightens up*
gestern *yesterday*
vergessen *to forget*

sofort *at once*
fertig *ready, finished*

Die Familie ist jetzt unterwegs. Sie fahren auf der Autobahn in die Alpen. Sie haben zelten gern. Sie gehen jedes Jahr in die Alpen zelten. Endlich kommen sie an den Campingplatz.

unterwegs *on the road*

endlich *finally*
der Campingplatz *the campground*

VATER: Ah! Frische Luft! Kein Lärm, keine Läden! Nur wir und die herrliche Natur! Karl, mach bitte ein Foto von uns!

KARL: Ich kann nicht, Vati.

VATER: Warum denn nicht? **Hast du** deine Kamera **vergessen?**

KARL: Die Kamera habe ich. Den Film **habe ich** leider **vergessen.**

MONIKA: Keine Sorge! **Ich habe** bei Meyers Film gekauft.

KARL: Vielen Dank, Monika.

MONIKA: Bitteschön. Vielleicht kannst du mir während dieser Ferien zeigen, wie man gute Aufnahmen macht.

frisch *fresh*
die Luft *the air*
herrlich *marvelous*

leider *unfortunately*
Keine Sorge! *Don't worry!*

während *during*
zeigen *to show*
die Aufnahme *the snapshot*

— ÜBUNG _____

B. Beantworte die Fragen:

1. Was macht die Familie in den Sommerferien?

   _____

2. Was hat die Mutter gemacht?

   _____

3. Wohin hat der Vater die Gartengeräte gestellt?

_____

4. Wo ist Karl?

_____

5. Wo ist Monika?

_____

6. Was darf Karl mitnehmen?

_____

7. Wohin fährt die Familie?

_____

8. Auf welcher Straße fahren sie?

_____

9. Wie oft gehen sie zelten?

_____

10. Warum kann Karl keine Aufnahmen machen?

_____

11. Was hat Monika bei Meyers gekauft?

_____

12. Was möchte Monika von ihrem Bruder lernen?

_____

_____

3 | Compare the following pairs of sentences:

Er *spielt* Klavier.   Er *hat* Klavier *gespielt*.
Er *hört* Radio.   Er *hat* Radio *gehört*.
Er *wartet* zu Hause.   Er *hat* zu Hause *gewartet*.
Er *telefoniert* mit Inge. Er *hat* mit Inge *telefoniert*.

What time do the sentences in the left column refer to, present or past?

_____ What time do the sentences in the right column refer to?

_____

The sentences on the right are in the conversational past tense. How many verb forms are used in the conversational past tense in each sentence?

_____ List them:

_____   _____

_____   _____

How does **spielt** differ from **hat gespielt?** _____

How does **hört** differ from **hat gehört?** _____

How does **wartet** differ from **hat gewartet?** _____

How does **telefoniert** differ from **hat telefoniert?** _____

___ ÜBUNG _____

C. Gestern oder heute? When did these events take place?

1. Ich arbeite im Garten. _____

2. Er hat ein Bild gemalt. _____

3. Wir machen unsere Aufgaben. _____

4. Die Jungen haben viel Bratwurst gegessen. _____

5. Mutti hat mir ein Buch gegeben. _____

6. Vater liest ein Buch. _____

7. Wir singen gern. _____

8. Hans hat mir einen Brief geschrieben. _____

4 Our story was in the conversational past tense, equivalent to these English past-tense forms:

ich habe gekauft	*I bought, I have bought*
wir haben gepackt	*We packed, we have packed*
sie hat gegessen	*she ate, she has eaten*
sie haben geschrieben	*they wrote, they have written*

The conversational past tense tells about events that happened or have happened in the past. To understand how the past tense works in English will help you understand how it works in German.

 You have already learned the present tense of many German weak and strong verbs. In the story of this lesson, you were introduced to both kinds of verbs in the conversational past tense. Read the story again and notice the verb forms in heavy type.

The conversational past tense consists of two verb forms for most German verbs: the present tense of the helping verb **haben** and a form called the PAST PARTICIPLE, which usually is the last word in the clause:

ich	**habe gespielt**	*I played, have played*
du	**hast gespielt**	*you played, have played*
er	**hat gespielt**	*he played, has played*
sie	**hat gespielt**	*she played, has played*
es	**hat gespielt**	*it played, has played*
wir	**haben gespielt**	*we played, have played*
ihr	**habt gespielt**	*you played, have played*
sie	**haben gespielt**	*they played, have played*
Sie	**haben gespielt**	*you played, have played*

 The past participle of weak verbs is formed by attaching the prefix **ge** to the verb stem. The **t** ending on the past participle tells you that the verb is weak:

gespiel**t**   **ge**kauf**t**

The past participle of verbs in **ieren** is the same as the **er**-form:

telefoniert   **fotografiert**

ÜBUNGEN

D. Your parents want to know how your day went. Tell them:

EXAMPLE: lernen / Deutsch
         Ich habe Deutsch gelernt.

1. üben / Klavier

_____

2. antworten / auf viele Fragen

_____

3. tanzen / bei Jürgen

_____

4. telefonieren / mit Erika

_____

E. Tell what the members of the Meyer family did today.

> EXAMPLE: Georg / spielen / Tennis
> Georg hat Tennis gespielt.

1. Der Vater / üben Gitarre

_____

2. Rudi und Karl / kochen / das Mittagessen

_____

3. Die Mutter / arbeiten / im Garten

_____

4. Die Mädchen / malen

_____

5. Susi / spielen / Klavier

_____

6. Die Eltern / fotografieren / die Kinder

_____

7 Now compare the following pairs of sentences:

Wir *kommen* sofort.	Wir *sind* sofort *gekommen*.
Die Münzensammlung *fällt* auf den Boden.	Die Münzensammlung *ist* auf den Boden *gefallen*.

Which sentences refer to the past, those on the left or on the right?

_____ . How many verb forms are used in these conversational

past tenses? _____

List them: _____   _____

How does **kommen** differ from **ist gekommen**? _____

How does **fällt** differ from **ist gefallen**? _____

__ ÜBUNG __

F. **Gestern oder heute?** When did these events take place?

1. Er kommt nach der Schule. _____

2. Sie sind zur Bibliothek gefahren. _____

3. Kurt schläft bis zehn Uhr. _____

4. Mutter ist mit uns ins Kino gegangen. _____

5. Der kleine Junge ist gefallen. _____

6. Ulrike reitet zum Campingplatz. _____

7. Im Winter tragen wir Mäntel. _____

8. Unsere Freunde haben uns im Zoo getroffen. _____

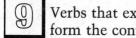 The past participle of strong verbs ends in **en.** In addition, many strong verbs have vowel and (sometimes) consonant changes in the verb stem (compare English *run* — [*has*] *run*; *go* — [*has*] *gone*):

INFINITIVE	PAST PARTICIPLE
essen	**gegessen**
schreiben	**geschrieben**

9 Verbs that express a change of place or condition use the helping verb **sein** to form the conversational past tense:

ich bin gefallen	*I fell, have fallen*
du bist gefallen	*you fell, have fallen*
er ist gefallen	*he fell, has fallen*
sie ist gefallen	*she fell, has fallen*
es ist gefallen	*it fell, has fallen*
wir sind gefallen	*we fell, have fallen*
ihr seid gefallen	*you fell, have fallen*
sie sind gefallen	*they fell, have fallen*
Sie sind gefallen	*you fell, have fallen*

The following strong verbs have appeared in this book. Verbs that use **sein** instead of haben as the helping verb are signaled by the word **ist**:

INFINITIVE	PAST PARTICIPLE
essen	gegessen
fahren	istgefahren
fallen	istgefallen
fressen	gefressen
geben	gegeben
gehen	istgegangen
helfen	geholfen
kommen	istgekommen
laufen	istgelaufen
lesen	gelesen
nehmen	genommen
reiten	istgeritten
scheinen	geschienen
schlafen	geschlafen
schreiben	geschrieben
schwimmen	geschwommen
sehen	gesehen
sein	istgewesen
singen	gesungen
sprechen	gesprochen
stehen	gestanden
tragen	getragen
treffen	getroffen
trinken	getrunken
tun	getan

NOTE: The past participle of **wissen** is irregular: **gewußt.**

__ ÜBUNGEN __

G. Tell what these people did or what happened yesterday:

1. du / laufen / in den Park

_____

2. wir / fallen / von dem Stuhl

_____

3. er / essen / eine Bratwurst

_____

4. du / kommen / nach Hause

_____

5. Marianne / tun / nichts

_____

6. die Sonne / scheinen

_____

7. die Lehrerin / stehen / vor der Klasse

_____

8. der Junge / schlafen / bis neun Uhr

_____

9. die Freundin / sprechen / mit ihrem Freund

_____

10. die Eltern / geben / den Kindern / das Geschenk

_____

11. Karl / sein / krank

_____

12. Susi / treffen / ihre Lehrerin

_____

H. Here's a description of what some people did yesterday. Complete the sentences by adding the correct German verb form in the conversational past tense:

1. (read) Die Mutter _____ ein Buch _____ .

2. (slept) Die Katze und der Hund _____ in der Ecke _____ .

3. (ate) Die Kinder _____ Bratwurst _____ .

4. (sang) Das Mädchen _____ auf deutsch _____ .

5. (swam) Karl _____ im Schwimmbad _____ .

6. (went) Susi und Hans _____ nach Hause _____ .

7. (sang) Erikas Freunde _____ gut _____ .

8. (drove) Gisela _____ nach Österreich _____ .

9. (wrote) Er _____ einen Aufsatz _____ .

10. (wore) Wir _____ unsere neuen Blusen _____ .

11. (drank) Die Eltern _____ Kaffee _____ .

12. (spoke) Die Großeltern _____ Englisch _____ .

13. (saw) Ich _____ den Film _____ .

14. (met) Du _____ deine Freunde bei Meyers _____ .

15. (came) Der Onkel _____ später _____ .

I. Ilse wrote a letter, but forgot to mail it. It is now a day later and she wants to rewrite it so that it describes accurately what happened yesterday. Help her rewrite this part of the letter:

Heute plane ich viel. Zuerst esse ich das Frühstück. Ich trinke dazu Orangensaft. Dann gehe ich zur Schule. Ich lerne heute Deutsch, Geschichte und Englisch. In Englisch schreibe ich einen Aufsatz, und in Geschichte lese ich im Textbuch.

Nach der Schule kaufen Erika und ich einige Schallplatten. Wir essen im Café zu Mittag. Dann spielen wir Tennis. Kurt und Udo treffen uns da. Wir gehen dann ins Restaurant zum Abendessen. Ich fahre mit dem Bus nach Hause, und ich plane dort eine Geburtstagsparty für Werner. Erika, Kurt und Udo kommen auch.

Ich mache heute soviel, daß ich sicher gut schlafe.

_____

_____

_____

_____

_____

_____

_____

_____

_____

_____

GESPRÄCH

Wortschatz

zelten gehen *to go camping*   **vorschlagen** *to suggest*

_____ DIALOG _____

You are discussing your plans for next summer with a friend. Respond to the questions in the conversational past tense:

PERSÖNLICHE FRAGEN

1. Was hast du zum Frühstück gegessen?

2. Was haben dir deine Eltern zum Geburtstag geschenkt?

3. Wohin bist du letzten Sommer gefahren?

4. Was hast du gestern gelesen?

5. Was hast du für die Sommerferien geplant?

_DU_

Think back over the past year in German class. Write a paragraph of at least five clauses describing what you did in German class:

KULTURECKE

Deutsche Spezialitäten

Over the centuries, German culture has produced many edible delectables, each one with its own history. For example:

Spekulatius, a molded spice cookie, originated in the Rhine area. It is said to have been created in honor of a bishop, St. Nicholas of Myra.

Pfeffernüsse, or pepper nuts, originated many centuries ago when sugar was prohibitively expensive. **Pfeffernüsse** are sweetened predominantly with honey.

Lebkuchen, or gingerbread, originated in the Black Forest. It is used as the building material for the Gingerbread House and is sometimes shaped like a heart and decorated for the Oktoberfest. Today, the most popular **Lebkuchen** is produced in the bakeries of the city of Nürnberg.

Here is a recipe for **Lebkuchen:**

½ cup honey	2¾ cup all-purpose flour
½ cup molasses	1 teaspoon each cinnamon, cloves, allspice, and nutmeg
¾ cup brown sugar (packed)	½ teaspoon baking soda
1 egg	⅓ cup cut-up citron
1 teaspoon grated lemon peel	⅓ cup chopped nuts
1 tablespoon lemon juice	Icing (below)

Mix honey and molasses in a large saucepan; heat to boiling. Cool thoroughly. Stir in sugar, egg, lemon peel, and juice. Mix in the remaining ingredients except the icing. Cover; chill at least 8 hours.

Heat oven to 400°. Roll a small amount of dough at a time ¼ inch thick on a lightly floured, cloth-covered board. (Keep remaining dough refrigerated.)

Cut dough into rectangles, each 2½ × 1½ inches. Place 1 inch apart on greased baking sheet. Bake 10 to 12 minutes or until no imprint remains when touched lightly with a finger. Brush icing lightly over cookies. Immediately remove from baking sheet; cool. Store in airtight container with slice of apple or orange.

Icing

Mix 1 cup of sugar and ½ cup of water in a small saucepan. Cook over medium heat to 230° on candy thermometer (or just until a small amount of mixture spins a 2-inch thread). Remove from heat; stir in ¼ cup of confectioners' sugar. If icing becomes sugary, reheat slightly, adding a little water.

Wiederholung VI (Aufgaben 21–24)

Aufgabe 21

a. To express:

	In German say:
I live in (name of country).	**Ich wohne *in*** (name of country).
I go to (name of country).	**Ich fahre *nach*** (name of country).
I come from (name of country).	**Ich komme *aus*** (name of country).

Examples:

> **Ich wohne *in Deutschland*.**
> **Ich fahre *nach Frankreich*.**
> **Ich komme *aus Spanien*.**

Note these exceptions:

> **Ich wohne *in den Vereinigten Staaten*.**
> **Ich wohne *in der Schweiz*.**
> **Ich fahre *in die Vereinigten Staatan*.**
> **Ich fahre *in die Schweiz*.**
> **Ich komme *aus den Vereinigten Staaten*.**
> **Ich komme *aus der Schweiz*.**

b. The verb **sprechen** (*to speak*) is a stem-changing verb. Memorize all its forms:

ich spreche	wir sprechen
du sprichst	ihr sprecht
er	
sie } spricht	sie sprechen
es	
	Sie sprechen

Aufgabe 22

Gender Clues:

Most nouns ending in **-er** are masculine.

Most nouns ending in **-e** are feminine.

Masculine nouns ending in **-e** in the nominative singular add **-n** to all other forms in the singular and plural.

der Elefant adds **-en** to all forms beyond the nominative singular.

Aufgabe 23

a. Dative pronouns replace nouns functioning as the indirect object of a verb or the object of a dative preposition:

mir	uns
dir	euch
ihm ⎫	
ihr ⎬	ihnen
ihm ⎭	
	Ihnen

b. **Wissen** (*to know*) is an irregular verb. Memorize all its forms:

ich weiß	wir wissen
du weißt	ihr wißt
er ⎫	
sie ⎬ weiß	sie wissen
es ⎭	
	Sie wissen

Aufgabe 24

a. The conversational past tense describes past events. It says that something "happened" or "has happened."

b. There are two verb patterns in the conversational past tense in German. Some verbs are weak and some are strong.

c. Weak verbs in the conversational past tense are conjugated according to the following pattern (example, **spielen**):

ich habe . . . gespielt
du hast . . . gespielt
er hat . . . gespielt
sie hat . . . gespielt
es hat . . . gespielt
wir haben . . . gespielt
ihr habt . . . gespielt
sie haben . . . gespielt
Sie haben . . . gespielt

The conversational past uses two words: a form of **haben** (or sometimes **sein**) and a past participle, which is usually the last word in the clause. The past participle of weak verbs is formed by attaching the prefix **ge** and the ending **t** to the verb stem. The past participle of verbs ending in **ieren** is identical to its **er**-form:

fotografiert   telefoniert

d. Strong verbs in the conversational past tense are conjugated according to the following patterns (examples, **geben, gefallen**):

ich habe . . . gegeben	ich bin gefallen
du hast . . . gegeben	du bist gefallen
er hat . . . gegeben	er ist gefallen
sie hat . . . gegeben	sie ist gefallen
es hat . . . gegeben	es ist gefallen
wir haben . . . gegeben	wir sind gefallen
ihr habt . . . gegeben	ihr seid gefallen
sie haben . . . gegeben	sie sind gefallen
Sie haben . . . gegeben	Sie sind gefallen

The past participle of strong verbs always ends in **en**, and the verb stem may also have vowel or consonant changes. Since it is impossible to predict these changes, memorize the past participles of strong verbs whenever you learn a new verb. The strong verbs already presented in this book and their past participles are listed on page 414.

e. The past participle of **wissen** is irregular: **gewußt**.

___ ÜBUNGEN _____

A. Hobby Jumble: Unscramble the words. Then unscramble the letters in the circles to find the message:

GENNIS   ☐ ☐ ☐ ⬭ ☐ ☐

STELBAN   ⬭ ☐ ⬭ ⬭ ☐ ☐ ☐

RUNNET   ☐ ⬭ ☐ ☐ ☐ ☐

LEERAMI   ☐ ⬭ ☐ ☐ ⬭ ☐ ☐

TAGRBIENEART   ⬭ ☐ ☐ ⬭ ☐ ☐ ☐ ☐ ☐ ⬭ ☐ ☐

Was alle einmal im Jahr haben: _____

B. Write the German word under the picture you see. Then find the German word in the puzzle on page 427. The leftover letters then form the answer to the clue at the end of the puzzle.

1. _____

2. _____

3. _____

4. _____

5. _____

6. _____

7. _____

8. _____

9. _____

10. _____

11. _____

12. _____

13. _____

14. _____

15. _____

16. _____

17. _____

T	A	U	D	N	U	H	U	H	N
I	F	T	D	R	S	H	C	U	F
G	E	E	N	M	E	A	E	K	S
E	F	Z	B	A	A	F	U	E	C
R	A	E	T	H	F	F	P	V	H
R	H	G	N	A	H	E	O	O	W
F	C	E	R	S	K	I	L	G	E
M	S	I	Z	E	L	E	S	E	I
O	G	Z	L	Ö	W	E	O	L	N

Wo man Tiere sieht: _____

und _____ .

C. Was hat Dorothea zum Geburtstag bekommen? Fill in the German words in accordance with the picture cues, then read down the boxed column to find what Dorothea got for her birthday:

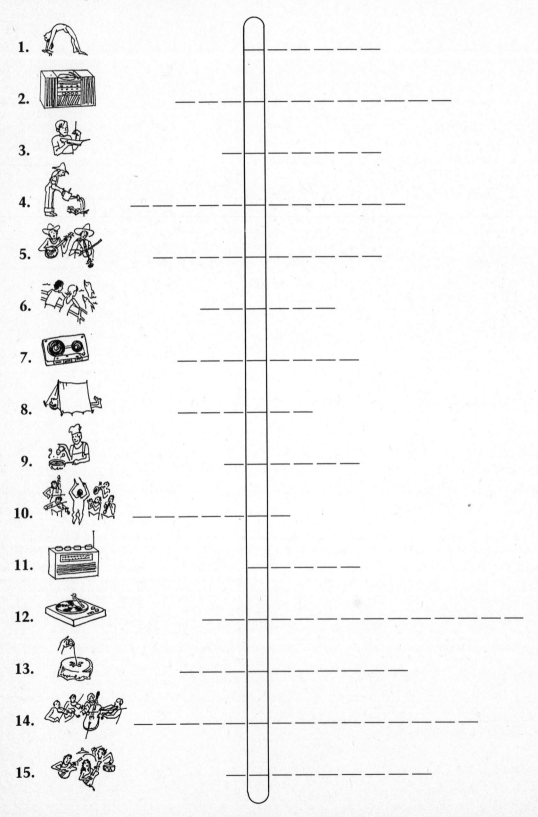

D. Hans is an export manager at **Import/Export Gesellschaft GmbH**. He is sending out catalogs to several important customers. The company puts out its catalogs in different languages. Help Hans send out the right one:

IMPORT/EXPORT GESELLSCHAFT GMBH

KUNDE	LAND	SPRACHE
1. Helmut Krause	Deutschland	_____
2. François La Mer	Frankreich	_____
3. Rick Jackson	Vereinigte Staaten	_____
4. Antonia Rossi	Italien	_____
5. Marco Perez	Spanien	_____
6. Andreas Schmidt	Österreich	_____
7. David Cantrell	England	_____
8. Ronald Fong	China	_____
9. Janice Dupont	Schweiz	_____
10. Georg Bauer	Schweiz	_____

E. Kreuzworträtsel:

WAAGERECHT

2. Wir sind gestern zur Schule _____ .
4. Inge _____ viel gegessen.
6. Ingrid hat ein Buch _____ .
8. Ich _____ morgens früh auf.
11. Michael hat mit Ilse _____ .
14. Susi braucht Film. Vati hat _____ Film gekauft.
15. _____ geht's?
16. Die Rucksäcke sind zu schwer für Monika. Hans hat ihr _____ .
18. Wann _____ Erich nach Österreich gefahren?
20. Ich habe sie seit zwei Monaten nicht _____ .
21. Im Sommer _____ wir gern am Strand.

SENKRECHT

1. Die Katze frißt die _____ .
3. Die Kinder sind letzte Woche sehr schnell _____ .
5. Ich _____ im Sommer nach Deutschland.
7. Der Kühlschrank _____ in der Küche.
9. Meine Freunde haben Deutsch gern. Deutsch gefällt _____ .
10. Wir haben gestern Tennis _____ .
12. Was machst du in den Sommer_____ ?
13. Ich habe Musik gern. Musik gefällt _____ .
14. Ich weiß nicht, wo mein Kuli ist. Hast du _____ gesehen?
15. Ich _____ nicht, wo er wohnt.
17. Die Eltern _____ die Zeitung.
19. Monika hat _____ Meyers Film gekauft.

F. Picture Story. Can you read this story? Much of it is in picture form. Whenever you come to a picture, read it as if it were a German word:

Meine hat immer viel vor. Zum Beispiel, letzten sind

wir alle in die gefahren. Mein hat einige und

gekauft. Mein hat und im Schallplatten-

laden gesucht. Er hat aber nichts gekauft, denn er hat nur einen zu

Hause. Aber die kleinen und gefallen ihm sehr, und er

hofft, daß jemand ihm einen oder zum Geburtstag schenkt.

ist im Reisebüro gewesen. Sie hat da Information über und

gesucht. Vielleicht reist die Familie in den Sommerferien in diese

Länder.

Nachher sind wir in den 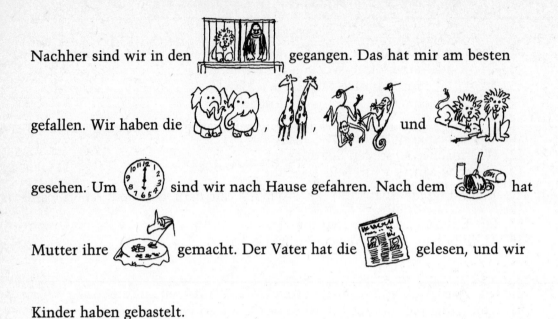 gegangen. Das hat mir am besten

gefallen. Wir haben die ⬚ , ⬚ , ⬚ und ⬚

gesehen. Um ⬚ sind wir nach Hause gefahren. Nach dem ⬚ hat

Mutter ihre ⬚ gemacht. Der Vater hat die ⬚ gelesen, und wir

Kinder haben gebastelt.

Culture Quiz

Having read the **Kulturecken,** you should have no problem with the blanks in this Quiz:

1. The ground floor of a house is called the _____ .

2. Children place a shoe on the window sill to receive gifts on _____ .

3. Germans measure temperature using the _____ scale.

4. The highest grade that German students can earn on their report cards is

   _____ .

5. The school recess during which German students may socialize and eat a mid-morning snack is called the _____ .

6. German television is funded by a fee (**Gebühr**), which is paid to the

   _____ .

7. To grab a quick bite at a snack bar, Germans go to the

   _____ .

8. Germans pay their telephone bills to the _____ .

9. The speed limit in German villages is _____ .

10. "Die Lorelei" is a famous German _____ .

11. _____ originated in the Rhine area. It is said to have been created in honor of a bishop, St. Nicholas of Myra.

12. _____ , sweetened with honey, originated many centuries ago when sugar was prohibitively expensive.

13. German is the official language of _____

   _____

14. In Germany, all children attend the first four years of school in the

   _____ .

15. At the end of high school (**das Gymnasium**), German students take a difficult

examination called the _____ , which determines eligibility for
university entry.

16. The _____ provides inexpensive food and overnight
lodging for students.

17. The monetary unit of Germany is the _____ .

18. If a German film started at 18 Uhr 45, you would expect the film to start when

your watch reads _____ .

19. German sizes are based on the _____ system.

20. The German sandwich is called _____ .

21. The most popular spectator sport in Germany is _____ .

22. Many Germans buy meat in a shop called _____ .

23. The German expressway system is called _____ .

24. The place where Germans fill their prescriptions for medicine is called the

_____ .

25. When entertaining dinner guests in Germany, the host or hostess may wish the

guests a _____ .

Vocabularies

The Vocabularies are complete for the purposes of this book.

Both the German-English and English-German vocabularies identify noun plurals [**der Affe, -n = der Affe, die Affen**] and verbs conjugated with **sein** in the conversational past tense [**kommen (er ist gekommen)** to come].

___ GERMAN-ENGLISH _____

A

der **Abend, -e** evening;
    heute abend tonight
das **Abendessen, -** dinner
    aber but
    **abfahren (er ist
    abgefahren)** to depart
    acht eight
    achtzehn eighteen
    achtzig eighty
der **Affe, -n** monkey
    alle all; everyone
    allein alone
    allgemein general
    als than, as, when
    also well, then
    alt old
der **Amerikaner, -,** die
    Amerikanerin, -nen
    American
    amerikanisch
    American
das **Amt, ̈er** office
    sich amusieren to
    enjoy oneself
    andere other
    angesehen respected
die **Angst, ̈e** fear
    antworten to answer
der **Anzug, ̈e** suit
der **Apfel, ̈** apple
der **Apfelsaft, ̈e** apple
    juice
der **Apparat, -e** machine;
    telephone
der **Appetit** appetite
der **April** April
die **Arbeit, -en** work
    arbeiten to work
der **Arm, -e** arm
    arm poor

die **Art, -en** kind, sort,
    type
der **Artikel, -** article
der **Arzt, ̈e,** die **Ärztin,
    -nen** doctor
    auch also, too
    auf on; **auf
    Wiedersehen**
    good-bye
die **Aufgabe, -n** lesson;
    assignment
die **Aufnahme, -n**
    snapshot, photo
    aufräumen to clean up
    aufregend exciting
das **Auge, -n** eye; die
    Augenfarbe, -n eye
    color
der **August** August
    aus out (of); from
der **Ausflug, ̈e** excursion
    ausgeben to spend
    (*money*)
    ausgezeichnet
    excellent
das **Auskunftsbüro, -s**
    information office
die **Ausrede, -n** excuse
    sich ausruhen to rest
die **Ausrüstung, -en**
    equipment
    aussehen to appear; to
    seem
    außerdem besides
die **Ausstrahlung, -en**
    radiation
das **Auto, -s,** das
    Automobil, -e
    automobile, car
der **Automobilhersteller, -**
    car manufacturer

B

das **Baby, -s** baby
die **Bäckerei, -en** bakery
der **Badeanzug, ̈e**
    swimsuit
die **Badehose, -n** bathing
    trunks
das **Badezimmer, -**
    bathroom
der **Bahnhof, ̈e** train
    station
    bald soon
der **Balkon, -s** *or* **-e**
    balcony
der **Ball, ̈e** ball
die **Banane, -n** banana
die **Bank, ̈e** bench
die **Bank, -en** bank
das **Basteln, -** handicraft
die **Bauarbeit, -en** road
    construction
der **Bauernhof, ̈e** farm
der **Baum, ̈e** tree
    beantworten to answer
    bedeuten to mean
    beginnen to begin
der/die **Behinderte, -n**
    handicapped (person)
    bei at, near, with
    beide both
das **Bein, -e** leg
das **Beispiel, -e** example
    bekommen to receive
    belegt covered
    beliebt popular
    benutzen to use
der **Bericht, -e** report
    beschäftigt busy,
    occupied

besitzen to own
besonder([e]s) special
sich besorgen to get
besser better
das **Besteck, -e** flatware
besuchen to visit
das **Bett, -en** bed
die **Bibliothek, -en** library
die **Biene, -n** bee
das **Bier, -e** beer
die **Biologie** biology
bis until
ein **bißchen** a little bit
bitte please;
    Bitteschön you're
    welcome
das **Blatt, ̈er** leaf
blau blue
bleiben to stay; to
    remain
der **Bleistift, -e** pencil
blitzen to sparkle; to
    lightning
blond blond
die **Blume, -n** flower
die **Bluse, -n** blouse
der **Boden, ̈** floor
das **Bogenschießen** archery
die **Bohne, -n** bean
böse angry; bad,
    naughty
die **Bratwurst, ̈e** fried
    sausage
brauchen to need
braun brown
braunhaarig
    brown-haired
die **Brezel, -n** pretzel
der **Brief, -e** letter
das **Briefmarkensammeln**
    stamp collecting
der **Briefträger, -,** die
    Briefträgerin, -nen
    letter carrier
die **Brosche, -n** brooch; pin
das **Brot, -e** bread
das **Brötchen, -** roll
der **Bruder, ̈** brother
das **Buch, ̈er** book
die **Buchhandlung, -en**
    bookstore
bunt colorful
das **Büro, -s** office
der **Bus, -se** bus
die **Bushaltestelle, -n** bus
    stop
die **Butter** butter

C

das **Café, -s** café
der **Campingplatz, ̈e**
    campground
der **CD-Spieler, -** CD
    player
der **Chef, -s,** die
    Chefin, -nen boss
die **Chemie** chemistry
(das) **China** China
der **Chinese, -n** Chinese
    (man),
die **Chinesin, -nen**
    Chinese (woman)
(das) **Chinesisch** Chinese
    (language)
chinesisch Chinese
der **Chor, ̈e** chorus, choir
die **Compact Disc, -s**
    compact disc (CD)
der **Computer, -** computer

D

da there
dabei with it, at the
    same time
der **Dachboden, ̈** attic
die **Dame, -n** woman, lady
damit with it; so that
der **Dank** thanks
danke thanks; thank
    you
danken to thank
dann then
der **Darsteller, -** actor,
    character
daß that
das **Datum,** *pl* die **Daten**
    date
dazu with it, to it
decken to cover; to set
    (*the table*)
dein your
denn because, for; *also
    used for emphasis
    without literal
    meaning*
des of the
deshalb therefore
(das) **Deutsch** German
    (language)
deutsch German;
    der/die **Deutsche, -n;**
    ein **Deutscher**/eine
    Deutsche German
    (man/woman)

die **Deutschklasse, -n**
    German class
(das) **Deutschland** Germany
der **Deutschlehrer, -,** die
    Deutschlehrerin,
    -nen German teacher
der **Dezember** December
dich you
dick fat, thick
der **Dienstag** Tuesday
das **Ding, -e** thing, object
dir you
doch but (still); yet; to
    be sure; *often used
    for emphasis
    without literal
    meaning*
donnern to thunder
der **Donnerstag** Thursday
drei three
dreißig thirty
dreizehn thirteen
dritte(r) third
du you (*familiar*)
dumm dumb
dunkeln to darken; to
    get dark
dünn thin
durch through; **Keine
    Durchfahrt** No
    Through-Traffic

E

die **Ecke, -n** corner
das **Ei, -er** egg
eigen own
der **Eilzug, ̈e** express train
ein a, an
einfach simple;
    one-way; simply
das **Einfamilienhaus, ̈er**
    one-family house
einig united
einladen to invite
eins one
einzig single
die **Eintrittskarte, -n**
    admission ticket
das **Eis, -e** ice; ice cream
eiskalt ice-cold
der **Elefant, -en** elephant
elegant elegant
elektrisch electric
der **Elektronikladen, ̈**
    electronics store
elektronisch electronic
elf eleven
die **Eltern** parents

empfehlen to recommend
endlich finally
der **Engel, -** angel
(das) **England** England
der **Engländer, -** Englishman
die **Engländerin, -nen** Englishwoman
(das) **Englisch** English (language)
englisch English; British
die **Engstelle, -n** narrowness (in the road)
die **Ente, -n** duck
die **Entfernung, -en** distance
er he
die **Erbse, -n** pea
die **Erdbeerbowle, -n** strawberry punch
die **Erde, -n** earth; world
das **Erdgeschoß, -sse** ground floor
die **Erdkunde** geography
ergreifen to seize; to grasp
erste(r) first
der/die **Erwachsene, -n** adult
es it; **es gibt** there is; there are
der **Esel, -** donkey
essen to eat
das **Eßzimmer, -** dining room
etwas something
euch you (*pl. familiar*)
euer your (*pl. familiar*)
ewig eternal
das **Examen, -** exam

F

die **Fabrik, -en** factory
das **Fach, -̈er** subject
die **Fahne, -n** flag
fahren (er ist gefahren) to drive; to travel
die **Fahrkarte, -n** ticket
das **Fahrrad, -̈er** bicycle
fallen (er ist gefallen) to fall
falsch false
die **Familie, -n** family
die **Farbe, -n** color

der **Februar** February
fehlen to be missing
feiern to celebrate
der **Feiertag, -e** holiday
das **Feinkostgeschäft, -e** delicatessen (store)
das **Fenster, -** window
die **Ferien** (*pl*) vacation
das **Fernsehen** television
fernsehen to watch television; **ich sehe fern** I watch television
der **Fernseher, -** television set
fertig finished; ready
der **Feuerwehrmann, -̈er** fireman
das **Feuerwerk, -e** fireworks
der **Film, -e** film
finden to find
der **Finger, -** finger
die **Firma,** *pl* die **Firmen** company; firm
der **Fisch, -e** fish
fischen to fish
das **Fleisch** meat
der **Fleischer, -** butcher
die **Fleischerei, -en** butcher shop
fleißig diligent
der **Flug, -̈e** flight
der **Flughafen, -̈e** airport
der **Flugplatz, -̈e** airport
das **Flugzeug, -e** airplane
die **Forschung** research
fotografieren to photograph
die **Frage, -n** question
fragen to ask
(das) **Frankreich** France
der **Franzose, -n** Frenchman
die **Französin, -nen** Frenchwoman
(das) **Französisch** French (language)
französisch French
die **Frau, -en** woman; lady; wife; Mrs.
frei free
das **Freibad, -̈er** outdoor pool
das **Freie** outdoors
der **Freitag** Friday
fressen to eat (*for animals*)

freuen: sich freuen to be happy; **ich freue mich** I am happy
der **Freund, -e,** die **Freundin, -nen** friend
frisch fresh
der **Frosch -̈e** frog
die **Frucht, -̈e** fruit
der **Frühling** spring
das **Frühstück, -e** breakfast
der **Fuchs, -̈e** fox
fünf five
fünfte(r) fifth
fünfzehn fifteen
fünfzig fifty
funkeln to sparkle
für for
der **Fuß, -̈e** foot
der **Fußball, -̈e** soccer (ball)
der **Fußgängerüberweg, -e** pedestrian crosswalk
füttern to feed

G

die **Gabel, -n** fork
ganz entire; whole
die **Garage, -n** garage
der **Garten, -̈** garden
die **Gartenarbeit** gardening
das **Gartengerät, -e** gardening tool
der **Gast, -̈e,** die **Gästin, -nen** guest
die **Gaststätte, -n** restaurant, inn
das **Gebäude, -** building
geben to give
gebrauchen to use
die **Gebühr, -en** fee
der **Geburtstag, -e** birthday
das **Gedicht, -e** poem
gefährlich dangerous
gefallen to be pleasing to
gehen (er ist gegangen) to go
gelb yellow
das **Geld, -er** money
der **Geldwechsel** money exchange
das **Gemüse, -** vegetable
der **Gemüseladen, -̈** vegetable store
genug enough
die **Geographie** geography

die **Geometrie** geometry
gerade just
das **Gerät, -e** tool
gern haben to like;
  gern (+ *verb*) to like
  (*doing*)
das **Geschäft, -e** store;
  business
die **Geschäftsfrau, -en**
  businesswoman
der **Geschäftsmann,** *pl* die
  Geschäftsleute
  businessman
die **Geschäftsreise, -n**
  business trip
das **Geschenk, -e** gift
die **Geschichte, -n** history;
  story
das **Geschirr** dishes
die **Geschwister** brothers
  and sisters
das **Gesicht, -er** face
gestern yesterday
die **Gesundheit** health
gewaltig powerful
gewinnen to win
gewiß surely; certainly
gewöhnlich usually
der **Gipfel, -** peak
die **Giraffe, -n** giraffe
die **Gitarre, -n** guitar
das **Glas, ̈er** glass
gleich immediately
das **Gleis, -e** track
das **Glück** luck
gold golden
Gott sei Dank! Thank
  God!
grau grey
die **Grippe** flu
groß large, big
der **Großbild(farb)fernseher,**
  - large-screen color
  TV
die **Großeltern**
  grandparents
größer larger, bigger
die **Großmutter, ̈**
  grandmother
der **Großvater, ̈**
  grandfather
grün green
die **Grundschule, -n**
  elementary school
die **Gruppe, -n** group
die **Gurke, -n** pickle
der **Gürtel, -** belt
gut good

Grusel- horror, scare
das **Gymnasium,** *pl* die
  Gymnasien
  academic high
  school

H

das **Haar, -e** hair; die
  Haarfarbe, -n hair
  color
haarig hairy
haben to have
der **Hahn, ̈e** rooster
Halt! Stop!
das **Handwerk** handicraft
hart hard
der **Haß** hatred
häßlich ugly
die **Hauptschule, -n**
  vocational school
das **Haus, ̈er** house
die **Hauswirtschaft** home
  economics
heißen to be called;
  ich heiße my name
  is
der **Herbst, -e** fall, autumn
der **Herr, -en** man; Mr.
herrlich magnificent
herzlich heaty, heartily
das **Hochhaus, ̈er** high rise
  (apartment house)
holen to get
hübsch pretty
der **Hubschrauber, -**
  helicopter

I

identifizieren to
  identify
imitieren to imitate
immer always
in in
intelligent intelligent
interessant interesting
interviewen to
  interview
(das) **Italien** Italy
der **Italiener, -,** die
  Italienerin, -nen
  Italian (man/woman)
(das) **Italienisch** Italian
  (language)
italienisch Italian

J

ja yes
die **Jacke, -n** jacket
das **Jahr, -e** year
die **Jahreszeit, -en** season
der **Januar** January
(das) **Japan** Japan
der **Japaner, -,** die
  Japanerin, -nen
  Japanese (man/
  woman)
(das) **Japanisch** Japanese
  (language)
japanisch Japanese
jawohl yes (indeed)
der **Jazz** jazz
jede, jeder, jedes each,
  every
die **Jugendgruppe, -n** youth
  group
der **Juli** July
jung young
der **Junge, -n** boy
die **Jungfrau, -en** maiden
der **Juni** June

K

der **Kaffee, -s** coffee
der **Kahn, ̈e** boat
kalt cold
die **Kamera, -s** camera
kämmen to comb
die **Kapelle, -n** band
kaputt broken
die **Karotte, -n** carrot
die **Karte, -n** card; ticket
die **Kartoffel, -n** potato
die **Kartoffelchips** potato
  chips
der **Käse, -** cheese
die **Kasse, -n** box office
die **Kassette, -n** cassette
der **Kassettenrecorder, -n**
  cassette recorder
die **Katze, -n** cat
kaufen to buy
das **Kaufhaus, ̈er**
  department store
kein no, not a
der **Keller, -** cellar,
  basement
kennen to know (*a*
  person); to be
  acquainted with

der **Ketchup** ketchup
das **Kino, -s** movie theater
die **Kirche, -n** church
die **Klarinette, -n** clarinet
die **Klasse, -n** class
die **Klassenarbeit, -en** test
der **Klassenkamerad, -en,**
die **Klassenkameradin,**
-nen, classmate
der **Klassenpräsident, -en,**
die **Klassenpräsi-**
dentin, -nen class
president
klassisch classical
das **Klavier, -e** piano
das **Kleid, -er** dress
die **Kleidung, -en** clothing
das **Kleidungsstück, -e**
article of clothing
klein small
das **Kleingeld** change
kochen to cook
der **Kollege, -n** colleague
kommen (er ist
gekommen) to come
können can; to be able
das **Konzert, -e** concert
der **Kopf, -e** head
der **Korb, -e** basket
das **Korn, -er** seed
der **Körper, -** body
der **Körperteil, -e** body part
korrigieren to correct
der **Kosename, -n** nickname
kosten to cost
der **Kram** junk
das **Krankenhaus, -er**
hospital
der **Krankenpfleger, -** die
Krankenpflegerin,
-nen nurse
die **Krawatte, -n** necktie
die **Kreide** chalk
die **Küche, -n** kitchen
der **Kuchen, -** cake
die **Kuh, -e** cow
kühl cool
der **Kühlschrank, -e**
refrigerator
der **Kuli, -s** ballpoint pen
die **Kunst, -e** art
das **Kunstwerk, -e** work of
art
der **Künstler,** die
Künstlerin, -nen
artist
kurz short

die **Kusine, -n** cousin
(female)

L

der **Laden, -** store
die **Lampe, -n** lamp
das **Land, -er** country;
auf dem Land in the
country
die **Landkarte, -n** map
das **Landschaftsbild, -er**
landscape picture
lang long
langweilig boring
der **Lärm** noise, clamor
der **Lastwagen, -** truck
(das) **Latein** Latin
laufen (er ist gelaufen)
to run
lausen to delouse
laut loud
leben to live
lebendig alive
das **Lebensmittelgeschäft,**
-e grocery story
lebhaft lively
der **Lehrer, -,** die **Lehrerin,**
-nen teacher
leicht easy; light
die **Leichtathletik** track
and field
leider unfortunately
leid tun to be sorry
legen to put
lernen to learn
lesen to read
die **Liebe, -n** love
lieben to love
lieber haben to prefer;
lieber (+ *verb*) to
prefer *(doing)*
der **Liebling** darling
das **Lieblingsfach, -er**
favorite subject
die **Lieblingsjahreszeit, -en**
favorite season
der **Lieblingsmonat, -e**
favorite month
liebsten: am liebsten
haben to like best;
am liebsten (+*verb*)
to like best *(doing)*
lila purple
die **Limonade** lemonade;
soda

das **Lineal, -e** ruler
die **Lippe, -n** lip
die **Liste, -n** list
der **Löffel, -** spoon
der **Löwe, -n** lion
die **Luft** air

M

machen to make; to do
das **Mädchen, -** girl
der **Magen, -** stomach
die **Mahlzeit, -en**
meal(time)
der **Mai** May
mal time(s)
die **Malerei** painting
man one
manchmal sometimes
der **Mann, -er** man
der **Mantel, -** coat
das **Märchen, -** fairy tale
die **Mark** mark (*German
monetary unit*)
der **März** March
die **Maschine, -n** machine
die **Mathe** math
die **Mathematik**
mathematics
der **Mathematiklehrer, -,**
die **Mathematik-**
lehrerin, -nen math
teacher
die **Maus, -e** mouse
der **Mechaniker, -**
mechanic
das **Medikament, -e**
medicine
mehr more
mein my
die **Melodie, -n** melody
der **Mensch, -en** human
(being)
das **Messer, -** knife
mich me
mieten to rent
das **Mietshaus, -er**
apartment house
der **Mikrowellenherd, -e**
microwave oven
die **Milch** milk
mindestens at least
der **Minifernseher, -**
minitelevision
minus minus
mir (to) me
die **Mischung, -en** mixture
mit with

der **Mittag, -e** noon
das **Mittagessen, -** lunch
die **Mitternacht** midnight
der **Mittwoch** Wednesday
   möchten would like
die **Mode, -n** fashion
   modern modern
die **Mohrrübe, -n** carrot
der **Monat, -e** month
das **Monster, -** monster
der **Montag** Monday
   morgen tomorrow
der **Morgen, -** morning
der **Motor, -en** motor
das **Motorrad, ¨er**
   motorcycle
der **Mund, ¨er** mouth
das **Münzensammeln**
   collecting coins
die **Münzensammlung, -en**
   coin collection
das **Museum,** *pl* die
   Museen museum
die **Musik** music
das **Musikinstrument, -e**
   musical instrument
   müssen must
   mutig brave
die **Mutter, ¨** mother

N

   na ja well
   nach to; after
   nach Hause home
   nachher afterward
der **Nachmittag, -e**
   afternoon
   nächste next
die **Nacht, ¨e** night
der **Nachtisch, -e** dessert
der **Name, -n** name
   naschen to snack
die **Nase, -n** nose
die **Nation, -en** nation
   natürlich of course
   neben next to
   nehmen to take
   nein no
   nett nice
   neu new
   neun nine
   neunzehn nineteen
   neunzig ninety
   nicht not
der **Nichtraucher, -**
   nonsmoker
   nichts nothing

   noch still; yet
   normal normal
die **Note, -n** grade, mark
   nötig necessary
der **November** November
   null zero
die **Nummer, -n** number
   nur only
   nützlich useful

O

   ob if; whether
das **Obst** fruit(s)
der **Obst- und**
   Gemüseladen, ¨
   fruit and vegetable
   store
   oft often
   ohne without
das **Ohr, -en** ear
der **Oktober** October
die **Oma, -s** grandmother
der **Onkel, -** uncle
der **Opa, -s** grandfather
   orange ¨e orange
der **Orangensaft, ¨e** orange
   juice
das **Orchester, -** orchestra
(das) **Österreich** Austria
der **Österreicher, -,** die
   Österreicherin, -nen
   Austrian (man/
   woman)
die **Ostküste** east coast
der **Ozean, -e** ocean

P

   packen to pack
das **Paket, -e** package
die **Panne, -n** breakdown
das **Papier, -e** paper
der **Paragraph, -en**
   paragraph
das **Parkverbot** No Parking
die **Party, -s** party
das **Pech** bad luck
   perfekt perfect
die **Person, -en** person
der **Pfeffer** pepper
der **Pfennig, -e** penny
das **Pferd, -e** horse
die **Pflanze, -n** plant
die **Physik** physics
das **Picknick, -s** picnic
der **Plan, ¨e** plan
   planen to plan

die **Platte, -n** record
der **Plattenspieler, -** record
   player
der **Platz, ¨e** place
die **Pleite, -n** bankruptcy,
   bust
(das) **Polen** Poland
der **Polizist, -en,** die
   Polizistin, -nen
   police officer
die **Pommes frites** french
   fries
die **Post** mail; post office
das **Postamt, ¨er** post office
der **Präsident, -en**
   president
   prima super
   probieren to try (on)
das **Programm, -e** program
der **Pullover, -** sweater
der **Pumpernickel, -**
   pumpernickel
die **Puppe, -n** doll

R

das **Radfahren** bicycle
   riding
der **Radiergummi, -s** eraser
das **Radio, -s** radio
der **Raucher, -** smoker
   räumen to clean
die **Realschule, -n**
   secondary school
die **Rechnung, -en** bill
   recht haben to be
   correct
der **Rechtsanwalt, ¨e,** die
   Rechtsanwältin,
   -nen lawyer
der **Redakteur, -e,** die
   Redakteurin, -nen
   editor
der **Regenmantel, ¨** rain
   coat
   regnen to rain
   reiben to rub
   reich rich
   reichen to reach; to
   pass
der **Reichtum** richess
das **Reihenhaus, ¨er** row
   house
die **Reise, -n** trip
der **Reiseführer, -,** die
   Reiseführerin, -nen
   tour guide
das **Reisen, -** travel

reisen (er ist gereist) to travel

reiten (er ist geritten) to ride

der Reparateur, -e repairman

reparieren to repair

das Restaurant, -s restaurant

das Rezept, -e recipe

richtig correct

riesig giant

der Ring, -e ring

das Ringen wrestling

der Rock, ¨e skirt

die Rockmusik rock music

das Roggenbrot, -e rye bread

rosa pink

rot red

die Rückfahrkarte, -n round-trip ticket

der Rucksack, ¨e backpack

die Ruhe rest

ruhig calm; peaceful

rund round; around

der Russe, -n, die Russin, -nen Russian (man/woman)

(das) Russisch Russian (language)

russisch Russian

das Rußland Russia

S

die Sackgasse, -n dead end

der Saft, ¨e juice

der Salat, -e lettuce

das Salz salt

sammeln to collect

der Samstag Saturday

das Sandwich, -es sandwich

das Schach chess

schade! what a pity!, too bad!

der Schädel, - skull

das Schaf, -e sheep

der Schal, -s scarf

die Schallplatte, -n record

der Schatz, ¨e treasure

schauen to look at

der Schauspieler, - actor

die Schauspielerin, -nen actress

die Scheibe, -n slice

scheinen to shine

das Schiff, -e ship

der Schiffer, - sailor

der Schinken, - ham

schlafen to sleep

das Schlafzimmer, - bedroom

die Schlagermusik hit music

das Schlagwort, -e slogan

schlecht bad

die Schleudergefahr danger of skidding

das Schloß, ¨sser castle; lock

schmecken to taste

der Schmuck jewelry

schneien to snow

schnell fast

schnurlos cordless

schön pretty; nice

die Schokolade, -n chocolate

schon already

der Schrank, ¨e closet

schrecklich awful

schreiben to write

die Schreibmaschine, -n typewriter

der Schriftsteller, - writer; author

schüchtern shy

der Schuh, -e shoe

die Schule, -n school

der Schüler, -, die Schülerin, -nen student

das Schulfach, ¨er subject

der Schultag, -e schoolday

schwach weak

der Schwamm, ¨e sponge; (blackboard) eraser

schwarz black

das Schwein, -e pig

die Schweiz Switzerland

der Schweizer, -, die Schweizerin, -nen Swiss (man/woman)

schwer heavy, difficult

die Schwester, -n sister

das Schwimmbad, ¨er swimming pool

schwimmen to swim

sechs six

sechste(r) sixth

sechzehn sixteen

sechzig sixty

der Seehafen, ¨ seaport

sehen to see

die Sehenswürdigkeit, -en sight

sein (er ist gewesen) to be

sein his; its

seit since

die Seite, -n page

der Seitenwind crosswind

der Sekretär, -e, die Sekretärin, -nen secretary

der Sekt champagne

selbstverständlich certainly

seltsam strange

der Senf mustard

der September September

die Serviette, -n napkin

der Sessel, - easy chair

sicher sure

Sie you (formal)

sie she; they

sieben seven

siebzehn seventeen

siebzig seventy

singen to sing

der Sinn, -e mind

Ski laufen to ski

die Socke, -n sock

das Sofa, -s sofa

sofort immediately

der Sohn, ¨e son

der Solarrechner, - solar calculator

sollen should

der Sommer, - summer

die Sommerferien (pl) summer vacation

die Sommersprosse, -n freckle

sondern but, on the contrary

der Sonnabend Saturday

die Sonne, -n sun

der Sonntag Sunday

sonst otherwise

die Sorge, -n worry

(das) Spanien Spain

der Spanier, -, die Spanierin, -nen Spaniard

(das) Spanisch Spanish (language)

spanisch Spanish

der Spargel, - asparagus

Spaß machen to be fun

spät late; später later

der **Speck, -e** bacon
spielen to play
der **Spieler, -** player
der **Sport** sports
der **Sportverein, -e** athletic club
die **Sprache, -n** language
sprechen to speak
das **Stadion,** pl die **Stadien** stadium
die **Stadt, ̈e** city
stark strong
statt instead of
der **Steckbrief, -e** "Wanted" poster
die **Stereoanlage, -n** stereo system
stimmen to agree
der **Stock, ̈e** floor, story
das **Stockwerk, -e** floor; story (of a building)
die **Strafarbeit, -en** punishment assignment
der **Strand, ̈e** beach
die **Straße, -n** street
die **Straßenbahn, -en** streetcar
streicheln to pet; to stroke
der **Strumpf, ̈e** sock
studieren to study
das **Studium,** pl die **Studien** study, studies
der **Stuhl, ̈e** chair
der **Stundenplan, ̈e** class schedule
der **Supermarkt, ̈e** supermarket
die **Suppe, -n** soup
süß sweet

T

die **Tafel, -n** chalk board
der **Tag, -e** day
die **Tagesrückfahrkarte, -n** same-day round-trip ticket
die **Tagestour, -en** day trip
die **Tankstelle, -n** gas station
die **Tante, -n** aunt
tanzen to dance
die **Tasse, -n** cup

tausend thousand
das **Taxi, -s** taxi
der **Tee** tea
das **Telefaxgerät, -e** fax machine
das **Telefon, -e** telephone
telefonieren to telephone
der **Teller, -** plate
die **Temperatur** temperature
(das) **Tennis** tennis
teuer expensive
der **Textautomat, -en** word processor
das **Theater, -** theater
die **Thermosflasche, -n** thermos bottle
das **Tier, -e** animal
der **Tiger, -** tiger
der **Tisch, -e** table
die **Tischdecke, -n** tablecloth
(das) **Tischtennis** table tennis
die **Tochter, ̈** daughter
toll crazy; great
die **Tomate, -n** tomato
die **Torte, -n** cake
die **Tour, -en** tour
der **Tourist, -en** tourist
tragen to wear; to carry
das **Transistorradio, -s** portable radio
die **Traube, -n** grape
der **Traubensaft, ̈e** grape juice
traurig sad
treffen to meet
treiben to pursue
die **Treppe, -n** staircase, stairs
trinken to drink
die **Trompete, -n** trumpet
die **Tschechoslowakei** Czechoslovakia
tschüß! good-bye!
tun to do
das **Tunnel, -e** tunnel
die **Tür, -en** door
das **Turnen** gymnastics
turnen to do gymnastics
der **Turnverein, -e** exercise club

U

die **U-Bahn, -en** subway
üben to practice
über over, above
die **Überraschung, -en** surprise
die **Übung, -en** exercise; practice
das **Ufer, -** bank, shore
die **Uhr, -en** clock
um around; about
und and
das **Ungeheuer, -** monster
die **Universität, -en** university
unmöglich impossible
uns us
unser our
unter under
unterwegs on the way
der **Urlaub, -e** vacation

V

die **Vase, -n** vase
der **Vater, ̈** father
die **Verabredung, -en** appointment; date
das **Verbot, -e** prohibition
verbringen to spend (time)
verdienen to earn
die **Vereinigten Staaten** United States
Verfügung: zur Verfügung stellen to place at (someone's) disposal
vergessen to forget
verkaufen to sell
der **Verkäufer, -** salesman
die **Verkäuferin, -nen** saleswoman
das **Verkehrsmittel, -** means of transportation
verrückt crazy
verschlingen to devour
die **Verspätung, -en** lateness
der/die **Verwandte, -n** relative
die **Verzeihung, -en** excuse
die **Verzierung, -en** decoration

der **Vetter, -n** cousin
die **Videokamera, -s** video camera
der **Videorecorder, -** videocassette recorder
viel much
viele many
vielleicht perhaps
vier four
das **Viertel, -** quarter
vierte(r) fourth
vierzehn fourteen
vierzig forty
die **Violine, -n** violin
der **Vogel, ⸚** bird
die **Volksmusik** folk music
der **Volleyball, ⸚e** volleyball
von from; of; by
vor in front of
vorbereiten to prepare; **vorbereitet** prepared
die **Vorliebe, -n** preference
vorschlagen to suggest
Vorsicht! Caution!
vorsichtig careful

W

wählen to choose
wahr true
während during
wandern to hike
das **Wandern** hiking
wann when
warm warm
warten (auf) to wait (for)
warum why
was what
was für what kind of
waschen to wash
der **Waschraum, ⸚e** washroom
das **Wasser** water

das **WC, -s** toilet, restroom
weg away
weh tun to hurt
(die) **Weinacht(en)** Christmas
der **Weihnachtsbaum, ⸚e** Christmas tree
weil because
der **Wein, -e** wine
weiß white
weit far
weiter further
welche(n) which
die **Welle, -n** wave
die **Welt, -en** world
wem (to) whom
wen whom
wenn when(ever); if
wer who
das **Wetter** weather
wichtig important
wie how
wieder again
wieviel how much
wie viele how many
wild wild
windig windy
der **Winter, -** winter
winzig tiny
wir we
die **Wirtschaft** economy
wissen to know (*facts*)
der **Wissenschaftler, -** scientist
wissenschaftlich scientific
wo where
das **Wochenende, -** weekend
woher from where
wohin to where
wohnen to live
die **Wohnung, -en** apartment
das **Wohnzimmer, -** living room
der **Wolf, ⸚e** wolf
die **Wolle** wool

wollen to want
das **Wörterbuch, ⸚er** dictionary
der **Wortschatz, ⸚e** vocabulary
wünschen to wish
die **Wurst, ⸚e** sausage
das **Würstchen, -** frankfurter, wiener

Z

die **Zahl, -en** number
der **Zahn, ⸚e** tooth
der **Zahnarzt, ⸚e,** die **Zahnärztin, -nen** dentist
das **Zebra, -s** zebra
zehn ten
der **Zehmarkschein, -e** ten-mark bill
zeichnen to draw
zeigen to show
die **Zeitung, -en** newspaper
das **Zelt, -e** tent
zelten to camp, go camping;
das **Zelten** camping
das **Zentrum,** *pl* die **Zentren** center; downtown
das **Zeugnis, -se** report card
die **Ziege, -n** goat
der **Zoo, -s** zoo
zu to
der **Zufall, ⸚e** coincidence
der **Zug, ⸚e** train
die **Zunge, -n** tongue
zurück back
zwanzig twenty
zwei two
zweite(r) second
zwölf twelve

__ ENGLISH-GERMAN

A

a, an ein(e)
about um
above über
actor der Schauspieler,
  -; der Darsteller, -
actress die
  Schauspielerin, -nen
admission ticket die
  Eintrittskarte, -n
adult der/die
  Erwachsene, -n
after nach
afternoon der
  Nachmittag, -e
afterward nachher
again wieder
agree stimmen
air die Luft
airplane das Flugzeug,
  -e
airport der Flughafen,
  ¨; der Flugplatz, ¨e
alive lebendig
all alle(s)
alone allein
already schon
also auch
always immer
American der
  Amerikaner, -, die
  Amerikanerin, -nen;
  amerikanisch
and und
angel der Engel, -
angry böse
animal das Tier, -e
answer antworten;
  beantworten
apartment die
  Wohnung, -en
appear aussehen;
  scheinen
apple der Apfel, ¨
appointment die
  Verabredung, -en
April der April
arm der Arm, -e
around rund; um
art die Kunst, ¨e

article der Artikel, -
artist der Künstler, -,
  die Künstlerin, -nen
as wie; als
ask fragen
asparagus der Spargel, -
assignment die
  Aufgabe, -n
at bei; um
athletic club der
  Sportverein, -e
attic der Dachboden, ¨
August der August
aunt die Tante, -n
Austria (das)
  Österreich
author der
  Schriftsteller, -
automobile das Auto,
  -s
autumn der Herbst
away weg
awful schrecklich

B

baby das Baby, -s
back zurück
backpack der
  Rucksack, ¨e
bacon der Speck
bad schlecht; böse; **too
  bad!** schade!
bakery die Bäckerei,
  -en
balcony der Balkon, -s
  or -e
ball der Ball, ¨e
ballpoint pen der Kuli,
  -s
banana die Banane, -n
band die Kapelle, -n
bank die Bank, -en
basket der Korb, ¨e
basketball der
  Korbball, ¨e
bathing trunks die
  Badehose, -n
bathroom das
  Badezimmer, -
be sein (er ist gewesen)

beach der Strand, ¨e
bean die Bohne, -n
because denn; weil
bed das Bett, -en
bedroom das
  Schlafzimmer, -
beer das Bier, -e
begin beginnen
belt der Gürtel, -
bench die Bank, ¨e
besides außerdem
better besser
bicycle das Fahrrad, ¨er
big groß
bill die Rechnung, -en
biology die Biologie
bird der Vogel, ¨
birthday der
  Geburtstag, -e
bit ein bißchen
black schwarz
blackboard die Tafel,
  -n
blackboard eraser der
  Schwamm, ¨e
blond blond
blouse die Bluse, -n
blue blau
boat der Kahn, ¨e
body der Körper, -
body part der
  Körperteil, -e
bold mutig
book das Buch, ¨er
bookstore die
  Buchhandlung, -en
boring langweilig
boss der Chef, -s, die
  Chefin, -nen
both beide
box office die Kasse, -n
boy der Junge, -n
bread das Brot, -e
breakfast das
  Frühstück, -e
British englisch
broken kaputt
brooch die Brosche, -n
brother der Bruder, ¨
brothers and sisters die
  Geschwister

brown braun
brunette brünett
building
das Gebäude, -
bus der Bus, -se
business das Geschäft,
-e
businessman der
Geschäftsmann, *pl*
die Geschäftsleute
businesswoman die
Geschäftsfrau, -en
busy beschäftigt
but aber; sondern;
doch
butcher der Fleischer, -
butcher shop die
Fleischerei, -en
butter die Butter
buy kaufen
by von

C

café das Café, -s
cake der Kuchen, -; die
Torte, -n
calm ruhig
camera die Kamera, -s
campground der
Campingplatz, ¨e
camping das Zelten
can können
card die Karte, -n
careful vorsichtig
carrot die Karotte, -n;
die Mohrrübe, -n
carry tragen
cassette die Kassette,
-n
cassette recorder der
Kassettenrecorder, -
castle das Schloß, ¨sser
cat die Katze, -n
CD player der
CD-Spieler, -
celebrate feiern
cellar der Keller, -
certainly gewiß;
selbstverständlich
chair der Stuhl, ¨e; der
Sessel, -
chalk die Kreide
change das Kleingeld
cheese der Käse
chemistry die Chemie

chess das Schach
China (das) China
Chinese der Chinese,
-n; die Chinesin,
-nen; chinesisch
chocolate die
Schokolade
chorus der Chor, ¨e
Christmas die
Weihnacht(en)
Christmas tree der
Weihnachtsbaum, ¨e
church die Kirche, -n
city die Stadt, ¨e
clarinet die Klarinette,
-n
class die Klasse, -n
class schedule der
Stundenplan, ¨e
classical klassisch
classmate der
Klassenkamerad, -en,
die Klassen-
kameradin, -nen
clean (up) (auf)räumen
clock die Uhr, -en
closet der Schrank, ¨e
clothing die Kleidung,
-en
coat der Mantel, ¨
coffee der Kaffee
coin collecting das
Münzensammeln
coin collection die
Münzensammlung,
-en
coincidence der Zufall,
¨e
cold kalt
colleague der Kollege,
-n, die Kollegin, -nen
color die Farbe, -n
colorful bunt
comb kämmen
come kommen (er ist
gekommen)
compact disc die
Compact Disc, -s
company die Firma, *pl*
die Firmen
computer der
Computer, -
concert das Konzert, -e
cook kochen
cool kühl
cordless schnurlos
corner die Ecke, -n

correct korrigieren;
richtig; **be correct**
recht haben
cost kosten
country das Land, ¨er;
in the country auf
dem Land
cousin die Kusine, -n;
der Vetter, -n
cover decken
covered belegt
cow die Kuh, ¨e
crazy verrückt; toll
cup die Tasse, -n
Czechoslovakia die
Tschechoslowakei

D

dance tanzen
dangerous gefährlich
darken dunkeln
darling der Liebling
date das Datum, *pl* die
Daten
daughter die Tochter, ¨
day der Tag, -e
day trip die Tagestour,
-en
December der
Dezember
decoration die
Verzierung, -en
dentist der Zahnarzt,
¨e; die Zahnärztin,
-nen
depart abfahren (er ist
abgefahren)
department store das
Kaufhaus, ¨er
dessert der Nachtisch,
-e
devour verschlingen
dictionary das
Wörterbuch, ¨er
difficult schwer
diligent fleißig
dining room das
Eßzimmer, -
dinner das
Abendessen, -
dishes das Geschirr
distance die
Entfernung, -en
do machen; tun

doctor der Arzt, ̈e; die Ärztin, -nen
donkey der Esel, -
door die Tür, -en
downtown das Zentrum, *pl* die Zentren
draw zeichnen
dress das Kleid, -er
drink trinken
drive fahren (er ist gefahren)
dumb dumm
during während

E

each jede, jeder, jedes
ear das Ohr, -en
earn verdienen
earth die Erde
east coast die Ostküste, -n
easy leicht
eat essen; fressen
editor der Redakteur, -e; die Redakteurin, -nen
egg das Ei, -er
eight acht
eighteen achtzehn
eighty achtzig
electric elektrisch
electronic elektronisch
electronics store der Elektronikladen, ̈
elegant elegant
elephant der Elefant, -en
eleven elf
England (das) England
English (das) Englisch; englisch
enjoy oneself sich amüsieren
enough genug
entire ganz
equipment die Ausrüstung, -en
eraser der Radiergummi, -s; der Schwamm, ̈e
every jede, jeder, jedes
everyone alle
exam das Examen, -

example der Beispiel, -e
excellent ausgezeichnet
exciting aufregend
excursion der Ausflug, ̈e
excuse die Verzeihung, -en; die Ausrede, -n
exercise turnen; das Turnen
exercise club der Turnverein, -e
expensive teuer
express train der Eilzug, ̈e
eye das Auge, -n

F

face das Gesicht, -er
factory die Fabrik, -en
fairy tale das Märchen, -
fall fallen (er ist gefallen)
false falsch
family die Familie, -n
far weit
farm der Bauernhof, ̈e
fast schnell
fat dick
father der Vater, ̈
favorite . . . Lieblings. . .
fax machine das Telefaxgerät, -e
fear die Angst, ̈e
February der Februar
fee die Gebühr, -en
fifteen fünfzehn
fifty fünfzig
film der Film, -e
finally endlich
find finden
finger der Finger, -
finished fertig
fireman der Feuerwehrmann, ̈er
fireworks das Feuerwerk
first erst
fish der Fisch, -e
five fünf
flag die Fahne, -n
flatware das Besteck, -e

flight der Flug, ̈e
floor der Boden, ̈; der Stock, ̈e, das Stockwerk, -e
flower die Blume, -n
flu die Grippe
folk music die Volksmusik
foot der Fuß, ̈e
for für
forget vergessen
fork die Gabel, -n
forty vierzig
four vier
fourteen vierzehn
fox der Fuchs, ̈e
France (das) Frankreich
free frei
French französisch
french fries die Pommes frites
Frenchman der Franzose, -n
Frenchwoman die Französin, -nen
fresh frisch
Friday der Freitag
friend der Freund, -e, die Freundin, -nen
from von; aus
fruit die Frucht, ̈e; das Obst
fun der Spaß; **be fun** Spaß machen
further weiter

G

garage die Garage, -n
garden der Garten, ̈
gardening die Gartenarbeit
gardening tool das Gartengerät, -e
gas station die Tankstelle, -n
general allgemein
geography die Geographie; die Erdkunde
geometry die Geometrie
German deutsch; **German class** die Deutschklasse, -n

Germany das Deutschland
gift das Geschenk, -e
giraffe die Giraffe, -n
girl das Mädchen, -
give geben
glass das Glas, ̈er
go gehen (er ist gegangen)
goat die Ziege, -n
golden gold
good gut
good-bye auf Wiedersehen; tschüß
grade die Note, -n
grandfather der Großvater, ̈, der Opa, -s
grandmother die Großmutter, ̈, die Oma, -s
grandparents die Großeltern
grape die Traube, -n
grasp ergreifen
great toll
green grün
grey grau
grocery store das Lebensmittelgeschäft, -e
ground floor das Erdgeschoß
group die Gruppe, -n
guest der Gast, ̈e, die Gästin, -nen
guitar die Gitarre, -n
gymnastics das Turnen; **do gymnastics** turnen

H

hair das Haar, -e
hairy haarig
ham der Schinken, -
handicraft das Basteln
have haben
he er
head der Kopf, ̈e
heavy schwer
helicopter der Hubschrauber, -
high school das Gymnasium, *pl* die Gymnasien

hike wandern
hiking das Wandern
his sein
history die Geschichte, -n
hit music die Schlagermusik
holiday der Feiertag, -e
home zu Hause; nach Hause
horse das Pferd, -e
hospital das Krankenhaus, ̈er
how wie;
how much wieviel
how many wie viele
hurt weh tun

I

ice (cream) das Eis
ice-cold eiskalt
if wenn; ob
imitate imitieren
immediately gleich; sofort
important wichtig
impossible unmöglich
in in; **in front of** vor
instead of anstatt
intelligent intelligent
interesting interessant
interview interviewen
invite einladen
it es
Italian der Italiener, -, die Italienerin, -nen; italienisch
Italy das Italien
its sein

J

jacket die Jacke, -n
January der Januar
Japan (das) Japan
Japanese der Japaner, -, die Japanerin, -nen; japanisch
jazz der Jazz
jewelry der Schmuck
juice der Saft, ̈e
July der Juli
June der Juni

junk der Kram
just gleich; gerade

K

ketchup der Ketchup
kind die Art, -en
kitchen die Küche, -n
knife das Messer, -
know kennen; wissen

L

lamp die Lampe, -n
landscape picture das Landschaftsbild, -er
language die Sprache, -n
large groß
large-screen (color) television der Großbild(farb)-fernseher, -
late spät
lateness die Verspätung
later später
Latin (das) Latein
lawyer der Rechtsanwalt, -e, die Rechtsanwältin, -nen
leaf das Blatt, ̈er
learn lernen
least: at least mindestens
leg das Bein, -e
lemonade die Limonade
lesson die Aufgabe, -n
letter der Brief, -e
letter carrier der Briefträger, -; die Briefträgerin, -nen
lettuce der Salat, -e
library die Bibliothek, -en
light leicht
lion der Löwe, -n
lip die Lippe, -n
list die Liste, -n
live leben; wohnen
lively lebhaft
living room das Wohnzimmer, -

lock das Schloß, ¨sser
long lang
look schauen
loud laut
love die Liebe; lieben
luck das Glück
lunch das Mittagessen,-

M

machine das Gerät, -e;
 die Maschine, -n; der
 Apparat, -e
maiden die Jungfrau,
 -en
mail die Post
make machen
man der Mann, ¨er
many viele
map die Landkarte, -n
March der März
Mark die Mark
math die Mathe
mathematics die
 Mathematik
May der Mai
me mich; mir
meal(time) die
 Mahlzeit, -en
mean bedeuten
**means of
 transportation** das
 Verkehrsmittel, -
meat das Fleisch
mechanic der
 Mechaniker, -
medicine das
 Medikament, -e
meet treffen
melody die Melodie, -n
microwave oven der
 Mikrowellenherd, -e
midnight die
 Mitternacht
milk die Milch
mind der Sinn, -e
minitelevision der
 Minifernseher, -
minus minus
missing: be missing
 fehlen
mixture die Mischung,
 -en
modern modern

Monday der Montag
money das Geld
monkey der Affe, -n
monster das
 Ungeheuer, -, das
 Monster, -
month der Monat, -e
more mehr
morning der Morgen, -
mother die Mutter, ¨
motor der Motor, -en
motorcycle das
 Motorrad, ¨er
mouse die Maus, ¨e
mouth der Mund, ¨er
movie theater das
 Kino, -s
much viel
museum das Museum,
 pl die Museen
music die Musik
musical instrument das
 Musikinstrument, -e
müssen must
der Senf mustard
mein my

N

name der Name, -n;
 my name is ich
 heiße
napkin die Serviette,
 -n
nation die Nation, -en
naughty böse
near bei
necessary nötig
necktie die Krawatte,
 -n
need brauchen
new neu
newspaper die Zeitung,
 -en
next nächste; **next to**
 neben
nice nett; schön
nickname der
 Kosename, -n
night die Nacht, ¨e
nine neun
nineteen neunzehn
ninety neunzig
no nein; kein

noise der Lärm, -e
noon der Mittag, -e
normal normal
nose die Nase, -n
not nicht
nothing nichts
November der
 November
number die Nummer,
 -n; die Zahl, -en
nurse der Kranken-
 pfleger, -, die
 Krankenpflegerin,
 -nen

O

ocean der Ozean, -e
occupied beschäftigt
October der Oktober
of von
of course natürlich
office das Amt, ¨er; das
 Büro, -s
old alt
on auf
one eins
one-family house das
 Einfamilienhaus, ¨er
one-way einfach
only nur
orange orange
orchestra das
 Orchester, -
other ander(e)
otherwise sonst
our unser
out (of) aus
outdoors das Freie
over über
own eigen; besitzen

P

package das Paket, -e
page die Seite, -n
painting die Malerei
paper das Papier, -e
paragraph der
 Paragraph, -en
parents die Eltern
party die Party, -s
pea die Erbse, -n

peaceful ruhig
peak der Gipfel, -
pencil der Bleistift, -e
penny der Pfennig, -e
pepper der Pfeffer
perfect perfekt
perhaps vielleicht
person die Person, -en
pet das Hobbytier, -e;
streicheln
pharmacy die
Apotheke, -n
photograph
fotografieren
physics die Physik
piano das Klavier, -e
pickle die Gurke, -n
picnic das Picknick, -s
pig das Schwein, -e
pink rosa
place der Platz, ̈e
plan planen; der Plan,
̈e
plant die Pflanze, -n
plate der Teller, -
play spielen
please bitte; gefallen
poem das Gedicht, -e
Poland (das) Polen
police officer der
Polizist, -en, die
Polizistin, -nen
pool das Schwimmbad,
̈er
poor arm
popular beliebt
post office die Post,
-en; das Postamt, ̈er
potato die Kartoffel, -n
potato chips die
Kartoffelchips
powerful gewaltig
practice üben; die
Übung, -en
preference die
Vorliebe, -n
prepared vorbereitet
president der
Präsident, -en
pretty hübsch; schön
pretzel die Brezel, -n
program das
Programm, -e
pumpernickel der
Pumpernickel, -
purple lila
pursue treiben

Q

quarter das Viertel, -
question die Frage, -n

R

radiation die
Ausstrahlung, -en
radio das Radio, -s;
portable radio das
Transistorradio
rain regnen
raincoat der
Regenmantel, ̈
reach reichen
read lesen
ready fertig
receive bekommen
recipe das Rezept, -e
recommend empfehlen
record die Schallplatte,
-n
record player der
Plattenspieler, -
red rot
refrigerator der
Kühlschrank, ̈e
relative der Verwandte,
-n
rent mieten
repair reparieren
repairman der
Reparateur, -e
report card das
Zeugnis, -se
rest die Ruhe; sich
ausruhen
restaurant das
Restaurant, -s
rich reich
ride reiten (er ist
geritten)
ring der Ring, -e
rock music die
Rockmusik
roll das Brötchen, -
round rund
round-trip ticket die
Rückfahrkarte, -n
rub reiben
ruler das Lineal, -e
run laufen
Russia (das) Rußland

Russian der Russe, -n,
die Russin, -nen;
russisch
rye bread das
Roggenbrot, -e

S

sad traurig
sailor der Schiffer, -
salesperson der
Verkäufer, -, die
Verkäuferin, -nen
salt das Salz
**same: at the same
time** dabei; **same-
day round-trip ticket**
die Tages-
rückfahrkarte, -n
sandwich das
Sandwich, -es
Saturday der Samstag,
der Sonnabend
sausage die Wurst, ̈e
scarf der Schal, -s
school die Schule, -n
schoolday der
Schultag, -e
seaport der Seehafen, ̈
season die Jahreszeit,
-en
second zweite
secretary der Sekretär,
-e, die Sekretärin,
-nen
see sehen
seize ergreifen
sell verkaufen
September der
September
set (the table) (den
Tisch) decken
seven sieben
seventeen siebzehn
seventy siebzig
she sie
sheep das Schiff, -e
shoe der Schuh, -e
short kurz
should sollen
show zeigen
shy schüchtern
sight die Sehens-
würdigkeit, -en
simple einfach
since seit

sing singen
single einzig
sister die Schwester, -n
six sechs
sixteen sechzehn
sixty sechzig
ski Ski laufen
skirt der Rock, ¨e
sleep schlafen
slice die Scheibe, -n
slogan das Schlagwort, ¨er
small klein
snack naschen
snapshot die Aufnahme, -n
snow schneien
so that damit
soccer (ball) der Fußball, ¨e
sock die Socke, -n
soda die Limonade, das Cola
sofa das Sofa, -s
solar calculator der Solarrechner, -
someone man
something etwas
sometimes manchmal
son der Sohn, ¨e
soon bald
sorry: I'm sorry es tut mir leid
sort die Art, -en
soup die Suppe, -n
Spain (das) Spanien
Spaniard der Spanier, -, die Spanierin, -nen
Spanish spanisch
sparkle funkeln; blitzen
speak sprechen
special besonder([e]s)
spend ausgeben (money); verbringen (time)
spoon der Löffel, -
sports der Sport
spring der Frühling
stadium das Stadion, pl die Stadien
staircase, stairs die Treppe, -n
stamp collecting das Briefmarkensammeln

stay bleiben
stereo system die Stereoanlage, -n
still noch
stocking der Strumpf, ¨e
stomach der Magen, -
store das Geschäft, -e; der Laden, ¨
story die Geschichte, -n; das Stockwerk, -e
strange seltsam
street die Straße, -n
streetcar die Straßenbahn, -en
stroke streicheln
strong stark
student der Schüler, -, die Schülerin, -nen
study studieren
subject das Fach, ¨er
subway die U-Bahn, -en
suggest vorschlagen
suit der Anzug, ¨e
summer der Sommer, -
sun die Sonne, -n
Sunday der Sonntag
supermarket der Supermarkt, ¨e
sure gewiß; sicher
surprise die Überraschung, -en
sweater der Pullover, -
sweet süß
swim schwimmen
swimming pool das Schwimmbad, ¨er
swimsuit der Badeanzug, ¨e
Swiss der Schweizer, -
Switzerland die Schweiz

T

table der Tisch, -e
table tennis das Tischtennis
tablecloth die Tischdecke, -n
take nehmen
taste schmecken

taxi das Taxi, -s
tea der Tee, -s
teacher der Lehrer, -, die Lehrerin, -nen
telephone das Telefon, -e; der Apparat, -e; telefonieren
television das Fernsehen, -
television set der Fernseher, -
temperature die Temperatur
ten zehn
tennis das Tennis
tent das Zelt, -e
test die Klassenarbeit, -en
than als
thank danken; thanks danke
that daß
theater das Theater, -
then dann
there da
there is, there are es gibt
therefore deshalb
thermos bottle die Thermosflasche, -n
they sie
thick dick
thin dünn
third dritte
thirteen dreizehn
thirty dreißig
thousand tausend
three drei
through durch
Thursday der Donnerstag
ticket die Karte, -n
tiger der Tiger, -
time die Zeit, -en
tiny winzig
to zu; nach; to it dazu
tomato die Tomate, -n
tomorrow morgen
tongue die Zunge, -n
too auch
tool das Werkzeug, -e; das Gerät, -e
tooth der Zahn, ¨e
tour die Tour, -en

tour guide der
Reiseführer, -; die
Reiseführerin, -nen
tourist der Tourist,
-en, die Touristin,
-nen
track das Gleis, -e
train der Zug, -e
train station der
Bahnhof, -e
travel fahren (er ist
gefahren); reisen (er
ist gereist)
traveling das Reisen
treasure der Schatz, -e
tree der Baum, -e
trip die Reise, -n
truck der Lastwagen, -
true weahr
trumpet die Trompete,
-n
try on probieren
Tuesday der Dienstag
tunnel das Tunnel, -e
twelve zwölf
twenty zwanzig
two zwei
type die Art, -en
typewriter die
Schreibmaschine, -n

U

uncle der Onkel, -
ugly häßlich
under unter
unfortunately leider
united einig; vereinigt;
United States die
Vereinigten Staaten
university die
Universität, -en
until bis
us uns
use benutzen;
gebrauchen
useful nützlich
usually gewöhnlich

V

vacation die Ferien
(pl); der Urlaub, -e
vase die Vase, -n
video camera die
Videokamera, -s
videocassette recorder
der Videorecorder, -
violin die Violine, -n
visit besuchen
vocabulary der
Wortschatz, -e
volleyball der
Volleyball, -e

W

wait (for) warten (auf)
want wollen
warm warm
wash waschen
watch television
fernsehen; **I watch
television** ich sehe
fern
water das Wasser
wave die Welle, -n
we wir
weak schwach
wear tragen
weather das Wetter
Wednesday der
Mittwoch
weekend das
Wochenende, -
**welcome: you're
welcome** Bitteschön
well also; na ja
what was
what kind of was für
when wann, als
whenever wenn
where wo
where from woher
where to wohin
whether ob

which welche,
welcher, welches
white weiß
who wer
whom wen; wem
why warum
wild wild
win gewinnen
window das Fenster, -
windy windig
wine der Wein, e
winter der Winter, -
wish wünschen
with mit; bei; **with it**
damit; dabei; dazu
without ohne
wolf der Wolf, -e
woman die Frau, -en
wool die Wolle, -n
word processor der
Textautomat, -en
work arbeiten; die
Arbeit, -en
world die Erde; die
Welt
worry die Sorge, -n
would like möchte(n)
write schreiben

Y

year das Jahr, -e
yellow gelb
yes ja
yesterday gestern
yet noch
you du; ihr; Sie; dich;
euch; dir; Ihnen
young jung
your dein; euer; Ihr
youth group die
Jugendgruppe, -n

Z

zebra das Zebra, -s
zero null
zoo der Zoo, -s

Grammatical Index

Topical Index